# THE SIEGE AT PEKING

Sir Claude MacDonald

# THE SIEGE AT PEKING

PETER FLEMING

*With an Introduction*
*by*
DAVID BONAVIA

HONG KONG  OXFORD  NEW YORK
OXFORD UNIVERSITY PRESS

Oxford University Press

Oxford  New York  Toronto
Petaling Jaya  Singapore  Hong Kong  Tokyo
Delhi  Bombay  Calcutta  Madras  Karachi
Nairobi  Dar es Salaam  Cape Town
Melbourne  Auckland

and associated companies in
Berlin  Ibadan

First published by Rupert Hart-Davis 1959
First issued, with permission and with the addition of
an Introduction, as an Oxford in Asia paperback 1983
Second impression 1984
Reissued in Oxford Paperbacks 1986
Third impression 1989

ISBN 0 19 583735 5

OXFORD is a trade mark of Oxford University Press

Printed in Hong Kong
Published by Oxford University Press,
Warwick House, Hong Kong

# Introduction

PETER Fleming, who died in 1971, was the epitome of the enlightened English gentleman adventurer, explorer and travel writer. His education — at Eton and Oxford — was the best available at the time. As a young man he travelled extensively in China in the capacity of a correspondent of *The Times*, then the most influential and famous newspaper in the world.

In the company of a young Swiss woman, Ella Maillert, Fleming crossed China from Peking to Sinkiang (Xinjiang) in 1935. He later related their journey in *News from Tartary*. Eastern Turkestan, as it was then known, was a huge and perilous land full of rugged mountains and deserts which could swallow up travellers without trace. The region — which had been declared a province of China in 1884 — was under strong Russian influence, and was infested with bandits. The Turks, Chinese and other races who inhabited Sinkiang were acutely suspicious of foreigners who might be spies masquerading as bona-fide travellers.

Fleming's journalistic work took him to many parts of China, and a marvellous portrait of him in pursuit of a story is given in the reminiscences of a 1937 trip there by the young English authors W.H. Auden and Christopher Isherwood. Fainting, they followed the robust Fleming, as he charged up steep tracks, setting a fast pace and pausing only to sleep, eat, or rattle away on his portable typewriter. He was a powerhouse of physical and professional energy, and obviously needed strong challenges to work it off.

*The Siege at Peking* was first published in 1959. By that time Fleming's wandering days were over and he had settled down to the life of a well-to-do English country gentleman with a sizeable estate to tend. As the author of a number of books, and with a wide knowledge of China, he was well placed to write about the events of the Siege. His bibliography for the book shows that he relied mainly on British, European and American sources (many of the survivors of the Siege wrote up their experiences afterwards), and he studied carefully the account of the episode by the leading Chinese scholar, Chester Tan. Among the most impressive figures behind the barricades was George Ernest Morrison, an Australian Scot and doctor-turned-journalist, the most renowned of all Peking correspondents of *The Times*; his articles and memoirs provide fertile material for the historian.

The author also had access to Foreign Office archives and to the papers of Sir Claude MacDonald, the British Minister in Peking, who assumed overall command of the motley garrison and the civilians living behind its defences. Fleming had evidently learnt enough Chinese to be able to comment intelligently on some of the ambiguities in the dealings of the Tsungli Yamen (the Chinese equivalent of a foreign ministry) with the Ministers of the foreign Legations.

The Siege of the Legations in 1900 was a landmark in the development of modern China. It brought to a head the crisis in the Celestial Empire's relations with the outside world in the most dramatic manner possible. The Chinese ruling class, from the Empress Dowager, Tz'u Hsi, to the humblest local magistrate, had long deeply resented the imposition on their country of a system of international law and binding treaties invented in remote, 'barbarian' countries — sometimes, it must have seemed, with the sole aim of subjecting China to foreign exploitation. Their own political and legal system might have been cruel, inefficient and corrupt, but it had worked, more or less, for more than two millennia. Confucianism, the official state creed, taught that ruler, officials and the common people should observe basic ethical principles in relations between one another.

For the first time in history, in the second half of the nineteenth century, the entire validity of Chinese culture was rudely challenged. China began losing parts of her territory to foreign powers. Most of these losses were by their nature

# INTRODUCTION

peripheral, and the Manchu court awoke too late to realize that from the point of view of the Western intruders, they were strategically important, both for trade and for naval domination. The land-orientated Manchus had little experience of naval warfare, apart from skirmishes with pirates.

The arrival of increasing numbers of missionaries, some of them capable of seemingly miraculous cures through surgery and drugs, presented an intellectual and spiritual challenge which the rough naval officers and merchants from the West did not.

The grabbing of land by Japan, France, Germany, and Russia, as well as Britain, went hand in hand with the growth of foreign 'concession' areas in Shanghai, Canton, Tientsin, Hankow and elsewhere. These were accompanied by the resented system of extraterritoriality, whereby foreigners were immune from the jurisdiction of Chinese courts. Certainly no European would have expected fair or objective rulings by the Chinese courts of the day, and punishments were unacceptably cruel even by the standards of European countries, some of which still practised public execution, and held jailed lawbreakers in conditions barely more tolerable than those of the Orient. As Fleming points out, no Oriental in a Western country would have been taken seriously had he or she demanded equivalent immunity there.

The Siege of the Legations marked the culmination of Chinese frustration and resentment at these foreign incursions and impositions. But it did not succeed in ridding China of the 'barbarian' Powers.

Instead the Siege exacerbated the political, cultural, military and economic decline of the Empire and the Manchu (Ch'ing, Qing) dynasty which had ruled China since 1644. And it intensified the competitive ambitions of Russia, the Western powers and Japan, as they strove to increase their control over parts of China which had hitherto been regarded mainly as 'spheres of influence'.

The incompetence shown during the Siege by the Chinese Imperial troops — they included Manchus, and Moslems from the north-west of the country — encouraged the Powers in

INTRODUCTION

their belief that the Chinese were and always would be inept at warfare, and that they were untrustworthy in diplomatic dealings.

The Siege also focussed attention on the need to build more railways, both for the shipment of Chinese imports and exports, and domestic commerce, and for the greater convenience and security of the foreigners living in China. The new railways were financed by loans floated by Western banks acting in consortia, and this burden of debt contributed further to the decline of the dynasty. The railways also contributed to the break-up of the old Chinese economic system, dependent on water transport, coolie labour and pack animals to exchange the rich products of the various provinces and regions. As a result, many transport workers lost their jobs. The gentry and merchant class, however, realized the possibilities for self-enrichment in the railways, and so they became the object of a patriotic anti-foreign movement to bring them under the full control of China. In addition, the coming of the railways ushered in the age of mass production and cheap consumer goods — especially cotton fabrics — from Western countries and British-ruled India.

Finally, the long delay in raising the Siege was due mainly to the lack of control over the land on either side of the permanent way from Tientsin to Peking; this helped convince warlords of the next generation, and the foreign Powers, of the importance of armoured trains and military control along the route of the track, and marked another step in the subjugation of China.

The Siege of the Legations in 1900 in some ways foreshadowed the violent antics of the Red Guard movement of the late 1960s. Both the Red Guards and the Boxers were the socio-psychological product of China's attempts to come to terms with the outside world and mend her own backwardness. Both grew out of high-level manipulation of gullible but patriotic young people, their impatience at what seemed to be the failure of the ruling class to cope with the problem of foreigners, and the destructive effects of the latter on Chinese society.

# INTRODUCTION

The Red Guards, it is true, professed to believe in proletarian internationalism, to the extent that any of them understood the concept. But the latent xenophobia of the Chinese led them to harass, abuse and even injure foreigners, most of whom had not wittingly done China any harm. At the same time, they were less violent than the Boxers in their dealings with foreigners — though sadistically cruel to those Chinese whom they considered tainted by foreign influence. The Boxers massacred thousands of Chinese Christian converts and several scores of foreigners. No foreigner, by comparison, died as a result of maltreatment at the hands of the Red Guards, and only a handful were seriously injured. Though they liked to vent their anger on foreigners — for instance, by burning down the British Embassy in 1967 — the young Maoist radicals usually preferred to fight among themselves, sometimes with firearms.

There were other important differences between the two movements. The Boxers took no action against the Chinese men of state whose ineptitude had let the situation develop so far. Mao, on the other hand, used the Red Guards to demolish the careers and reputations, and even brutally end the lives, of hundreds of his former friends and comrades-in-arms. He created havoc in Chinese society in his own name and in that of the continuous revolution. He stood to a large degree aloof from the upheaval he had caused, issuing ambiguous statements which, like those of the Empress Dowager and the Tsungli Yamen, served mainly to confuse the fighters and activists, and split them into factions.

Both movements encouraged belief in totems and charms. For the Red Guards, it was the 'little red book' of Mao's quotations, believed to hold the key to all problems and the strength to win endless victories. The Boxers thought themselves invulnerable against bullets. And in the end, both the Boxers and the Red Guards were put down by armed might when they had outlived their usefulness to the ruling clique, and had become a disruptive embarrassment.

Both movements cost China dear in prestige and money. The outside world — already prejudiced against China — was shocked by the seemingly irrational behaviour of the Court and the Boxers, especially when the lives of women and children were at stake. When the fiasco was over, China was made to pay huge sums in indemnities. The Red Guards, 67 years later, brought industry and education almost to a halt. The damage wrought by both movements lasted for years to come.

Yet the desire of the foreigners to retain some foothold in one of the world's biggest market-places soon induced them to return to correct relations with the Court in Peking. In the same way foreign statesmen flocked to meet the dying Mao, who just a few years previously would have denounced them as imperialists and bourgeois exploiters. Fleming's closing scene — with the diplomatic corps archly applauding the woman who was responsible for the death or injury of many of their friends a year and a half earlier — brings home humanity's ability to forgive, if not forget, especially when there are good pickings to be had from the hulk of a dying adversary.

Fleming notes, but does not try to explain, that the Boxers and Imperial guards died in their hundreds before the Peking Wall or in the gardens and alleyways of the Legation Quarter, when they could quite easily have overwhelmed the defenders with sheer numbers and fire-power. To my mind this is a characteristically Chinese attitude towards warfare. According to ancient precepts, war should be used as an implement of politics and diplomacy, and used sparingly, while counter-vailing tactics of conciliation and even tribute to the enemy are employed to soften his determination. An example was the Court's gift of flowers, fruit and vegetables to the foreigners during a truce. And in the end the Empress Dowager and her immediate entourage saw the merit of the old Chinese saying: 'Of the thirty-six stratagems, flight is the best.'

The court escaped lightly. The £60-million Boxer Indemnity levied on China was mostly ploughed back to modernize Chinese education, and for other worthy causes. But by then the dynasty's fate was sealed. In 1908 the Empress Dowager died, and three years later a revolution toppled the Manchu rulers and set China on its long road to modernization.

# INTRODUCTION

Modern Chinese historians have re-evaluated the Boxers as Chinese patriots opposed both to Manchu rule and to the presence in China of the imperialist powers — Russia, Britain, Japan, France, Germany, the United States, Austro-Hungary, Holland, Belgium and Spain. An official account, published in Peking in 1958 and still in print, gives the following extra-ordinary summary of the Siege: 'In June 1900 the Manchu Government declared war on the imperialist powers [quite un-true]. The Manchu troops, in collaboration with the Yi He Tuan [Boxer] compatriots, launched onslaughts on the Lega-tions in Peking. The attacks lasted over five days but they [the Legations] were not taken.'

No less fatuous were some contemporary European and American accounts of the Siege, which portrayed the Chinese as heathen, diabolical, cowardly anti-Christs, deserving no understanding or quarter. The German Emperor fitted out a so-called East Asiatic Corps with ponies and Australian-style bush-hats to fight the wars of Christendom on pagan ground. They arrived too late to take part in the rescue and the best part of the looting, in which the British and French distinguished themselves by their greed.

A direct result of the Siege was the enforced agreement of the Chinese Government to the stationing of stronger military guards in the Legations, and secure lines of communication and reinforcement with Tientsin. From then on foreigners in danger from, say, bandits, could call on a machine squad from their Legation, and the murder of missionaries and other foreigners became rarer (with the exception of the killing of six people by Nationalist soldiers at Nanking in 1926).

Over the decades, China's rulers have come to see the counter-productive nature of acts of violence against foreigners. Most non-Chinese residents were treated correctly by the victorious communists from 1949 on, though some — especially missionaries and suspected spies — were subjected to physical and mental cruelty in order to extract 'confessions' before their expulsion from China. In recent memory, the only serious outbreaks of anti-foreign sentiment were in 1967 when diplomats and others were harassed and, in a few cases, injured by the Red Guards. Nearly all foreigners in Peking nowadays are cooped up together in special hotels and housing compounds, which would make it easy for the authorities to protect them in the event of another xenophobic upheaval. But all who value China, and wish her well, hope that such futile mass paranoia will never arise again. Perhaps the most important message of Fleming's account of the Siege is that it need never have happened in the first place.

Though the book is of value to the historian, it is essentially a brilliant work of historical journalism. It is as readable as a good novel, and its subject-matter is unfailingly gripping. It is also a very witty book, containing many dry observations on both the Chinese and the foreigners. Fleming neither spares the clowns nor over-embellishes the heroes. He was a soldier of distinction himself and his own military record gave him the right to condemn the cowards and doff his hat to the brave.

It is futile to pretend that Fleming was not affected by the prejudices of his day. Though he is knowledgeable about the Chinese, he lacks sympathy for them. He shows compassion for the plight of the Chinese Christian converts, but passes no judgement on the rationing in the latter days of the Siege, when the converts nearly starved whilst the foreigners and their families survived tolerably well on a diet of horse-meat, rice and champagne. He lists no unusual cases of dash on the part of the Chinese besiegers, evidently sharing the contempt in which most foreigners held them. When Chinese soldiers show cowardice he accepts it as typical; when a Western diplomat shows equivalent cowardice, Fleming belittles him, as though assuming that bravery should be the prerogative of the Occidental.

Fleming shows particular disgust at the conduct of the French Minister, the Jonah of the entire operation. But he marvels at the courage and determination of a few dozen French and Italian fighting men under the command of a heroic young Breton lieutenant at the Beitang Cathedral, where they miraculously protected their bishop and priests, together with hundreds of Chinese converts, most of whom were schoolgirls.

# INTRODUCTION

Seeking an explanation of the Siege of the Legations, Fleming confesses that he has drawn a blank. There are plenty of hypotheses, none of them fully convincing. The key question remains: why did the Chinese Government not press home the attacks with artillery (as they could easily have done), but instead gave the impression of not really wanting the hated foreigners to be slaughtered after all? (The Empress Dowager and the Tsungli Yamen sent solicitous messages enquiring whether the ladies and gentlemen were not suffering unduly from the heat, and there is no sign that this was meant sarcastically.) Why kill and maim a hundred or two, rather than wipe them out, together with the even more hated Chinese converts? Certainly, the results of the way the affair was handled were disastrous for China and the dynasty, and it is in some ways surprising that the republican revolution did not take place earlier than 1911.

DAVID BONAVIA

# THE SIEGE AT PEKING

# THE SIEGE AT PEKING

## Peter Fleming

RUPERT HART-DAVIS
SOHO SQUARE LONDON
1959

To
**RUPERT  HART-DAVIS**
my old friend

**ERRATUM**

For *Hsia Kuo Men* (Chapter Thirteen *passim*) read *Sha K'ou Men*

# Contents

# Illustrations

# ILLUSTRATIONS

# MAPS

*Drawn by K. C. Jordan*

# Foreword

'IN view of the tremendous interests involved,' wrote a leading American missionary when the Siege was over, 'it is very unlikely that mankind will venture to forget its experiences in the Chinese Empire during the closing year of the nineteenth century.' His cautious prophecy has hardly been fulfilled. The Boxer Rising is one of those episodes in history—like, for instance, the Boston Teaparty and the Black Hole of Calcutta— which we all remember to have occurred. Their picturesque qualities, acting as a preservative, have converted them into part of the iron rations of general knowledge which everyone carries in his head.

But not even the best iron rations improve with keeping. Should we have cause to reappraise our memories of these events, we are apt to find that almost everything about them that was not unforgettable has been forgotten.

At Boston tea-chests were thrown into the harbour; at Calcutta Europeans were barbarously imprisoned. But by whom? Why? When? What happened afterwards? An enviable few can reel off all the answers; the rest can only maintain that it was once within their power to do so.

So it is—or so I suspect it to be—with the Boxer Rising. The foreign Legations in Peking were besieged; the people in them were rescued by an international force; there was a great deal of looting. That much almost everybody remembers. But who the Boxers were, and why these things happened, and when, many people have quite forgotten and some perhaps never clearly understood.

Yet it all took place less than sixty years ago. Survivors of the Siege are still scattered thinly over the world. In 1950 about thirty of them met in London to celebrate the fiftieth anniversary of the Relief. In Peking there must be old men alive who, as striplings, donned the fantastic uniforms of the Imperial Army, manned the enclosing barricades, and emptied their Mausers or Mannlichers at the loopholes behind which the detested foreigners stubbornly held out.

The diplomatic representatives of eleven countries were besieged in the Legations; the armed forces of eight took part in their relief. As a glance at the bibliography will show, neither the besieged nor their rescuers were backward in writing accounts of their experiences; in addition to the published recollections of private individuals, the Ministers, the Admirals and the Generals compiled their official despatches; and from the archives of the Manchu Dynasty and other vernacular sources it is today possible to reconstruct the strange sequence of events in the Chinese camp.

The participants in this affair fall into three main categories: the besieged, their assailants, the relief forces. There was no wireless in 1900, and all the relevant telegraph lines were destroyed at an early stage. Each category was thus insulated from the other two and had only a vague—often a wholly erroneous—idea of what they were doing and why they were doing it. Each category left copious records. Virtually all were written immediately after, or even during, the events which they describe. We are left with the numerous pieces of a large jigsaw puzzle which has never been put together.

The purpose of this book is, by assembling all these pieces, to show a picture which has not been seen before. It can scarcely be presumptuous to claim that the picture is an extraordinary one, for it was bound to be so; but I should like, with due diffidence, to claim for it a general accuracy. Just as in a jigsaw puzzle many blue bits of different shapes and sizes go to make up the sky, many green bits the grass, so my narrative has been formed by fitting together the testimony of many eye-witnesses of the same events, many authorities on the same subject.

# FOREWORD

Where divergent viewpoints have produced a conflict of evidence, I have done my best to resolve the conflict fairly, in favour of the truth; and I have nowhere been under the temptation to dramatise the story of events which are dramatic enough in themselves.

I must acknowledge, with regret, my failure through linguistic disability to study Japanese sources; for the same reason I have been able to read only such Russian material—it is not much—as has been translated into English or French. I have on the other hand been lucky in gaining access to two very valuable sets of unpublished documents—the miscellaneous private papers of Sir Claude MacDonald, the British Minister in Peking who assumed the duties of Commander-in-Chief during the Siege, and the diary kept by Dr G. E. Morrison, *The Times* Correspondent, who took a leading part in the defence of the Legations.

I have given sparse references in footnotes for my quotations from published and unpublished sources. In a book intended for the general reader the proliferation of *op. cit.* and *ibid.* at the foot of the page is a tiresome and unnecessary distraction. Nor would it here be of much value to the specialist. To pinpoint references to private papers which have not been catalogued is impossible. Many of the published works (virtually all now out of print) to which I refer appeared in more than one edition, many of the editions were revised, and sometimes the title was changed. I have therefore used my own judgment in this matter, burdening the text only with such references as it seemed to me the reader's curiosity might demand, or my debt to a particular source exact.

It remains only for me to hope that from his contemplation of the completed jigsaw the reader will derive some part at least of the interest and enjoyment which I have found in putting it together.

PETER FLEMING

*Nettlebed, Oxfordshire,* 1959.

# Acknowledgments

A BIBLIOGRAPHY of published sources will be found at the end of the book. For granting me access to unpublished material I am indebted to the following:

Miss Stella MacDonald, younger daughter of the late Sir Claude MacDonald, GCMG, KCB, for placing at my disposal her father's personal papers.

The Trustees of the Mitchell Library, Sydney, New South Wales, for allowing me to see Dr G. E. Morrison's diary for the period May to October 1900.

Mrs M. L. Poole, widow of the late Lt-Colonel F. G. Poole, DSO, OBE, the Middlesex Regiment, for lending me the diaries kept by her husband and his brother, Dr Wordsworth Poole.

Mrs Violet Garnons Williams for lending me the diary of her mother, the late Mrs B. G. Tours.

Besides these, several survivors or descendants of survivors have kindly provided me with a miscellany of documents and photographs. To all of them I am most grateful.

I am indebted for a variety of kindnesses to Mr Duncan Wilson, CMG, HM Chargé d'Affaires in Peking: to Mr C. C. Parrott, CMG, OBE, and the staff of the Foreign Office Library: to Mr J. S. Maywood, head of *The Times* Intelligence Department: to Brigadier-General Samuel B. Griffith II (retd.) and Colonel R. D. Heinl, Jr., of the United States Marine Corps; and to Captain Robert Asprey.

I would also like to thank Mrs Joan St George Saunders, of Writers' and Speakers' Research, for her patience, ingenuity and resource, and Miss Barbara Bellamy for her services at the typewriter.

# CHAPTER ONE

# The Ostriches

*A characteristic of foreign communities in Eastern lands is their incredulity concerning the danger of an attack from the population among which they live.*

Daniele Varè: *The Last of the Empresses.*

ON the evening of 24 May 1900 Queen Victoria's eighty-first, and last, birthday was celebrated in the British Legation at Peking. Her Minister at the Manchu Court, Sir Claude Mac-Donald, entertained the British community to dinner; he was a tall, thin, canny man of forty-eight, with a Highlander's narrow head, Ouidan moustaches, and serious, faintly censorious eyes. There were some sixty guests, the gentlemen outnumbering the ladies by two to one. The meal was served in a small theatre which, like the adjacent fives-court, provided solace and distraction in the long cold winter months.

After dinner there was dancing on the tennis-court. To this guests from the ten other Legations had been invited, and soon a cosmopolitan throng was waltzing, gossiping or drinking champagne by the soft warm light of paper lanterns which hung from the branches of the trees. Music was dispensed by a Chinese band under a Portuguese conductor. It had been lent for the occasion to Lady MacDonald by the Inspector-General of the Imperial Maritime Customs, an elderly Irish bachelor called Robert Hart, whose administrative achievements in China his Queen had acknowledged by a baronetcy. Sir Robert Hart had lived in China for forty-six years, during which time he had paid only two short visits to Europe. His band, whose members he himself had trained in the use of their unfamiliar Western instruments, made an important contribution to the amenities of life on Legation Street, where it gave weekly concerts in the Customs compound. Rightly, though for the wrong reasons, most of Sir Claude MacDonald's guests did not expect to hear it perform again for some months. The *soirée* at the British Legation, wrote the Peking Correspondent of the *North China Daily News*, 'practically ends our cool season.' Soon a dry, oppressive heat would lie over the North China plain. Peking society was preparing for its annual migration to the beaches at Peitaiho and Weihaiwei or to the Western Hills, fifteen miles away, where the diplomats and their families would pass the insalubrious season in temples converted into villas. Those few obliged to stay behind in the foetid sweltering capital and, as they put it, 'hold the fort' were the objects of sympathy or chaff.

The number of foreign residents in Peking was probably about five hundred. They did not however form a single compact community in either the topographical or the social sense, as did foreigners living, behind the deer-fence of extra-territoriality, in the settlements and concessions of the Treaty Ports. They comprised three separate microcosms, tenuously related to each other.

About half of them were missionaries, whose lives centred round cathedrals, churches, chapels, hospitals, dispensaries, orphanages and schools scattered widely over the rectilinear network of grey streets enclosed by the huge walls of the Tartar City.* Physically isolated from each other and from the Legations, the missionaries were yet more decisively sundered by the doctrinal gulf fixed between the Roman Catholics and the various Protestant denominations; across this gulf social contacts, though not invariably held inadmissible, were always

---

* Peking (of which there is a plan on p. 18) comprised the Tartar City and the Chinese City; the southern wall of the first formed the northern boundary of the second. In the centre of the Tartar City stood the Imperial City, which in its turn enclosed the Forbidden City; this was not really a city but a great walled pleasaunce in which the Winter Palace was the principal building.

Legation Street in 1900: a party of foreigners on Mongol ponies, with outriders and grooms

The Grandstand on the Peking Racecourse, summer 1899
A scene during the visit of Prince Henry of Prussia, who is seen in the centre of the picture

rare. So there were in effect two missionary bodies, not one; for the Deity whom both adored, the godless Chinese, puzzled but accommodating, were at this period being taught no less than five different names.*

The third, secular, microcosm revolved round the Diplomatic Corps. In 1900 the Legation Quarter did not exist as such; it was the events of that year which brought into being the semi-citadel, self-contained and self-administered, in which the foreign envoys, their staffs and their military guards resided for the next three and a half decades, and in which, though control of its affairs was handed back to the Chinese Government in 1945, a third of them still reside today.

In Peking, as in other Oriental cities, custom had always favoured the concentration of crafts and trades in particular localities; the silversmiths were to be found in one street, the saddlers in another, the jewellers in a third. This principle, reinforced by the Manchu Court's wish to facilitate surveillance and control of the barbarians, had been followed with the diplomats. The eleven Legations (they were those of America, Austria-Hungary, Belgium, Great Britain, France, Germany, Holland, Italy, Japan, Russia and Spain) occupied an enclave roughly three-quarters of a mile square. It was bounded on the south by the crenellated wall of the Tartar City, forty feet high and more than forty feet thick; on the north and west by the equally high but slightly less minatory wall of the Imperial City, coloured pink and crowned with yellow tiles; and on the east by the great thoroughfare to which the Ha Ta Men † gave access through the Tartar Wall. It was roughly bisected by a shallow canal running north and south.

---

* The conception of a Supreme Deity was, before the advent of Christianity, already embodied in two separate Chinese words, the rarer being used only by the Moslem minority. The Jesuits coined a third and the earliest Protestants a fourth; but as rival Protestant denominations entered the field fresh names for the object of their faith had to be invented to differentiate their brands of Christianity from those of their rivals. The delicate and confused problems thus created were known in missionary circles as the Term Question.
† *Men* means gate.

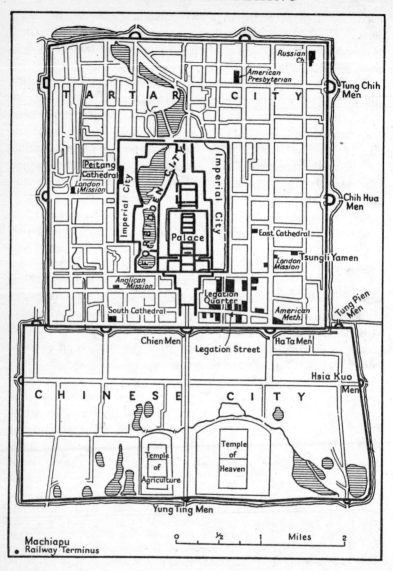

Alongside the Legations a number of other foreign enterprises and concerns had established themselves. The Hongkong
and Shanghai Bank, the Russo-Chinese Bank and the offices

of Jardine Matheson formed part of the enclave; there were
two shops, Imbeck's and Kierulff's; a resourceful Swiss named
Chamot managed, with the help of his American wife, the Peking
Hotel; there was the inevitable club. Foreign employees of the
Post Office and the Customs and a few teachers at the newly-
founded University swelled the small community of exiles.

A certain unreality is inherent in the social life of diplomats.
This is enhanced when, as in Peking, they form the predominant
element in a small expatriate community whose members are
insulated from all save the most formal contacts with the native
population. The very expression 'diplomatic corps,' with its
undertones of solidarity, has an ironic ring, and conveys a
wholly inadequate notion of the cross-currents of rivalry and
distrust which in 1900 animated the representatives of the
Powers in China.

It is true that M. de Giers, the Russian Minister, shared
with his French colleague a partial and precarious identity of
purpose (to which in the matter of one railway concession
M. Joostens, the Belgian Minister, also adhered). It is true that
Sir Claude MacDonald had no cause to view the Japanese
with the profound suspicion which they aroused in M. de Giers,
and that from the American Legation Mr Conger, whose
Government had no designs on Chinese territory and only small
commercial interests to further or safeguard, could afford to
survey with lofty disapproval the symptoms of European
rapacity. In general, nevertheless, behind their outward show
of comity and despite the close entwinement of their social
lives, the basic attitude to each other of the foreign envoys in
Peking differed in few essentials from the relationship between
gold-prospectors in a Klondyke saloon. Their vigilance was
stimulated and their suspicions were nourished by surmise, by
rumour, by probability, and not infrequently by fact.

The old hands lamented the old days. Since, five years
earlier, China's humiliating and unexpected defeat by Japan
had revealed the true extent of her weakness, the small diplomatic world of Peking had been transformed from a backwater

into a cockpit. 'Peking,' wrote one observer,* 'has never been what it was before the Japanese war. In the old days we were all something of a happy family. There were merely the eleven Legations, the Inspectorate of Chinese Customs . . . and perhaps a few favoured globe-trotters or nondescripts looking for rich concessions. Picnics and dinners, races and excursions, were the order of the day, and politics and political situations were not burning. Ministers Plenipotentiary and Envoys Extraordinary wore Terai hats, very old clothes, and had an affable air—something like what Teheran must still be. By 1900,' he went on, 'there were always ominous reports . . . of great things being done secretly.'

A remarkable series of 'great things' had been done, secretly and otherwise, by the Powers between 1894 and 1900; the following chapter contains an account of them.

Such, then, was the texture of the cosmopolitan society whose leading members gathered on 24 May to drink the health of the octogenarian queen who, at Balmoral, was enjoying 'some nice music after dinner' and who possibly derived even

* B. L. Simpson. Under the pen-name of B. L. Putnam Weale he wrote a number of books on Far Eastern affairs, and notably *Indiscreet Letters from Peking* (1906). This strange, rather odious work purports to describe the Siege of the Legations through the eyes of an anonymous diplomat. Though perfunctorily maintained, the pretence that he is relating experiences other than his own gives the author a dramatic licence to 'slant' his narrative for the purposes of indirect self-glorification or hostile innuendo against those individuals—and they were many—whom he wishes to criticise. The book enjoyed a *succès de scandale*. Although irredeemably tainted as a source of facts, Putnam Weale can be followed, with caution, as a guide to the atmosphere of the period.

Simpson was employed in the Chinese Customs Service. In a despatch written immediately after the Relief of the Legations, the British Minister included Simpson's name, with eight others, in a list of Customs employees whose conduct deserved commendation. During the Allied occupation of Peking, however, Simpson went in for organised looting on a scale open only to those who could speak Chinese. Sir Claude MacDonald issued a warrant for his arrest. This was counter-signed by the Commander-in-Chief of the British forces but was never executed because Simpson was operating outside the sector of Peking garrisoned by the British. (*MacDonald Papers*, hereafter referred to in footnotes as M.P.) After a stormy and equivocal career Simpson was assassinated by Chinese political agents in Tientsin in 1930.

greater pleasure from the fact that six men had to be sent to assist the two local telegraphists to deal with a spate of birthday greetings.

It is tempting, and would on the evidence of the preceding weeks be logical, to imply that this outwardly carefree gathering was clouded, if not by a sense of doom, at least by grave misgivings. The known facts present a less haggard but a more surprising picture.

Sir Claude MacDonald and his staff accepted from their *chers collègues* congratulations on the relief of Mafeking; this had been effected a week earlier after a siege lasting seven months. That they themselves would shortly be subjected to an ordeal in comparison with which Mafeking's would seem commonplace occurred to nobody.

There was however a good deal of talk about the rebels known as Boxers, who had been sporadically active in North China for two years and whose latest outbreaks, directed at this stage mainly against Chinese converts to Christianity, had been reported from places uncomfortably close to the capital. Among the British Minister's guests interest centred chiefly on a reported rift in the Corps Diplomatique; this had been caused by disagreement about the measures to be taken in a situation which some of its members viewed more gravely than others.

The Corps Diplomatique was the title formally assumed by the heads of the eleven foreign missions when they met in council. One of these periodical meetings had taken place four days earlier; although its proceedings were in theory confidential, everybody knew that a proposal to send to Tientsin for naval detachments to guard the Legations in case of trouble had been rejected after an acrimonious discussion. The French Minister, it was understood, had been the chief advocate of this precaution, which had been taken with excellent effect when in October 1898 minor anti-foreign disturbances occurred in Peking after the deposition of the Emperor Kuang Hsü by his aunt the Empress Dowager. M. Pichon's early departure (which he was at no pains to make unostentatious) from the festivities at the British Legation stimulated the flow of speculation about the clash of ministerial views and personalities; but when, later, Sir Claude's other guests were carried homeward in their sedan chairs through the straight, silent, empty streets, few saw in this pother about the guards anything more than yet another storm in the diplomatic tea-cup. 'Nobody worries much about the Boxer stories,' a journalist wrote to his paper in Shanghai next day. Six weeks later, when nothing had been heard of the foreigners in Peking for a month and the worst was feared, *The Times* found worthy of comment the fact that up to 24 May private correspondence from Peking reflected 'no premonition of the storm which was so soon to burst;' one long letter from a senior Customs official (probably Sir Robert Hart) had contained no reference to the Boxers.

As the last guests went home, dawn began to break over the great parched plain. In the British Legation the golden lanterns paled; the auspicious characters painted on them became less easy to decipher.

It was to be another cloudless day. There had been no rain at all that spring, and throughout North China no corn had been sown. In a despatch to the Marquess of Salisbury, reporting the outcome of the conference at which it had been decided not to send for guards, the British Minister had written on 21 May: 'I am now convinced that a few days' heavy rainfall, to terminate the long-continued drought which has helped largely to excite unrest in the country districts, would do more to restore tranquillity than any measures which either the Chinese Government or foreign Governments can take.'

It was a conviction which reflected more credit on Sir Claude's imperturbability than on his political acumen; 'he possesses as little wisdom as judgment,' Morrison, who liked him, wrote in his diary on 13 July. It needed more than a cloudburst to quench the fires banked round Peking. And the drought, in any case, was not broken for another five weeks. By then it was painfully clear—and this the diplomats can hardly be blamed for failing to foresee—that the Chinese Government was not interested in the restoration of tranquillity.

CHAPTER TWO

# The Vultures

*The Celestial Kingdom itself had been too devoid of organisation, coherence and solidarity even to possess, let alone enforce, a collective will. But the encroachment of the Powers upon the Chinese State, the extensive diminutions of Chinese Sovereignty, the extraordinary concessions that had been wrung from China on the most unreasonable pretexts, the de jure privileges and the de facto abuses of extraterritoriality, the special position of the foreign missionary and of the native converts to Christianity— they all gave to large groups in these vast regions the common bond of a fierce resentment at common grievances which developed into a venomous hatred of everything foreign, and resulted in the Boxer Rising of 1900.*

Philip Joseph: *Foreign Diplomacy in China, 1894–1900.*

THE Boxer Rising was a spontaneous, semi-clandestine popular movement which began in 1898 among the sturdy peasantry of Shantung, smouldered across the border into the metropolitan province of Chihli, and in the early summer of 1900 burst into a conflagration from whose savage heat the world flinched back in dismay.

Yet, though the movement was purely indigenous, we must seek its ultimate causes in the chanceries of Europe. It was not to right their own wrongs, grievous though these were, that the peasants of North China took up their swords and spears and muskets, but to put an end to the spoliation of their country by the *yang kuei-tzu*, the foreign devils, the barbarians from without. Their Manchu rulers, besides being oppressive, extortionate and inept, were themselves aliens; but the Boxer watchword was '*Protect the Ch'ing dynasty. Exterminate the foreigners.*' It was to this slogan that the masses rallied; and it was their espousal of a primarily xenophobe cause which earned

23

the rebels, first, immunity from suppression and, later, the open support of the Imperial authorities in their bloody crusade.

The Boxer Rising and the Peking Court's connivance at it can be understood only in the light of actions taken by the European Powers and by Japan over the previous sixty years. These actions, and the virtual certainty that sequels to them impended, had placed the Chinese Government in an intolerable position and had opened its mind to counsels of frenzy and despair.

At the end of the nineteenth century anti-foreign feeling in China stemmed from two main causes. One was the conduct of the foreigners, which was often deplorable and always open to misconstruction; the other was the policy of the Manchu Dynasty, which was deluded and out of date.

When in 1644 the Manchus swept down over the Great Wall and ousted the Mings, China had little experience of, and no regular contacts with, the outside world. Her inbred contempt for it was founded partly on pride of race and partly on her acquaintance with the primitive, often aboriginal tribes who— to the north in deserts, to the west in mountains, and to the south in jungles and islands—formed a fringe round her extensive frontiers.

The Chinese, however, are by nature curious, tolerant and hospitable; and their commercial instincts are highly developed. Down the centuries these attributes had led to spasmodic but on the whole auspicious exchanges with younger civilisations. There had been a trickle of trade with the Roman Empire. A Chinese army had marched to the Caspian. From India the doctrines of Buddhism had been welcomed and characteristically adapted to suit the national temperament. The Moslem faith had taken root in the north-western provinces, and the Jesuits had won respect in Peking. Marco Polo, after seventeen years in Kublai Khan's service, was only with great reluctance permitted to depart. Despite difficulties over the protocol of the kowtow, European envoys had had audience of Ming Emperors.

# THE VULTURES

Along the coast, it is true, the barbarians had behaved with barbarity. From the early sixteenth century small parties of European adventurers inflicted on the Chinese colossus pinpricks which were not forgotten; the Dutch were a particularly alarming race, with feet one cubit and two-tenths long, and a Spanish embassy of twenty-three men had to be tortured to death as a reprisal for outrages committed by their countrymen. It cannot however be said that Chinese history before 1644 foreshadows the deliberate isolationism in which for the next two centuries the country was plunged.

It was the instinctive, unwavering aim of Manchu statecraft to keep the people in purdah. The analogy between this policy and that of contemporary Soviet Russia is unwittingly brought out by Clements, writing in 1915: 'The Manchurian conquerors of one of the most favoured regions of the globe were not slow in realising that, being relatively few in numbers, it was to their interest, as overlords of an intelligent and law-abiding though passive race constituting one-fourth of the world family, to interdict all efforts at change, to seal the country so that a repetition of their own exploit, or disaffection with their own rule resulting from outside influences, would be impossible.' *

Thus the fact, for instance, that until 1842 the only part of the Chinese Empire on which foreign merchants were permitted to set foot—and then only between October and March —was a plot of land on the Canton waterfront measuring 1100 by 700 feet was not due to bitter memories of excesses committed by foreigners in the past. It was the expression of a two-hundred-years-old policy which would have been in force however impeccably Western merchants and seamen had conducted themselves on their visits to China.

This policy was bound to fail in the long run. Under the Manchus the whole structure of Chinese society was an anachronism, which as time went on became increasingly ill-qualified to survive outside the vacuum in which the dynasty strove, against increasing difficulties, to preserve it. Forces were

* Paul H. Clements: *The Boxer Rebellion.*

25

at work which, one day, could not but make it impossible for China to live any longer in a world of her own. In 1842 those forces made their first decisive impact on this huge, mysterious land whose riches were a legend and whose strength was a fable.

In that year Britain defeated China in the Opium War. Although embarked on under severe provocation, this war was by any standards a discreditable affair, for the British were fighting to protect an illegitimate and shameful traffic; that opium-smuggling would never have become a major British interest if China had allowed foreign merchants to trade in the ordinary, legitimate ways is probable but beside the point. By the Treaty of Nanking China ceded to Britain the barren islet of Hongkong, paid a swingeing indemnity, removed the most vexatious restrictions on commerce at Canton, opened four other ports to trade and granted foreigners the right to reside in them. 'It is impossible to exaggerate the importance of this treaty, which was a turning-point in the relations between China and the West.' * Europe had got a toe in the door which had been closed against her for so long.

A couple of years later America got hers in, too, with the Treaty of Wanghia. This instrument was negotiated, not imposed by force, and involved China in no territorial concession; it wears thus a more virtuous aspect than the Treaty of Nanking. But it would never have been concluded if Britain had not fought and won the Opium War. If American idealism was quick to condemn the imperialists for summarily shaking the tree, American opportunism was not behindhand in picking up the fruit.

The purpose of this book is to record and interpret the events of a few crowded weeks in the summer of 1900, and I can here do no more than tabulate the long sequence of aggressions committed on China by the Powers in the preceding decades, without some knowledge of which the frantic attempt to mass-

* Henri Cordier: *Histoire des Relations de la Chine avec les Puissances Occidentales.*

acre their representatives in Peking cannot be seen in its true perspective.

In 1858 Russia seized vast territories north of the Amur.

In 1860 Britain and France, alleging—correctly—that China had violated the Treaty of Tientsin (1858), stormed the Taku Forts at the mouth of the North River and took Peking, where the Summer Palace was razed as a reprisal for Chinese brutality to envoys captured under a flag of truce. China was forced to grant Britain a ninety-nine-year lease of Kowloon, on the mainland opposite Hongkong.

In 1862 Portugal was confirmed in her occupation of Macao.

In 1862 France occupied a large part of Annam.

In 1862 Britain annexed Lower Burma.

In 1867 France annexed three provinces of Lower Cochin-China and gained control of the Mekong basin.

In 1871 Russia occupied Ili, a big tract of territory in Chinese Turkestan.

In 1879 Japan took the Liuchiu Islands.

In 1880 Russia, in return for a massive indemnity, handed back part but not the whole of Ili.

In 1886 Britain annexed Upper Burma.

In 1887 the whole of Annam, Cochin-China and Cambodia were sequestered to form French Indo-China, with a population of 18,000,000.

Impressive though it is, this list is incomplete, for it records only the most striking violations of Chinese sovereignty. During the same period an endless series of treaties, in theory negotiated, in effect dictated, secured for the lesser as well as for the leading Powers a wide range of privileges and concessions. The Celestial Kingdom had become a Tom Tiddler's Ground.

As the century drew to its close there were signs that the tempo of outright territorial exactions was slowing down. All the Powers (save Japan, whose designs on Korea and Formosa remained high on her agenda) had more pressing pre-occupations nearer home. Their rivalries in China, where their

interests were luxuries rather than necessities, had reached a
point beyond which it behoved them to step warily for fear of
provoking an internecine clash. They were moreover obsessed
with a vague, almost superstitious fear of their victim, so vast,
so populous, so overweening even in adversity.

These inhibitions were largely dispelled by the Sino-Japanese
War of 1894–95. China's crushing defeat by her small neigh-
bour revived the flagging cupidity of Europe. As one authority
has put it: 'The Balkan scramble over and the partition of
Africa nearly complete, the disclosure of China's weakness by
Japan served as an invitation to the colonizing Powers to stake
their claims in China.'* And it was not only greed that impelled each Power to grab, but the fear that, if she held back,
others less scrupulous might unduly advantage themselves; for
it was now almost universally believed that it was China's
destiny to be carved up, as Africa had been. The competition
became keener than ever.

By 1895 most of its outlying dependencies had been lopped off
the Chinese Empire. Manchuria, across which Russian engineers were pioneering a railway which would link the Trans-
Siberian line with Vladivostok, was still ruled from Peking by
the dynasty whose homeland it was, and Chinese suzerainty
over Tibet had not yet been directly challenged; but the events
of the past sixty years had sharply contracted China's frontiers.
She now marched with Russian territory for 5000 miles, with
British territory for about half that distance, and with French
territory for 700 miles. The age of supercilious isolation was at
an end. 'It is an unprecedented situation in the history of more
than three thousand years,' wrote Li Hung-chang, the leading,
if not indeed the only, Chinese statesman of the period.

For a variety of motives, none of them creditable, Russia,
France and Germany combined to deny Japan the full fruits of
her victory over China. Russia, who throughout the period was
at some pains to cloak her policies in an aura of benevolence,
granted China on generous terms a loan with which she was
able to pay half the war-indemnity to Japan. In return Russia

* Joseph.

28

gained a number of valuable economic concessions. In 1896 she attempted further to improve her position, especially in Manchuria, by a secret agreement known as the Cassini Convention.* But the news leaked, and Russia's rivals, apprised of the far-reaching benefits which she stood to obtain, raised such a hullaballoo that both signatories of the Convention were constrained to deny its existence.

France exacted her *quid pro quo* by redrawing in her own favour various disputed sections of the Annamite frontier, where China had to open three new 'Treaty Ports' † and lower certain transit dues.

It was however Germany who, by seizing the port of Kiaochow in Shantung, supplied what had been justly called 'not the sole but the principal cause' ‡ of the Boxer Rising and its sponsorship by the central authorities. The lease of Kiaochow to Russia was understood to have been provided for in the Cassini Convention, and when, in 1897, the murder of two German missionaries in a nearby part of the interior supplied a convenient pretext, the Kaiser struck at once, 'instead,' as *The Times* of 16 November 1897 wistfully noted, 'of wasting time making remonstrances at Peking, which would assuredly have been met as usual by the innumerable dilatory devices of Chinese diplomacy.' By her *coup de main* Germany gained a ninety-nine years' lease of Kiaochow Bay and the city of Tsingtao, an indemnity for the two heaven-sent martyrs, and extensive railway and mining concessions in Shantung. The Boxers made their first appearance in that province a few months later.

In her rivals Germany's peremptory action aroused a mortified envy. 'The experiment,' wrote *The Times*, whose clinical

---

* Cassini was the name of the Russian Minister in Peking.

† Treaty Ports—i.e. places where foreign merchants were permitted to reside and trade—were not necessarily coastal or riverine cities. As time went on several were established on China's landward frontiers, and the Maritime Customs had on its pay-roll many 'tide-waiters' (as certain subordinate officials were called) who had never seen salt water and performed their duties several thousand feet above sea-level.

‡ Cordier.

choice of a word to describe this violent and high-handed act epitomises the European attitude to China, 'is one which we ourselves have tried on one or more occasions, with results so excellent as compared with any obtainable by diplomatic negotiation that there is reason to wonder why we do not always follow the more effectual method.' Russia, discountenanced by the Cassini affair and forestalled at Kiaochow by Germany, quickly took up the running. Demands were served on China for the lease of Port Arthur and Dairen and the construction of a railway which would link both places with the Trans-Siberian system. China, encouraged by Britain, tried evasive tactics. Russia's reaction was an ultimatum; if her requirements were not met by 27 March 1898 she would 'take hostile measures.' China gave in.

In the following month France, Russia's ally, demanded among other things the important anchorage of Kwangchouwan in the extreme south of China. Following the German precedent she put a force ashore. The decapitation of two sailors during the landing operations gave her, belatedly, martyrs to avenge, and the subsequent murder of a missionary enlarged the scope and the importunacy of her requisitions on Peking. By June 1898, besides securing a valuable naval base and important railway concessions, she had pegged out a 'sphere of influence' covering the three provinces of Kwantung, Kwangsi and Yunnan and the island of Hainan; her right to this sphere was based on a Chinese undertaking not to alienate any part of it to another Power.

Spheres of influence were now all the rage. Germany claimed exclusive privileges in Shantung, Russia in Manchuria, Japan in Fukien (opposite Formosa, which had come to her as the spoils of war) and Britain in the Yangtse valley. In all, thirteen out of the eighteen provinces of China were pre-empted in this way, as well as the three provinces of Manchuria. Into the greater part of these vast territories no representative of their putative lessees or suzerains had ever penetrated; but although within them the Powers' rights were shadowy and in the last analysis unenforceable, sharp rivalries sprang up as the Euro-

Foreign 'Spheres of Influence' in China, c. 1900.
(From a map widely reproduced at the time.)

pean nations forced the moribund dynasty to write codicil after codicil into its will. France's stake in Yunnan conflicted with British interests in Upper Burma; a nominally Belgian railway concession threatened to bisect the British Yangtse sphere with a line of which France and Russia, who had in fact financed it, would be the effective controllers; Japan watched in a glum silence the steady progress of Russian aspirations in Manchuria. As for China, she could do little but sign, again and again, upon the dotted line.

Britain, who had set the whole unbecoming process in motion half a century earlier, was no longer leading when the runners came up the straight. Once the requirements of her naval strategy were satisfied at Hongkong, her interests in China, of whose foreign trade she handled over sixty per cent, were essentially commercial; she disliked the idea of a partitioned China, not from motives of altruism but because she instinctively feared its effects on the balance of power. However, just as Germany's seizure of Kiaochow had sparked off Russia's occupation of Port Arthur, the establishment of German and Russian naval bases in North China was a development which she could not view with passive unconcern. When the Japanese evacuated Weihaiwei under the terms of the Chefoo Convention, Britain pressed for, and inevitably obtained, a lease of the place. She did so in a rather shamefaced manner, for a short time before she had declined Peking's offer of this port on the grounds that she 'aimed at discouraging any alienation of Chinese territory' as long as other Powers practised a similar abstinence; and she took over Weihaiwei with a verbal promise that she would 'give it up tomorrow' if Russia gave up Port Arthur.

Writing in 1928, a thoughtful student of the period recorded his opinion that 'one is forced to conclude on the present available evidence that throughout the 1894–1900 crisis the conduct of the British Government coincided more completely with the best interests of China than did that of any other Power.' * If for 'coincided more completely with' were

* Joseph.

substituted 'outraged less flagrantly,' this verdict could be allowed to stand.

The cumulative effect of these encroachments, following each other pell-mell on the heels of a major defeat in war and making their successive impacts in the short space of five years, would have driven any ordinary Government, even if it was constitutionally irremovable, into a state of distraction. But the Manchu Court was not an ordinary Government. It was dominated by the strong, capricious will of the Empress Dowager, who deposed her nephew, the Emperor Kuang Hsü, in September 1898. Her overt resumption of supreme power as Regent ended a short interlude of higgledy-piggledy reform (known as The Hundred Days) during which the weakling Emperor and his progressive associates sought to strengthen China by a process of overnight Westernisation. The reactionaries, back in the saddle, embodied all that was worst in the traditions of the ruling class, whether Manchu or Chinese. Orgulous, corrupt, ignorant and fantastical, ridden by absurd protocols and blinded by infantile superstitions, the hierarchy who controlled China's destinies in this hour of crisis were wholly incapable of facing realistically, let alone of averting, the mortal dangers which beset their country. Down the years the high-flown language of contemporary Edicts and Memorials echoes the pompous futility of turkeys gobbling at the rumble of distant thunder.*

With this outlook prevailing at Peking, it is perhaps not surprising that China's single diplomatic success during the period should have gone to her head. In 1899 Italy, actuated almost as much by the wish to be modish as by pure greed, demanded the lease of San Men Bay in Chekiang, one of the only five remaining provinces for which nobody had as yet made a bid.

* Cf. Valentine Chirol, the Foreign Editor of *The Times*: 'A more hopeless spectacle of fatuous imbecility, made up in equal parts of arrogance and helplessness, than the central Government of the Chinese Empire presented after the actual pressure of war [with Japan] had been removed, it is impossible to conceive.' (*The Far Eastern Question*.)

Italy's naval forces in the Far East were not impressive; Peking rejected her demand. The dilettante aggressor essayed an ultimatum. When this was ignored, she had second thoughts about the project, from which she extricated herself by recalling her Minister from Peking on the grounds that he had exceeded his instructions.

A square meal may have serious consequences for a starving man, and this small but undeniable success revived all China's most dangerous illusions about her innate superiority over the barbarians. 'The results to China were, perhaps, more serious than if the Italian demands had been acceded to.' * 'The rejection of the Italian demands did not impress the European Powers as deeply as it should have done.' † In a series of Edicts the Empress Dowager put an end to appeasement. An extract from that circulated to the Provinces on 21 November 1899 is typical:

> Recently the Viceroys and Governors of the various Provinces, when facing important international events, often had the word 'peace' in their minds with the result that they were not in the least prepared. This persistent habit is the worst kind of disloyalty to the Throne and the worst kind of betrayal of the country. . . . Never should the word 'peace' fall from the mouths of our high officials, nor should they harbour it for a moment in their breasts. With such a country as ours, with her vast area stretching out for several tens of thousands of *li*, her immense natural resources and her several hundreds of millions of inhabitants, if all would prove their loyalty to their Emperor ‡ and love of their country, what indeed is there to fear from any strong invader?

The idea of resistance to the foreign Powers, and the delusion that it could be successful, had simultaneously obsessed the

---

* Arthur H. Smith: *China in Convulsion.*
† William L. Langer: *The Diplomacy of Imperialism, 1890–1902.*
‡ For constitutional reasons, his aunt always issued Edicts in the name of the Emperor whom she had deposed.

minds of the country's rulers. And this occurred at a time when, within a short distance of the capital, there was coming into prominence a powerful and rapidly expanding organisation of armed fanatics, vowing loyalty to the Throne and death to the alien intruders. Already the foreign envoys were demanding that the Boxers be suppressed. To do so would be a difficult and highly invidious task; its completion—necessarily by violent means—might in those tense times entail grave consequences for the Manchu régime.

To the members of this quaint régime, protesting an empty defiance with their backs to the wall, their arsenals ill-stocked and their armies deficient alike in martial ardour and in skill at arms, the Boxers commended themselves by their numbers, by their savage zeal, and by the magic powers which (it was widely believed) conferred on them invulnerability in battle; they had also, by contrast with other sinews of war, the considerable virtue of costing the exchequer nothing.

They were, it could be foreseen, a double-edged weapon; but double-edged weapons are better than none, and no serious attempt was made to subdue or control the Boxer Rising. In less than two years it spread across the hungry North China plain, creeping from village to village as a heath fire creeps through the sere grass between one clump of gorse and the next. By the last week of May 1900 the Boxers were at the gates of Peking.

# CHAPTER THREE

# The White Peril

*The Catholic and Protestant religions being insolent to the gods, and extinguishing sanctity, rendering no obedience to Buddha, and enraging Heaven and Earth, the rain-clouds no longer visit us; but eight million Spirit Soldiers will descend from Heaven and sweep the Empire clean of all foreigners. Then will the gentle showers once more water our lands; and when the tread of soldiers and the clash of steel are heard heralding woes to all our people, then the Buddhist Patriotic League of Boxers will be able to protect the Empire and to bring peace to all its people.*

*Hasten, then, to spread this doctrine far and wide, for if you gain one adherent to the faith your own person will be absolved from all future misfortunes. If you gain five adherents your whole family will be absolved from all evils, and if you gain ten adherents your whole village will be absolved from all calamities. Those who gain no adherents to the cause shall be decapitated, for until all foreigners have been exterminated the rain can never visit us.*

*Those who have been so unfortunate as to have drunk water from wells poisoned by foreigners should at once make use of the following Divine Prescription, the ingredients of which are to be decocted and swallowed, when the poisoned patient will recover:*

> *Dried black plums . . . half an ounce.*
> *Solanum dulcamara . . half an ounce.*
> *Liquorice root . . . . half an ounce.*

From a Boxer Edict, 'issued by the Lord of Wealth and Happiness.'

THE fully-fledged Boxer was a colourful figure, a demon in some Grand Guignol pantomime. But it would be wrong to describe the flummery and hocus-pocus with which he drugged himself, or the atrocious cruelties which he practised, without first trying to explain why he was so ready to join a movement dedicated to the extermination of all foreigners and all Chinese converts to Christianity, even if these latter included neighbours whom in some different crisis he might have risked his life to succour.

In nine cases out of ten the Boxer was a Chinese peasant in fancy dress. More recent rebels in more politically sophisticated states have donned coloured shirts as a symbol of loyalty to their cause; but the Boxer's fancy dress was not merely sartorial. The symptoms of his dedication were more various, and came from greater depths in his nature, than the impulse to wear scarlet finery. He had no Führer, no supreme commander, no figurehead. He had no advantage for himself in view. His battle-cry was '*Sha! Sha!*' ('Kill! Kill!'), yet he was not a bewildered savage in the jungle, but a member of the oldest civilisation in the world. Rites and incantations, trances and cataleptic fits nerved him, before altars hitherto but lackadaisically revered, for the insensate struggle. Why did he so readily take part in it?

The answer can be found only by reading between, or beyond, the lines of the preceding chapter. 'China's troubles' (wrote a wise missionary who, while he withstood the Siege, pondered deeply the events leading up to it) 'came directly through a network of treaties which she did not want, the meshes of which were steadily becoming smaller in size and more closely drawn.' We have seen how this network, with its arbitrary and opportunist design, was imposed on Peking. It is of equal importance to establish how the narrowing mesh affected the small fry; for of these, at its origin, the Boxer Society was almost exclusively composed.

China's population at the end of the nineteenth century has been loosely estimated at 350,000,000. Of this total only a very small fraction had ever set eyes on a foreigner. Almost equally few were those, at the level of society from which the Boxers sprang, who understood the significance of the aggressions committed on their country by the Powers. Yet throughout the land there existed a powder-train of emotional prejudice against the *yang kuei-tzu* to which rumour or agitation could at any moment put a match with dire results. This state of affairs had two main causes. The first was the missionaries; the second was the economic impact of the West on the Chinese economy.

In 1860 the French Government, by virtue of a treaty with the text of which it was suspected of having tampered in the process of translation, secured what amounted to a charter for missionaries. They were granted rights of residence in the interior (at this date the merchants, though permitted to travel inland, were still tethered to domiciles in the Treaty Ports); they were guaranteed protection by the Chinese authorities; and the legality of the Christian religion, which until 1842 had been proscribed, was officially recognised. Though they had been obtained for the benefit of Roman Catholics, these concessions were interpreted as applying to all denominations of the Christian faith.

The consequences were far-reaching. The purely administrative problems involved in grafting the far-flung missionary establishments on to the centres of population which they had chosen as their fields inevitably generated friction and misunderstanding. At first most of the missionaries were ignorant of the Chinese language and Chinese customs; upon the latter they looked with scant sympathy as the expression of a pagan way of life. Their treaty rights made them the *protégés* of officialdom and, since officialdom was invariably corrupt and frequently oppressive, this did not endear them to the common people. Further friction was created by their need for land on which to build their houses, churches and chapels. These tall edifices produced a disturbing impression, for they were held to invade the realms and to jeopardise the composure of the *feng-shui*. These were the spirits of wind and water, a nebulous but influential relic of the geomancy which had dominated Chinese beliefs before the advent of Buddhism; all that needs to be said about them here is that they were extremely temperamental and easily took umbrage if the delicate balance of their interests was upset. The spires of Christendom seemed only too likely to discommode them, and it became a common thing for local disasters to be blamed upon the missionaries, who in their teaching expressed views about the *feng-shui* which could hardly be called propitiatory.

The susceptibilities of these gremlins were often invoked more from a desire to obstruct the unwelcome foreigner than from any geomantic fervour; but once they were invoked the people felt strongly about them. 'Their disturbance by a church spire,' wrote a contemporary pamphleteer, 'is considered as much a grievance as the erection of a hideous tannery beside Westminster Abbey would be.' * In a circular addressed to missionary societies the British Legation recommended that 'Chinese prejudice and superstitions should be more carefully considered in the forms and heights of the buildings erected.'

The Chinese are not a naturally religious people. A vague piety is cultivated, but the frontiers of faith are ill-defined. A marzipan effect is produced by the superimposal, on a basis of Shamanism and myth, of Buddhism, Taoism and Confucianism; the precepts of pre-Buddhist sages are still valid, and it is difficult to make out where the gods take over from the spirits, or to fit the philosophers in with the fertility rites. But in this amalgam the most important ingredient—regarded as such by everyone from the Emperor to the common thief—was ancestor-worship; and against this the nineteenth-century missionaries, following a lead originally given by Rome in the time of the great Emperor K'ang Hsi, set their faces.

The effect of this embargo was not merely to debar their converts from taking part in idolatrous rites; it was to exclude them from—and to prevent them from helping to finance—ceremonies and entertainments which played an important part in communal life. The more Christians there were in a village, the more money each of the other villagers had to pay into the fund from which the performance of Taoist high mass, seasonal festivals, theatrical performances and the upkeep of the temple were financed. Leaving ancestral piety and racial prejudice on one side, the Chinese viewed the situation in much the same way as the missionary societies would have viewed the conversion to Buddhism of a small but growing minority of their subscribers.

The parochial frictions so far described were not in themselves acute; but they helped to lay the powder-train which led

* Wen Ching: *The Chinese Crisis from Within.*

to the ultimate explosion by creating a stock of petty grievances against the missionaries and making enemies for them all over the country. A more dangerous, more emotional source of anti-foreign feeling was the allegation against the missionaries of horrible malpractices.

In China female children were often exposed at birth or—later in life, and if times were hard—offered for sale; no organisation, and indeed no impulse, existed to care for waifs and strays. The missionaries, accordingly, opened orphanages. 'It is,' wrote Smith in 1901, 'impossible for the Chinese to understand the motive for beneficence of this sort; and the presence of so many helpless infants, especially when the mortality is large, is immediately connected with the invincible superstition that foreigners wish to mutilate the bodies for the purpose of alchemy, thus turning lead into silver.'

Similar fables abounded, and plausibility was lent to them by garbled accounts of such rites as extreme unction and the baptism of the dying. The medical work done by many of the missionaries earned the gratitude of sufferers all over China, but the ill-disposed (including, for obvious reasons, the native doctors and pharmacists) saw to it that the most gruesome interpretation was put on any cure or operation that failed. When the Boxers began their attacks on mission property, the hospitals and dispensaries were often the first buildings to which the torch was applied.

As the aggressions of the Powers continued, and more and more Treaty Ports and Concessions were established on her coasts, China came to feel that all foreigners in the interior were 'like prolongations of the sea: inasmuch as wherever they penetrate they carry with them the waves and powers of the great unknown foreign ocean.'

This was true of all missionaries, but particularly of the Roman Catholics. All missionaries lived on their treaty rights, which they relied on the officials to enforce. Their converts, the *protégés* of *protégés*, clung to the same apron-strings and were tarred with the same brush. Often they were victimised for embracing the foreigner's religion; but whether they suffered for their faith or were merely caught up in the harshness and injustice of Chinese life, the missionary felt bound to use his influence on their behalf (there were places where the loss of a single convert would reduce his flock by a quarter or a third). The missions, whose less spiritually minded adherents were known as 'rice-Christians,' thus tended to become centres of privilege, auspicious bases from which to conduct litigation.

Trouble from these and cognate causes had long been foreseen. After the Tientsin riots of 1870, when some twenty Europeans (including the nuns in charge of an orphanage) and many converts were massacred, a senior official of the Tsungli Yamen, or Foreign Affairs Board, addressed to the French Legation a restrained and objective appreciation of the risks which the Roman Catholic missionaries were courting by 'founding, as it were, among us an undetermined number of States within the State.' After surveying with perspicuity the main causes of friction and misunderstanding, the memorandum ended: 'How, under these conditions, can we hope to prevent the governors and the governed uniting against the missionaries in common hostility? . . . The members of the Yamen fear, in all sincerity, that so much accumulated bad feeling, causing a sudden explosion, will bring about a catastrophe.'

But the missionary empire, like the other Western bridgeheads in China, continued to expand, and anti-foreign feeling (for it was really no more anti-Christian than the resentment inspired by traders in the Treaty Ports was anti-commercial) continued to grow in intensity and to spread. There were frequent riots, occasional murders. Tracts, pamphlets and pictures of a gross kind, in which Christianity was vilified, made their appearance. These were the work, not of the small fry who later supplied the rank and file of the Boxer cohorts, but of scholars, writing for the *literati* and the official class. For all their virulence, these productions were essentially cynical. The writers' aim was not to refute or discredit the Christian doctrine, about which they cared nothing, but, by blaspheming it, to ridicule and if possible to wound its proponents.

THE WHITE PERIL

A short book called *Death to the Devil's Religion* was a typical example of this murky literature. It was given, free of charge, to the customers of pawnshops in a city near Hankow and had a considerable circulation in the province of Hunan. 'It is impossible,' wrote an intelligent missionary, 'to convey in print any adequate conception of the vile nature of this production.' It included pornographic representations of the crucifixion of a hog; the Chinese term—or one of the terms—for Christianity (*T'ien Chu Chiao*) was written in characters which have the same sound but which mean 'The Squeak of the Heavenly Pig.' * Propaganda of this type was ominous, because it declared the interest of a section of the educated class, and dangerous, because some of it would reach the officials on whose goodwill the missionaries relied.

During the last ten years of the nineteenth century local anti-missionary outbreaks occurred in every one of the eighteen provinces of China proper.

Though the sources of anti-missionary prejudice were diverse, far the most important were the secular pretensions of the Roman Catholic Church. These have a long history, for there were Roman Catholic missions in China before the Manchus came; but their efforts to consolidate their position vis-à-vis the Chinese authorities were not crowned with complete success until the Boxers were already on the move. By that time the French Legation was acting as an agent or intermediary for the Vatican, because France held a protectorate over Catholic missions in China; and on 15 March 1899, following a series of representations made through that Legation to the Tsungli Yamen, there was addressed to the Throne a 'Memorial as to Official Intercourse between Chinese Local Authorities and Roman Catholic Missionaries.'

This document recognised, unconditionally and in full, the political rights and privileges which the missionaries had long claimed for themselves. The trappings of rank customarily assumed by Roman Catholic bishops—the mandarin's button,

* One of these cartoons is reproduced opposite page 65.

41

the appropriate retinue of chair-bearers, outriders and foot-men, the umbrella of honour, the discharge of a cannon on arrival or departure—were now granted them as a right. Henceforth Bishops would rank with Governors-General and Governors, Provicaires with Treasurers, Judges and Taotais, and so on down the respective hierarchies. The effect of this measure on Chinese opinion can approximately be gauged by imagining nineteenth-century British reactions to an announce-ment in the Court Circular that senior witch-doctors were to have equal precedence with Lords Lieutenant.

The British Legation felt that 'this formal recognition of the status of Roman Catholic Bishops . . . is likely to add greatly to their influence in Chinese affairs.' Six months later a con-ference of Anglican bishops in Shanghai passed the following resolution: 'We cannot view without alarm, both on behalf of our own flock and of the Chinese population generally, the rapidly growing interference of French and other Roman Catholic priests with the provincial and local government of China.' It is true that the Anglicans and the other Protestant sects lacked the unity and the political backing to wrest major concessions from the Chinese authorities. Nevertheless their disapproval of the Roman mandarins was not an affair of sour grapes; it was caused by genuine concern at the dangers im-plicit for all missionaries in the political self-aggrandisement of the Roman Catholics.

When the storm broke, the fury of the Boxers was virtually indiscriminate. There is however much evidence, from provinces where the Boxers were not strongly established but where in the general frenzy missionaries were hunted down and killed, that the Roman Catholics were regarded as a more important quarry than the Protestants. Time and again, in the harrow-ing accounts of the overland journeys which brought some of the persecuted evangelists to safety, passages like this recur: 'We found in passing through Honan that it was our greatest protection from the wrath of the people to let them know that we were Protestants.' Children, for as long as they survived the hardships and maltreatment which their fugitive parents under-

went, had a talismanic value, being ocular proof that the party
were not Roman Catholics.*

It is time now to turn from the religious to the economic
aspects of the West's intrusion into China, for these made a
parallel contribution to the nation-wide resentment against
foreigners. Another fleeing missionary came near to putting
the causes of the Boxer Rising in a nutshell when he wrote:
'The enmity of people and officials alike seemed to be chiefly
directed against two classes—Roman Catholics and mining and
railroad engineers—and we had all along the road to prove
that we were neither the one nor the other.' †

In 1900 only three railways, all comparatively short, were in
full operation in China; but concessions for many more had
been granted, and a score of lines were being surveyed or were
under construction. The ingredients of their unpopularity,
which was intense, embody almost all the reasons which the
Chinese found for disliking foreign economic enterprise in
almost all its forms.

Earlier in the century European countries had viewed the
advent of railways with mistrust and alarm; and China could
hardly be expected to welcome what she still calls the 'fire-
cart.' But the grounds on which she objected to it were much
more diverse and fanciful than those on which the early
European critics of the railway took their stand, and some
account of them may help to explain the mentality of the Boxers
and the pattern of their outbreaks.

That the railway was an innovation was bad; that it was
a foreign thing was worse. Because of the haphazard ubiquity
of Chinese burial-places, scarcely a mile of track could be laid
without desecrating the graves of somebody's ancestors. Serious
and frequent offence was caused to the *feng-shui*. The well-
known foreign custom of burying Chinese babies in the foundations of important structures, like cathedrals, gave rise to
macabre suspicions about the permanent way.

---

* M. Broomhall: *Martyred Missionaries of the China Inland Mission.*
† *Ibid.*

These were some of the objections on what may be called the ideological plane. Others were more concrete and easier to sympathise with.

The foreign businessmen who negotiated the concessions were often boors; the overseers who supervised the work were often bullies. Though the railway might on a long view bring prosperity as well as progress, it immediately threatened the livelihood of thousands. Carters, chair-bearers, muleteers, camel-men, innkeepers and other humble folk faced, or thought they faced, ruin. Junks and the ponderous houseboats of officials could not pass under the bridges, so that riverine trade-routes which had flourished for centuries were interrupted. Minor functionaries who controlled and preyed on traffic using the roads and waterways found their importance and their illicit revenues sharply reduced. Although the rolling-stock itself, and especially the locomotives, excited wonder and delight in a people who have an inborn relish for ingenuity and loud noises, the railways aroused deep misgivings in the districts through which they passed or were projected; and in parts of the Empire where they were as yet only a bogy, rumour saw to it that the bogy was very alarming indeed.

Similar feelings were evoked, and similar distress and dislocation caused, by the steamships which made their appearance on the Yangtse and other inland waterways. In cotton-growing districts the importation of foreign piece-goods killed the market for native products; the hand-loom or the spinning-wheel could no longer be relied on to keep the wolf from countless doors. Mining concessions exacerbated the *feng-shui*. In commerce and industry, one shrewd observer noted, 'the idea of a real reciprocity, in which what is advantageous to one party may be in a different way not less so to another, is completely alien to Chinese thought.' The spectacle of minerals being dug out of the bowels of their homeland and taken away by foreigners was not one of which the Chinese could be expected to take a detached view.

Telegraph lines were a further source of alarm and despondency. To the countrypeople across whose patchwork fields the tall poles strode, their purpose was unfathomable and their appearance forbidding. When the wind blew, a low moaning, very piteous to hear, diffused itself from the wires. As these rusted, the rainwater dripping from them acquired a gruesome tinge of red and strengthened the belief that the spirits were being tortured by these alien contraptions. The official class, who knew better, disliked the telegraph because it was an agent of remote control and narrowed the area of legitimate delay which, seemly and expansive as a well-kept lawn, surrounded every yamen in the Empire.

Then there was opium. The importation of opium was forbidden by the Throne; was keenly desired by the bulk of the Chinese people (and in particular by the official class who were supposed to prevent it); and was carried out, contrary to both Chinese and international law, by British merchants, who either sold to smugglers or smuggled in themselves huge quantities of the drug bought in bulk from the East India Company. It was this state of affairs which led to the Opium War of 1842, the immediate after-effect of which was to increase the trade and to lessen its hazards.

This is not the place to discuss the rights and wrongs of the business. It can be argued that if the Manchu policy towards foreign commerce had not been unreasonably harsh and restrictive the British would not have been forced to build up an illegitimate trade till it became so valuable—to India, to Hongkong and to the merchants—that no British Government could afford to suppress it. It can be argued that by the middle of the nineteenth century the Chinese, despite drastic prohibitions, were cultivating opium poppies on a vast and steadily increasing scale, and that to call the drug 'foreign earth' was invidious and unfair. But these were niceties beyond the grasp of the Boxers, who were mostly too poor to indulge even (as the Empress Dowager regularly did) in moderation; and opium, which was generally recognised as a national scourge even by those who found most pleasure or most profit in it, was resentfully associated in the public mind with the barbarians from without.

Thus many things, from the church-spires of well-meaning missionaries to the mine-shafts of self-seeking concessionaires, combined to reinforce in the hidebound but volatile minds of the Chinese their traditional dislike of foreigners. A climate not only of opinion but of emotion was created in which everyone was an extremist, everyone shared a common lust for retribution and revenge. After referring to the Powers who 'cast upon us looks of tiger-like voracity, hustling each other in their endeavours to be the first to seize upon our innermost territories,' a Secret Edict issued by the Empress Dowager on 21 November 1899 ended: 'Let each strive to preserve from destruction and spoliation at the ruthless hands of the invader his ancestral home and graves. Let these our words be made known to each and all within our domain.' The Manchus, in their time, had issued many high-falutin exhortations to their subjects; none had so closely coincided with their mood or found them so responsive.

Of the wrongs under which China smarted some were fancied but most were real. It would however be unfair to close this short account of them without noting that the foreigners, too, had a lot to put up with.

They came to China to trade; the motive may not have been lofty, but it was natural and legitimate. When the Chinese refused to let them trade, the foreigners could hardly be expected to understand, let alone to sympathise with, the reasons for this refusal. They were in hard fact very silly reasons, based on a conception of the world which was self-centred, obsolete and doomed, and they were normally explained—if at all—in a gratuitously offensive manner.

No one can say that the Manchus were not within their rights in enforcing a policy of isolationism, however misguided. But they were wrong, by any standards of behaviour and notably by those laid down by the Chinese sages, in seizing every opportunity to insult, humiliate and trick the foreigner. His aggressions were deplorable, but they were not unprovoked. To insist that he should have submitted to the insults, taken the hint, accepted his *congé* and sailed away, is surely to demand too much of nineteenth-century morality, or indeed of human nature in any epoch. It is equally unrealistic to argue that the Manchu Dynasty, sunk in ignorance and conceit, should have adopted a more enlightened attitude towards the West.

It was inevitable that the Powers would come, with selfish aims, to China. It was inevitable that they would be prepared to use force to further those aims. What, as we look back down history, does not seem wholly inevitable is that China's rulers should have immured the country for so long in a cocoon of childish bigotry that her first important encounters with younger civilisations were bound to end in tears.

# CHAPTER FOUR

# The Boxers and their Patrons

*One might profitably use them to inspire, by their fanaticism, the martial ardour of our regular troops. As a fighting force they are quite useless, but their claims to super- natural arts and magic might possibly be valuable for the purpose of disheartening the enemy.*

From a letter written by Jung Lu, the Commander-in-Chief at Peking, to his friend the Viceroy of Fukien in early July 1900.

THERE had always been secret societies in China. They gave the ordinary people, who had no voice in affairs, some hope of bringing pressure to bear on the officials, the wealthy merchants and the landlords. They suited alike the Chinese taste for mystery and the Chinese talent for small-scale combination. The mumbo-jumbo with which they surrounded themselves— the magic rites, the charms, the incantations—appealed strongly to a superstitious peasantry and brightened their drab lives with a lurid, tawdry glow. But they remained secret; they left no written records, and we know no more about them than the Chinese knew about the *feng-shui*. Throughout Chinese history we are aware of them, as in an old house one is aware of mice; but like the mice they elude scrutiny.

To explain therefore, as several authorities have, that the Boxers were an offshoot of the Eight Diagram Sect, were associated with the White Lotus and the Red Fist Societies, and had affiliations with the Ta Tao Hui or Big Knives, will scarcely enlighten even the most learned reader. It seems best to leave the Boxers' cloudy pedigree on one side, and to set down such facts as are known about their eruption in 1898.

THE BOXERS AND THEIR PATRONS

These are not many. I Ho Chüan means literally 'The Fists of Righteous Harmony.' 'The idea underlying the name,' the British Minister—or more probably his Chinese Secretary, Mr Cockburn—informed the Foreign Office, 'is that the members of the Society will unite to uphold the cause of righteousness, if necessary by force.' The sobriquet 'Boxers' was first applied to the movement in its early days by one or two missionaries in the interior who acted as local correspondents of the *North China Daily News* of Shanghai, the principal foreign-language newspaper in China; the name stuck.

When in the summer of 1900 the rebels were virtually embodied in the government forces, Manchu grandees were given charge of them. But from the two preceding years, during which the Rising found its feet and should in theory have been most likely to need and to throw up its own leaders, no names of note come down to us. Indeed, no names come down to us at all. The fact indirectly confirms the thesis, outlined in earlier chapters, that China was ready to rally to any anti-foreign banner, no matter who raised it.

As the movement spread, scraps of evidence that it was centrally organised and directed came to light. Some of the placards and handbills (like that printed at the beginning of Chapter Three), which the Boxers used for the purposes of recruiting and intimidation, appeared in identical wording in widely separated districts; and the pattern of their outbreaks showed, as they gained in audacity and violence, a consistency which suggested a central control. But whether this control in fact existed, or how it was exercised, nobody knows.

'It was [as Smith put it] the supernatural element in the Boxer claims which gave the sect its powerful hold upon the popular imagination and the popular faith.' Because it gained, if only for a time, credence at the Manchu Court as well as in the villages, far the most important of these claims was the claim to invulnerability. This useful asset was conferred on the Boxers by the spirits of the heroes, demi-gods and other legendary beings to whom they addressed their incantations, of which the following is a fair example:

The Instructions from the God Mi T'o to his Disciples—proclaiming upon every mountain by the Ancient Teachers—reverently inviting the Gods from the central southern mountains, from the central eight caves—your Disciple is studying the Boxer art, to preserve China and destroy Foreigners. The Iron Lo Han, if cut with knife or chopped with axe, there will be no trace. Cannon cannot injure, water cannot drown. If I urgently invite the Gods they will quickly come, if I tardily invite them they will tardily come, from their seats in every mountain cave. Ancient Teachers, Venerable Mother, do swiftly as I command.

This abracadabra was uttered to the accompaniment of gestures and posturings. Facing towards the south-east (nobody knows why) the worshipper genuflected, stamped on a cross, knocked his head on the ground, bowed and made cabalistic signs with his hands.

These rituals were for preference performed in a Buddhist temple or before a shrine. If all went well the celebrant became 'possessed.' Violent spasms, during which his limbs twitched, his mouth foamed and his eyes rolled, were succeeded by a trance-like state; when he emerged from this his initiation was complete. These magical goings-on made a deep impression on the spectators, whose descriptions of them to their friends lost nothing in the telling.

Public demonstrations of the Boxers' invulnerability were frequent. The audiences were large, and seem never to have been disappointed. Sword-cuts and pike-thrusts were seen to make no impression on bodies which the spirits had entered; bullets were deflected by a wave of the hand. Accidents were, inevitably, caused by failures in the chicanery and legerdemain without which these tests must have proved either unconvincing to the audience or fatal to the actors; one keen fellow had the ill luck to be blown in two by a cannon-ball. But these miscarriages were glossed over by explaining that their victims had been lax in performing their devotions or had transgressed one of the numerous bye-laws of the Society. Smith, who heard many first-hand accounts of invulnerability-tests, concluded that 'by the Chinese themselves they were almost universally regarded as real and solid evidence of supernatural power, while the native Christians had a tendency to attribute them to the direct agency of the Devil.'

The Boxers are first mentioned by name in Chinese official documents in May 1898, although just under two years earlier the then Governor of Shantung, Li Ping-hêng, referred in a Memorial to 'the riots now stirred up by the secret societies' which 'have their origin in the conflicts between the people and the Christians.'

Shantung was a logical background for their first appearance. Its people, like those of Hunan, have always had a reputation for independence and resource, and the German seizure of Kiaochow, whence their prospectors and an occasional punitive expedition made forays into the interior, had brought the 'tiger-like voracity' of the Powers more vividly home to Shantung than to any other province.

The Boxers' first main sphere of activity was along the border between Shantung and Chihli (provincial frontiers have always offered attractions to Chinese law-breakers who, by slipping across them at need, can cause the responsibility for police action to be passed to and fro between one Governor and the next for an almost indefinite period). The Boxers in Shantung soon discovered that there was small necessity for these tip-and-run tactics. When Yü Hsien became Governor in March 1899, the movement gained notable impetus. The word got round that the rebels had the tacit support of the Governor, and this gossip was strikingly confirmed in October by the sequel to a clash in which twenty-seven Boxers were killed by provincial troops. Yü Hsien removed the district magistrate, cashiered the local commander and imprisoned a police official who had arrested some of the rioters. For the rest of that year the Boxers were immune from interference.*

A series of sharp diplomatic protests, in which the German Legation took a leading part, brought about Yü Hsien's

* Chester C. Tan: *The Boxer Catastrophe.*

removal in December 1899. But after an audience with the Empress Dowager, who bestowed on him marks of esteem, he was transferred to Shansi, where in the following summer he personally supervised the butchery, in the course of one day, of forty-five European missionaries, including a number of women and children.

His successor in Shantung, Yüan Shih-k'ai, was a strong and able man. He immediately issued a proclamation laying down measures which, had they been carried out, would have put an end to the disturbances. But within a month of taking office he received no less than three Edicts from Peking warning him, in a pointed manner, to be 'extremely careful' and not to 'rely solely upon military force.' These Edicts made it clear which way the wind was blowing; Yüan trimmed his sails to it, and the Boxers continued to grow in strength and reputation.

Over the border, in Chihli, it was much the same story, except that the Viceroy, Yü Lu, was a weaker man and, being closer to Peking, was even more susceptible to its reactionary influence. The situation was already well on its way to getting out of hand when on 11 January 1900 the whole Empire learnt, by reading between the lines of an Edict, that the Empress Dowager meant to give the Boxers their head.

The Edict did not say this in so many words. But no official, however anxious to restore order in his district, could ignore the implications of the following passage:

> Of late in all the Provinces brigandage has daily become more prevalent, and missionary cases have recurred with frequency. Most critics point to seditious societies as the cause, and ask for rigorous suppression and punishment of them. But reflection shows that societies are of different kinds. When worthless vagabonds form themselves into bands and sworn confederacies, and relying on their numbers create disturbances, the law can show absolutely no leniency to them. On the other hand when peaceful and law-abiding people practise their skill in

mechanised arts for the preservation of themselves and their families, or when they combine in village communities for the mutual protection of the rural population, this is in accord with the public-spirited principle (enjoined by Mencius) of 'keeping mutual watch and giving mutual help'. Some local authorities, when a case arises, do not observe this distinction, but listening to false and idle rumours regard all alike as seditious societies, and involve all in one indiscriminate slaughter. The result is that, no distinction being made between the good and the evil, men's minds are thrown into fear and doubt. It means not that the people are disorderly, but that the administration is bad.

Some, but not all, of the diplomats recognised this decree as ominous. Sir Claude MacDonald did not judge it worth telegraphing home about. In a written despatch, which took the normal two months to reach the Foreign Office, he reported on 17 January that it was 'regarded in some quarters with misgiving' but that, 'in view of the divergence of opinion as to its effects,' he did not for the time being propose to raise the matter with the Tsungli Yamen. He did however join his American, French, German and Italian colleagues in protesting about it ten days later. Their conjoint *démarche* produced no result whatever.

By this time wide areas of North China were in a state of anarchy. A sequence of natural calamities, spread over two years, had prepared the ground only too well. Two successive harvests had failed, so that there had been two famines running. There had been a plague of locusts. The Yellow River had inundated hundreds of villages; at one time 150,000 people were squatting, like cormorants on some endless reef, on the breached dykes above swirling waters which covered the land as far as the eye could see. They were the fortunate ones, for they at least had not been drowned.

Relief measures were concerted from Peking. But 'what made the situation more unbearable was the corruption and inefficiency with which the local authorities handled the relief. People living in districts a short distance away from the provincial capital received hardly any aid, although the Imperial Government had appropriated large sums of money and directed large quantities of food to be shipped to the area for relief purposes.' * The Boxers' rabid xenophobia offered an outlet for discontents which might well have expressed themselves in ways more directly dangerous to the dynasty. No evidence survives to show that this obvious contingency helped to obtain for them Imperial patronage; but it can scarcely have been left out of account by the Empress Dowager and her advisers.

In their campaign against the Christians, the Boxers began merely by pillaging the 'secondary devils,' as they called the converts. They went on to arson and after that to murder, often preceded by torture. On 31 December 1899 they killed their first foreign missionary, a young Englishman called Brooks. His murderers were arrested, tried in the presence of a British consular official and executed; the Tsungli Yamen expressed the Government's formal regret. This was the last occasion on which the normal amenities of diplomatic intercourse, to say nothing of its treaty obligations, were observed in full by the Chinese Government.

Thereafter things went from bad to worse. Butchering the Christians and burning their churches and chapels, the Boxers steadily extended their influence throughout the troubled land. They were joined by bandits and deserters, and gained influential sympathisers among officials who sensed the favourable feeling towards them in Peking. On 17 April a further equivocal Edict renewed the charter given by implication to the rebels in that of 11 January. Diplomatic protests on the subject met with as little response as had those objecting to its predecessor.

Early in May the Imperial Court toyed with the idea of embodying the Boxers in a militia which could be deployed against 'great enemies.' The Viceroy of Chihli and the Gover-

* Tan.

54

nor of Shantung, asked to comment on this project, laced their opposition with some forthright criticism of the Boxers. The mild Yü Lu revealed as openly as he dared his view that the Boxers were criminals and charlatans. Yüan Shih-k'ai said roundly that the I Ho Chüan was a predatory and heretical organisation, led by bad elements. 'Devoid of any skills and defeated repeatedly by government troops, how can the Boxers be prepared for great enemies?' The scheme for a militia was dropped, but the adverse opinions of the men on the spot did nothing to undermine the Court's faith in their turbulent minions.

This survey of the events which led up to the Siege of the Legations has now brought us back to the point in time—the end of May 1900—at which my narrative began. But it would be a mistake to close this preamble without including in it a sketch of the remarkable woman who was ruler, in all save name, of the Manchu Empire; for it was by the Empress Dowager's will that the Boxers were encouraged instead of being suppressed, and it was by her will that the foreign envoys were doomed (as she supposed) to massacre.

Yehonala was born in 1836. Accounts of her parentage differ and are for the most part derogatory; but it seems probable that her father was a captain in the second of the eight Banner Corps, which may be loosely described as the household troops of the Manchu Dynasty. A striking beauty, she was one of twenty-eight Manchu girls selected for the harem of the Emperor Hsien-feng, and began her political career as a third-grade concubine.

Despite formidable competition she became a favourite of the Emperor, who was weak, sickly and vicious, and bore him (or anyhow produced) a son. This gained her promotion to the first grade. Her personal ascendancy over the Emperor made her, while barely in her twenties, a force to reckon with in the tortuous precincts of the Court.

This is not the place to try to unravel the conflicting and unreliable tales of the plots and counter-plots, intrigues and betrayals, which kept the Empress Tzŭ Hsi * in a position of great and often supreme power for nearly half a century. She became Regent on Hsien-feng's death in 1861, continuing in that office until her son, the Emperor Tung Chih, was declared to be of age in 1872.

Tung Chih died three years later and was succeeded by the infant Kuang Hsü. Tzŭ Hsi, who was his aunt, once more assumed the Regency, and although the young Emperor ascended the Dragon Throne in 1889 Tzŭ Hsi continued to dominate affairs at Court. In 1898 she put herself at the head of the reactionary party, who were perturbed by Kuang Hsü's well-meant but iconoclastic reforms, and deposed her nephew, who became virtually her prisoner. For the last ten years of her life her authority was not seriously challenged.

This bald summary does less than justice to a fabulous tale which, since most of its turning-points are recorded only in hearsay or in documentary sources of a suspect kind, is nearer to legend than to history. Its heroine emerges as a strange, compelling figure. From girlhood the Empress Dowager had lived in a world whose outward unrealities are too many and too complex to describe, and whose inner realities elude the most adroit imagination.

The high walls of the Forbidden City enclosed her, and were themselves enclosed by the higher walls of Peking. Eunuchs, a mephitic clique, were her janissaries, ministering to Imperial needs and mulcting the bearers of Imperial tribute. Her public life was paved with ceremony and roofed with superstition. Of her private life we know little save that she was fond of amateur theatricals,† water-picnics, painting and pugs; in old age she expressed a warm admiration for Queen Victoria, an engraving

---

* This, her official name, meant 'Motherly and Auspicious.' To it, before death closed her long career in 1908, had been added a string of honorifics: Orthodox, Heaven-Blessed, Prosperous, All-Nourishing, Brightly Manifest, Calm, Sedate, Perfect, Long-Lived, Respectful, Reverent, Worshipful, Illustrious, Exalted. By her subjects she was generally called 'the Old Buddha,' a term which is more respectful than it sounds.

† Her favourite part in *tableaux vivants* was that of Kwang-yin, the Goddess of Mercy.

of whose portrait hung in her private apartments. She preserved her early beauty with care and success. 'Had I not known she was nearing her sixty-ninth year, I should have thought her a well-preserved woman of forty,' wrote Miss Carl, an American artist who in 1903 shared Tzü Hsi's life for several weeks while painting her portrait. She invariably captivated foreigners and may be said to have bowled over the ladies of the Corps Diplomatique whom, with Lady MacDonald as bellwether, she received for the first time in 1899, the year before she did her best to put them to the sword.

'All one family!' she constantly murmured throughout a protracted social function (it went on for five hours) unique in the history of China. In that country women had always been excluded—with one or two disastrous omissions—from positions of power; foreigners were tabu. To open the gates of the Forbidden City to the wives of the barbarian envoys flouted not only the precedents of the Manchu Court but the traditions, indeed the very instincts, of its subjects. Yet the Empress Dowager, behind whose Lady-Macbeth-like reputation one detects a certain cosiness, carried off with perfect aplomb a gesture prompted rather by feminine curiosity than by any political motive.

The diplomatic ladies, each of whom was given a valuable ring before leaving the Presence, were enchanted with the Empress Dowager. It was no easier for them than it is for us to fathom the nature of a woman accustomed, since her twenties, to take a hand in the drafting of Edicts like the following, which dates from 1860:

> As to Su Shun, his treasonable guilt far exceeds that of his accomplices [*two of whom had been permitted to commit suicide, and two imprisoned for life*] and he fully deserves the punishment of dismemberment and the slicing process. But we cannot make up our mind to impose this extreme penalty and therefore, in our clemency, we sentence him to immediate decapitation.

Though doubtless kindly meant, the Empress Dowager's description of herself and her guests as 'all one family' might have

sounded ambiguous, if nothing worse, to anyone acquainted
with the course of events in her own domestic circle. When her
young son became Emperor, she encouraged him in the de-
baucheries which hastened his death and her return to power;
his pregnant widow died, in mysterious circumstances, shortly
afterwards. When her sister and rival 'ascended the fairy
chariot for her distant journey,' Tzü Hsi was strongly suspected
of having helped her into it. She deposed her nephew and,
while keeping him in semi-captivity, is thought to have practised on his life with poison.

These are some only of the more unnatural crimes imputed
to the Empress Dowager. There is not a shred of proof that
she committed them. There can be almost equally little doubt
that she was capable of them.

In statecraft her undeniable talents were those of a tactician
rather than a strategist. As one of her biographers puts it, she
had what chess-players call 'a quick sight of the board.' She
was essentially an opportunist. Yet in the cold light of reason it
is difficult to understand why she saw an opportunity in the
Boxer Rising.

It is true that she was desperate, at the end of her tether: that
she could draw on no other reserves in her unequal struggle
with the Powers. It is true that the Boxers, if promptly and
bloodily suppressed, would almost certainly have been succeeded by rebels of a less esoteric kind, upon whose banners pro-
dynastic slogans would have been unlikely to appear. It is true
that many of her closest advisers were intemperate fools.

Even so, the decision to rely on a rabble of uncontrollable
heretics was far below her usual standards of shrewdness; and
it was not merely rash but suicidal to encourage the Boxers in
courses which were bound to unite the squabbling Powers, as
nothing else could possibly have done, in joint action against
China. Why did she adhere—covertly at first, more openly as
time went on—to a policy so oddly unsophisticated?

In 1900 the Empress Dowager was sixty-four. She had always
been superstitious, and now it was the Boxers' magic powers
that established the same sort of hold on her mind that, in the

West, spiritualism sometimes exerts on elderly ladies with no shamanistic background to their upbringing. 'Little by little she became fascinated with the thought of adding the supernatural to the infranatural (and the unnatural).' * Like millions of her subjects, she believed in the Boxers' claims to invulnerability. She listened to eye-witness reports of the spectacular demonstrations at which these claims were tested, and is said to have attended one herself.

It was useless for clear-sighted officials to urge in memorials that: 'Never can heretical formulae resist enemies, nor can rebels protect the country.' The Empress Dowager had convinced herself that both things were possible. 'It is futile to memorialise,' the Viceroy at Nanking wrote to the Governor of Anhui; 'the Imperial Court has decided to appease the Boxers.'

Tzü Hsi was playing her last card. Her armies were useless. She had spent the money for her navy on rebuilding the Summer Palace. She would call in the dark forces of the spirit world.

* Smith.

# CHAPTER FIVE

# Portents in Peking

*What no European had foreseen, certainly none in Peking, was that the Chinese Government would be so influenced by the pretensions of the Boxers to supernatural powers as to believe that they could safely defy the rest of the world.*

Sir Claude MacDonald to Lord Salisbury, 20 September 1900.

ON 28 May, four days after the loyal festivities at the British Legation, two American ladies stood on the balcony of a temple in the Western Hills which had been converted into a villa. They were very frightened. On the plain below them flames and dense clouds of smoke rose from the railway station and locomotive sheds of Fengtai. The nearby houses of the foreign engineers were burning. The steel bridge appeared to have been blown up. Smoke darkened the sky.

The ladies were Mrs Squiers, the wife of the First Secretary of the American Legation, and her guest, a pretty girl called Polly Condit Smith. With them in the temple were three small children, two governesses—one German, the other French —and some apprehensive Chinese servants. On the previous day a guard of twelve Chinese soldiers, armed with rusty spears, had been provided by the authorities in view of the threatening situation; of these there was now no sign.

The women waited; there was nothing else to do. Presently 'our reward came when we saw down in the valley a dusty figure ambling along on a dusty Chinese pony, coming from the direction of Fengtai and making for our temple.' * The knight

* Mary Hooker (Polly Condit Smith): *Behind the Scenes in Peking.*

errant, whose entry into these pages is made in characteristic style, was *The Times* Correspondent in Peking, Dr G. E. Morrison. He had ridden out from Peking—a distance of about fifteen miles—to verify for himself reports of the burning of Fengtai, which, since it was the Boxers' first attack on government property, marked an important new phase in the Rising.* He had started back to Peking but, remembering the American ladies in their hot-weather retreat, had decided that the demands of chivalry must have precedence over his duties at the cable office.

Dr George Ernest Morrison was thirty-eight years old. The son of a Scottish emigrant to Australia, he had been, as he once wrote, 'a wanderer from my eighteenth year.' He began his journalistic career with a pungent exposure of the traffic in native labour between the South Sea Islands and the Queensland sugar plantations. He walked, alone and unarmed, across Australia, covering 2043 miles in 123 days. He led an expedition to New Guinea and was left for dead with two spears in his body. He qualified as a doctor, served as medical officer at the Rio Tinto copper mines in Spain and as court physician to a Moroccan sheikh, then walked across China from Shanghai to the Burma frontier, and in 1895 joined *The Times*, becoming its Peking Correspondent two years later. He combined flair with scrupulous accuracy to an extent which sometimes irked the Foreign Office in London; it was he who provoked Lord Curzon to coin his phrase about 'the intelligent anticipation of events before they occur,' which (wrote *The Times*), 'though not primarily intended as a compliment, was perhaps the most genuine tribute ever wrung from unwilling lips to the

---

* The havoc at Fengtai (where incidentally a railway coach specially built for, but never used by, the Empress Dowager was destroyed) was largely the work of men from the nearby city of Tungchow. Tungchow, whose prosperity depended on its status as an entrepot for tribute-rice brought by canal from the interior, had economic as well as ideological motives for disliking the railway. Cf. a despatch to the *North China Daily News* from its Tungchow Correspondent, May 1900. 'Since the railway came into actual operation three years ago, the occupation of the carriers has dwindled away, and with starvation in sight they are ready for anything.'

highest qualities which a correspondent can bring to bear upon his work.' *

The ladies were much relieved at Morrison's appearance. Shortly afterwards Mr Squiers arrived with a Cossack borrowed from the Russian Legation (the Russians were the first Power to establish—by the Treaty of Nertchinsk in 1689—diplomatic relations with China and were allowed to keep a small guard of Cossacks in Peking; its strength in 1900 was seven). After an anxious night the cosmopolitan party set out at dawn, the women and children travelling in carts; and five hours later they safely reached Peking.

It seems scarcely credible that, in so volcanic a situation, ladies from the Legations should have been allowed to occupy their isolated summer residences in the Western Hills. Yet a week later, on 3 June, Miss Condit Smith recorded that 'the heat is becoming insufferable, and the children of the diplomatic corps are showing the bad effects of this enforced confinement. Lady MacDonald has sent her little girls [they were aged five and three] back to their Legation bungalow in the hills, in the charge of her charming sister, Miss Armstrong, with a guard of Marines.' (The first Legation guards had reached Peking on 31 May.) Miss Armstrong 'most fortunately' brought the children back two days later. Shortly afterwards the British Legation bungalow was burnt to the ground.

It is worth pausing to examine the insouciance of which these domestic arrangements were a symptom; for not only did it dangerously blur the judgment of the Corps Diplomatique as to the nature and extent of their predicament, but it indirectly reflects the contempt in which the Chinese were held by the foreigners—a contempt which, as the *Spectator* put it, 'is sometimes kindly but never tolerant.'

Several chapters could be filled with a rehearsal of the evidence which, reaching the Legations during the five pre-

---

* Morrison's eldest son, Ian, followed in his father's footsteps. As a *Times* Correspondent in the Far East he had laid the foundations of a brilliant career when he was killed in the Korean War.

ceding months, indicated clearly that the Boxer Rising threatened the whole foreign position in North China. Two days before the ominous Edict of 11 January missionaries at Taiyuan had telegraphed to the British Minister: 'Outlook very black ... secret orders from Throne to encourage [Boxers].' A month earlier the American Legation had been warned in a telegram from missionaries in north-west Shantung that 'unless Legations combine pressure, Americans consider situation almost hopeless.'

These warnings were echoed by the *North China Daily News* and the *Peking and Tientsin Times*. In the diplomats' view missionaries were apt to be more alarmist, and newspapers more sensational, than the facts warranted. But it cannot have been easy to dismiss as a mere *canard* an undated despatch from its 'native correspondent' in Peking which the former paper published on 10 May. This correspondent, a minor official of good family whom foreigners respected, addressed his readers as followers: 'I write in all seriousness and sincerity to inform you that there is a great secret scheme, having for its aim to crush all foreigners in China, and wrest back the territories "leased" to them.' After naming the leaders and enumerating the military forces to be employed (in both cases correctly) he went on: 'All Chinese of the upper class know this, and those who count foreigners among their friends have warned them, but have to my own knowledge been rather laughed at for their pains than thanked.' He ended his prophetic dispatch with a circumstantial account of favours shown by the Empress Dowager to the Boxer movement.

Although there was nothing new about them, the evasive tactics of the Tsungli Yamen should have seemed suspicious. The diplomats could not expect the Imperial Court to lose face by admitting the gravamen of their charges; but it was (they at first imagined) even more in the interests of China than of the Powers that the rioters should be dispersed and the Rising suppressed, and they went on expecting something to happen as a result of their indignant and often united protests. They were disappointed.

The news got worse, and came from places closer to the capital. In March the idea of a naval demonstration by the Powers was canvassed, then abandoned; but Britain, America and Italy sent warships to Taku, and a German squadron was on call at Kiaochow. In April the Empress Dowager issued what Sir Claude MacDonald called 'a satisfactory Imperial Decree denouncing by name the Boxers' Societies,' and the naval precautions were relaxed.

The Edict had ended 'Let all tremblingly obey!' but nobody did. Still the Boxers came on. On 17 May the French Legation learned that three villages had been destroyed and sixty-one converts massacred at a place ninety miles from Peking. On 18 May a London Mission chapel was burnt to the ground within forty miles of the capital. On 19 May Monseigneur Favier, the Vicar-Apostolic of Peking, addressed a grave warning to the French Minister. He summarised the casualties, the damage, the thousands of refugees. He found in the situation a striking resemblance to that which had prevailed on the eve of the Tientsin massacres, thirty years earlier: 'the same placards, the same threats, the same warnings, the same blindness.' 'I implore you, M. le Ministre, to believe me; I am well informed and I do not speak idly. This religious persecution is only a façade; the ultimate aim is the extermination of all Europeans. ... The Boxers' accomplices await them in Peking; they mean to attack the churches first, then the Legations. For us, in our Cathedral, the date of the attack has actually been fixed. Everybody knows it, it is the talk of the town.' The Bishop ended with a fervent plea for 'forty or fifty sailors, to protect our lives and our property.'

In the Legations Monseigneur Favier was known and respected; he 'had by general admission the best sources of information.' The contents of his letter, which were quickly bruited about, produced the first faint quirk of alarm. Yet the meeting of the Corps Diplomatique on 20 May, at which the letter was considered, decided (as has been briefly told in Chapter One) not to send for guards from Tientsin. 'I confess,' Sir Claude MacDonald wrote to the Foreign Office on the

大清國當今慈禧端佑康頤昭豫莊誠壽恭欽獻崇熙聖母皇太后

The Empress Dowager

Anti-Christian Propaganda

A mandarin presides over the execution of a crucified pig (identified in the margin as Christ) while goat-headed foreigners are decapitated

following day, 'that little has come to my own knowledge to
confirm the gloomy anticipations of the French Father.'

Seven weeks later, and fifteen years before he died, _The
Times_ printed Sir Claude's obituary. It included this sentence: 'How the British Minister and his colleagues, together,
it must be added, with Sir Robert Hart and all the leading
members of the foreign community in Peking, failed altogether
to see any signs of the coming storm, is a mystery which will
probably now remain for ever unsolved.' With only one important exception, all the leading members of the foreign community survived to tell their tales, which most of them did
in considerable detail; but on their failure to read the writing
on the wall none threw any light.

It is impossible not to suspect that the counsels of Sir Robert
Hart contributed to their myopia. He had spent nearly fifty
years in China. He was a trusted servant of the Chinese
Government and controlled an organisation with ramifications
all over the Empire.* He was the local expert to whom diplomats had long been accustomed to turn for information and
advice. 'For a quarter of a century at least' (_The Times_ wrote
in his premature obituary) 'the final instructions given succes-
sively to every British Minister on his appointment to Peking
might have been summed up in half a dozen words: "When in
doubt, consult Sir Robert Hart." ' In 1885 he had even been
offered the post of British Minister; he accepted, but resigned
without taking up the appointment. He was very much the
elder statesman of the Legation Quarter; no other foreigner—
not even Bishop Favier—was so well placed to know what was
going on and which way the wind would blow.

But Sir Robert was an invincible optimist (five years earlier
he had wildly overestimated China's chances in her war against
Japan) and he had an intense personal admiration for the
Empress Dowager. He was not only China's servant; he had
undergone what _The Times_ called 'that strange fascination
which a Chinese environment so often exercises over the

* In 1899 the Imperial Maritime Customs employed 993 foreigners
(of whom 503 were British) and 4611 Chinese.

European mind,' and was intellectually her slave. Even after his experiences in the Siege, he remained an apologist for the Boxers, whose movement he curiously described as 'patriotic in origin, justifiable in its fundamental idea, and in point of fact the outcome of either foreign advice or the study of foreign methods.'

There survive among Sir Claude MacDonald's personal papers an interesting series of letters written to him, almost daily, by Sir Robert between the 11th and the 20th of June. The advice tendered in the later ones, when the danger was becoming acute, can only be called astonishing; it will be examined when we reach the events with which it deals. But this is perhaps the place to note the views expressed in the first letter of the series, for they throw a revealing light on Hart's interpretation of events.

News had just reached him of the appointment to the Tsungli Yamen of four thorough-paced reactionaries, of whom the most notoriously anti-foreign, Prince Tuan, had replaced the urbane Prince Ch'ing as President. It was an ominous development.

Hart's comment was: 'We have had several cases of rabid critics and anti-foreign men brought into the Yamen, and most of them turned out well under the load of responsibility and in the light of fuller knowledge; they began with an honest hatred and ended with an honest appreciation. So I think Prince Tuan's appointment will [one word illegible] work well.'

A fortnight later Prince Tuan had ample opportunity to work off his honest hatred. His load of responsibility was increased. He was placed in supreme command of the Boxer hordes.

Fengtai, where the Boxers made their first attack on the railway, was the junction of the Peking–Tientsin Railway with the line destined to link Peking and Hankow; in 1900 this ran only as far as Paotingfu.* The main headquarters of the

* See map on page 76.

66

staff and the construction engineers, most of whom were Belgian, was at Ch'anghsintien, about sixteen miles from Peking. After the attack on Fengtai on 28 May, in the course of which the telegraph lines were cut, grave fears were entertained for the foreigners at Ch'anghsintien. Those at Fengtai had escaped by train to Tientsin, but the damage done at the junction meant that Ch'anghsintien was cut off, withdrawal by rail to either Peking or Tientsin being no longer possible.

The diplomats showed few signs of derring-do, but on 29 May a small unofficial rescue-party, armed with rifles and revolvers, set out on ponies through the unquiet countryside. It was led by the Swiss proprietor of the Hôtel de Pékin, M. Auguste Chamot, and his young American wife; with them rode four Frenchmen and a young Australian. Their bold mission was successful, and they returned the same evening escorting twenty-nine Europeans, of whom nine were women and seven children; an hour after these people left Ch'anghsintien their houses were looted and burnt by the soldiers sent to protect them. 'This prompt and daring rescue was one of the best incidents of the Siege,' wrote Morrison afterwards in *The Times*.*

* The Chamots behaved throughout the Siege with gallantry and resource. Madame Chamot may not have manned the barricades as continuously as some authorities suggest; and it is unlikely that for her appearances in the firing-line she donned a zouave uniform 'doubtless borrowed from the small French garrison,' which was after all made up of sailors. But she was certainly a plucky woman. The Hôtel de Pékin formed part of a dangerous sector of the outer defences; she never left it to join the other ladies in the comparative safety of the British Legation.

Her thirty-three-year-old husband played a major part in victualling first the besieged and later the relieving forces; his local knowledge and contacts made him pre-eminent among the serious looters. He was loaded with honours and financial rewards by the Governments whose representatives he had served so ably, and after amassing a considerable fortune retired to San Francisco, where he built two large houses, established a private menagerie, and kept a yacht. Both houses were destroyed in the earthquake of 1906 and Chamot died a pauper at the age of forty-three. He had divorced his wife and on his deathbed married his mistress, a manicurist called Betsy Dollar. (Dr P. Campiche: 'Notes sur la Carrière d'Auguste Chamot' in the *Revue Historique Vaudoise*, March 1955.)

Though not yet alive to the full gravity of the situation, the Corps Diplomatique decided on 28 May to send for guards; the French Minister revealed that he had already done so. The Tsungli Yamen, notified of this decision, at first refused to grant the necessary permission; even though the precedent of 1898 existed, the entry of foreign troops into the capital involved a serious loss of face for the Chinese authorities, and indeed for the whole country. But the diplomats were insistent, and the first contingents, after virtually commandeering a train in the face of local obstruction, left Tientsin on 31 May.

These contingents were all made up of sailors or marines from the foreign warships lying off the Taku Bar, where a sizeable armada was now assembled. Admiral Seymour wrote to Sir Claude MacDonald on 1 June: 'There are seventeen men of war of sorts here now. It reminds me of 1860.' * The Taku Bar was some twelve miles offshore. The detachments for Peking had to tranship into destroyers, gunboats, lighters and other shallow-draught vessels, which ferried them past the forts guarding the mouth of the Pei Ho, or North River, to the small riverine port of Tangku. Thence the railway took them thirty miles to Tientsin, which is eighty miles from Peking.

There was much tension and anxiety among the foreigners in Peking on the afternoon of 31 May. It was known that the first detachments were on their way, but their numbers—about 300 officers and men—were regarded as dangerously small. They could not arrive until after dark. The railway terminus at Machiapu was outside the walls of Peking; the gates were normally closed at dusk; between the station and the Yung Ting Men (the gate by which the guards would enter Peking) 6000 truculent Mohammedan soldiers from the remote province of Kansu had been concentrated. It was strongly rumoured that the small force from Tientsin was to be annihilated outside the walls.

* (M.P.) Seymour had served as a midshipman in the Anglo-French force which had captured the Taku Forts and marched to Peking forty years earlier.

# PORTENTS IN PEKING

In the streets round the Legations a competent witness reported that by 7 p.m. 'the mob was prodigious, and the common speech threatening.' *  In more than one missionary compound in the city carts were prepared for an attempt at flight, and the Europeans put on native dress.†

But all went well. The Kansu soldiery were withdrawn at the last moment. The train arrived. The gates were kept open. At about 8 p.m. 337 officers and men, comprising guards for the American, British, French, Italian, Japanese and Russian Legations, marched up Legation Street with fixed bayonets; they were led (Polly Condit Smith noted with pride) by a detachment of the United States Marine Corps, one of whose officers found 'the dense mass of Chinese which thronged either side of the roadway more ominous than a demonstration of hostility would have been.' On 3 June a further contingent of fifty-two German and thirty-seven Austrian sailors arrived without incident.

The advent of this tiny, lightly-armed, polyglot force had an almost magical effect. The mobs dispersed, the tension eased, missionaries who had taken refuge in the Legations returned to their compounds. This interlude of normality was short-lived, but it lasted long enough to revive complacency among the diplomats. On 2 June Sir Claude MacDonald telegraphed to Admiral Seymour: 'No more ships wanted at Taku unless matters become more complicated which I do not think they will;' ‡ and in a letter to Seymour written on the following day, after referring to the 'wholesome calm' prevailing in the capital, he made clear his view that a need for further British forces to be sent to Peking would arise only if the central authority disintegrated, the Court fled, and it became necessary to compete with Russia and France in an

* The Rev. R. Allen: *The Siege of the Peking Legations.*

† The ladies disguised themselves as Manchus, because the women of this race did not bind their feet; it would thus be possible for the fugitives to walk with a normal gait without attracting suspicion. Chinese women, their feet having been deliberately deformed in infancy, could only hobble.

‡ M.P.

international scramble for the spoils. Whatever happened, he concluded, the Legations 'would be the last place attacked.' *

While there was a lull in Peking, the storm raged ever more fiercely in the surrounding countryside. On 2 June news reached the capital that between thirty and forty railway personnel, mostly Belgian, from Paotingfu were trying to escape to Tientsin by river and had suffered casualties; seven were missing when they reached their destination in a state of terrible distress. A guard of twenty-five Cossacks permanently stationed at Tientsin had been sent to their rescue, but had been surrounded during the night and forced to return without making contact with the fugitives. The opportunity to claim a victory over foreign troops, and cavalry at that, was not lost by the Boxers.

On the following day the murder of two British missionaries was reported from a place forty miles south of Peking; and on 4 June the railway to Tientsin, traffic on which had been precariously restored after the attack on Fengtai, was decisively cut. Stations were burning, the troops guarding them had deserted, the staff had bolted and the Boxers were tearing up the rails. A meeting of the Corps Diplomatique was hastily summoned, and the Ministers, to whom M. Pichon pointed out that telegraphic as well as rail communications would shortly be interrupted, wired to their respective Governments a request that the commanders of the naval squadrons should be ordered to undertake their rescue if things got worse.

Some apprehension of their impotence and isolation began at this stage to influence the outlook of the diplomats, who, on top of everything else, were receiving disquieting news about the situation at Tientsin. The Chinese authorities now abandoned their perfunctory attempts to dupe or reassure them. On 4 June a member of the Tsungli Yamen, one of the four present, was seen to be fast asleep while the British Minister was delivering a protest about the murder of the two missionaries.

* M.P.

On 5 June Prince Ch'ing's manner at a further interview convinced Sir Claude that his worst suspicions were correct, that the Empress Dowager was in league with the Boxers, and that the Tsungli Yamen 'had ceased to represent effectively the ruling power of China.' On 6 June this impression was confirmed by the most forthright (or the least ambiguous) of a long series of Edicts dealing with the Boxers; it violently disparaged the Christians as trouble-makers and absolved the Boxers from all blame for such disturbances as might be going on.

More and more missionaries converged, often with large numbers of converts, upon Peking. The Americans among them were dissatisfied with the negative attitude of Mr Conger, the United States Minister, and after a conference sent to President McKinley a telegram which ended: 'Thirty Americans convened regard outlook practically hopeless.' *

The Legations (whose staffs were small or, where minor Powers were concerned, virtually non-existent) depended almost entirely on the missionaries for intelligence about what was happening in North China, and even in Peking itself. But the missionaries—dim, dedicated, sacrificial figures—lived in a world to which the diplomats were strangers, and of whose social standards they instinctively disapproved. To grow (as many missionaries did) a pigtail, to eat Chinese food, to travel by wheelbarrow, to descend readily into the sea of squalor which the Legation Quarter, on its tiny atoll, was at pains to keep at bay—all these things interposed between the missionaries and the diplomats the kind of barrier which in 1900 separated the social classes in their countries of origin.

If this is understood, we can see why, as the British Minister recorded, the burning of the grandstand on the race-course

---

* This telegram included a passage in which the Imperial Edicts were described as 'double-faced,' and there was some doubt whether the Imperial Post Office would accept the epithet for transmission overseas. No student of the Chinese character will be surprised to learn either that it did, or that the epithet had to be paid for as two words, not one.

three miles outside Peking, which occurred on 9 June, 'brought home more vividly [than any previous incident] to the minds of all Europeans in Peking a sense of the perilous position in which they stood.' It is true that a native Christian was roasted alive in the ashes; but the Legations had, after all, been receiving for several weeks well-authenticated reports of far worse holocausts. The destruction of the grandstand was an attack on the small artificial world of privilege which the diplomats had, quite naturally, striven to create; it was followed on the same day by an incident in which some young Englishmen, riding out towards the race-course, had to fire their pistols in self-defence; and it made a deeper impression than the reports from missionary sources of infinitely worse outrages committed farther afield.

It was the straw that broke the camel's back. The Corps Diplomatique had considered (on 6 June) demanding a collective audience with the Empress Dowager: had postponed making the demand until authorised by their respective Governments to insist (how?) that it must be complied with; and had meanwhile learnt that the Boxers had seized and were destroying the railway bridge at Yangtsun, the one irreplaceable link in the railway communications between Peking and Tientsin.

The Corps met on the afternoon of the 9th to discuss the advisability of asking the Admirals to send up a relief force. The British Minister, acting on information from Chinese sources, had already telegraphed to Admiral Seymour that unless reinforcements came quickly they might come too late; but his colleagues—headed, surprisingly, by the congenitally alarmist M. Pichon—decided to postpone the taking of so drastic a step.

Later that day still more alarming information reached Sir Claude. His appeal to the Admiral, countermanded two hours previously, was renewed. He reported that 'the situation in Peking is hourly becoming more serious' and asked that 'troops should be landed and all arrangements made for an advance on Peking at once.'

## PORTENTS IN PEKING

Next morning five trains, carrying 2000 armed men of eight nationalities, steamed out of Tientsin. They were expected to reach Peking that night. In the Legations a convoy of carts stood ready to go out to meet them at the railway station as soon as the city gates were opened in the morning.

CHAPTER SIX

# Five Trains and Four Forts

*Sea power, when properly understood, is a wonderful thing.*
            Winston Churchill: *Their Finest Hour.*

ADMIRAL SIR EDWARD SEYMOUR assumed personal command of the expedition to Peking. 'I could never understand,'
he once wrote, 'why anyone minds responsibility. You have
only to do what seems proper, and if it turns out badly it is the
fault of Nature for not having made you cleverer.' * The
words are a fair guide to the character of a gallant, distinguished
but not very imaginative officer. He had been given a wide discretion by the Admiralty. Since they dropped anchor off Taku,
the commanders of the foreign squadrons had done little save
discuss the action to be taken if the situation in Peking got out of
control. It had occurred to none of them (least of all, perhaps,
to Seymour) that there was any alternative to an immediate
dash to Peking with the strongest forces they could scrape
together. They discerned no great hazards in the operation;
the officers took their full-dress uniforms with them. They were
acting on what the *Spectator*, on the day before they set out,
called 'the assumption that any force of Europeans however
small can beat any force of Chinamen however large.'

The international bickering which preceded their departure
was on a minor scale. On 6 June the French Admiral recommended that a Russian, Colonel Vogak, should command any
force that might have to be put ashore. The German Admiral

* *My Naval Career and Travels.*

74

objected. The Austrians asked privately to serve under British command. On 9 June the French and the Russians announced that they were not coming. Everybody, however, turned up at the station on the 10th, and throughout their trying experiences Seymour handled his small force with remarkably little friction.

Its final composition was as follows:

| | |
|---|---|
| British | 915 |
| Germans | 512 |
| Russians | 312 |
| French | 157 |
| Americans | 111 |
| Japanese | 54 |
| Italians | 42 |
| Austrians | 26 |

Total Strength 2129

The force had seven field-guns and ten machine-guns.

The leading train, in which the Admiral travelled, carried about half the British, all the Americans and Austrians, and a gang of coolies with materials for repairing the line. (A reconnaissance four days earlier had found Boxers burning the sleepers at Lofa.) The fifth and last train carried supplies. The foreign community at Tientsin gave the men a demonstrative send-off. 'We looked forward to a journey of a few hours,' recalled a junior diplomat attached to Seymour's staff, which included Captain John Jellicoe.*

Soon after midday they crossed the steel bridge over the Pei Ho at Yangtsun. Here was encamped General Nieh Shih-chêng, whose well-found, foreign-trained army had fought a

* Clive Bigham: *A Year in China.* Commander David Beatty was also serving under Seymour. Both officers were wounded in the fighting, Jellicoe severely.

75

successful action against the Boxers a week earlier and who had been sharply reminded from Peking that 'the Boxers are the children of China.' The demeanour of the Imperial troops was friendly.

Beyond Lofa minor damage had been done to the line, but

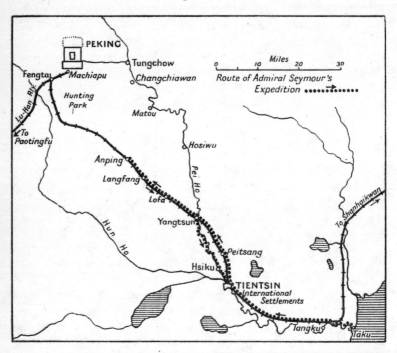

the sailors repaired it as they went along, and Langfang, half-way to Peking, was reached on the evening of the second day, 11 June. Here things looked less promising. The station and the water-tanks had been destroyed, and the engines had to be watered with buckets; the burning of the sleepers had buckled the rails. The weather was intensely hot. The wells were reputed poisoned and drinking-water was scarce. On the third day only four miles were covered. Yet on 14 June Seymour wrote to Sir Claude MacDonald from Langfang, where he had received news from Peking by the hand of a courier: 'Am confident of entering city. Hope in a few days.' A postscript, added at 10 p.m., struck a less sanguine note but ended 'All will yet be well.' *

It was on the afternoon of the third day that the Boxers launched their first attack on the trains. Their reckless courage made a profound impression on the Europeans. 'They came on us in a ragged line, advancing at the double from a village some quarter of a mile to the left flank. Not more than a couple of hundred, armed with swords, spears, gingals † and rifles, many of them being quite boys. To anyone who has been some little time in China it was an almost incredible sight, for there was no sign of fear or hesitation, and these were not fanatical "braves," or the trained soldiers of the Empress, but the quiet peace-loving peasantry—the countryside in arms against the foreigner. As they approached they dropped to their knees, lifting up their hands to heaven to invoke the God of War. Then they charged until they dropped again as our volleys began to tell. In twenty minutes they were in full retreat, leaving some sixty dead on the field.'

Bigham, who thus described the action, tried after it was over to convince his Chinese servant that the Boxers' claims to invulnerability were moonshine. The man's reactions were typical of the stubborn credulity often displayed on such occasions even by those who were not adherents of the Boxers. 'These,' he insisted, when shown some badly wounded prisoners, 'are not real Boxers, only make-believe; or if they are real,' he added as an afterthought, 'in a few days they will get up healed, disappear miraculously, and then come and fight again.' The dead were deliberately left unburied in the hope that the piles of corpses might give rise at least to a reasonable doubt regarding the Boxers' pretensions.

This first attack was followed by others in much greater strength. Supplies, particularly of ammunition, began to run short. On 14 June the rearmost train, whose role was to keep

* M.P.
† A kind of two-man blunderbuss, generally fired from a wooden tripod.

up a continuous shuttle-service between the by now almost stationary expedition and its advanced base at Tientsin, was unable to pass Yangtsun. General Nieh had disappeared, the bridgehead was strongly held by Boxers, and attempts were being made to demolish the steel bridge.

By now Seymour's force was dangerously strung out, for almost every station had to be garrisoned to prevent the Boxers drawing the net even tighter. The expedition had become a sort of military amphisbaena, which needed to fight its way back as much as it needed to fight its way on. The isolated detachments were called on to withstand an increasing weight of attack with a diminishing stock of ammunition. The burden of the wounded was becoming a serious matter.

Nothing (fortunately for Seymour's peace of mind) was known about the situation at Tientsin, which had deteriorated sharply since he left; it was vaguely hoped that the small garrison there would find some means of restoring rail communications through Yangtsun.

Langfang was only thirty-two miles from the Legations as the crow flies and, further progress along the railway being clearly out of the question, an advance across country was briefly considered. But there was no road and, apart from the problem of the wounded, the naval expedition had no transport or pack-animals. The only alternative was to fall back on Yangtsun and strike north up the river—the route followed by the Anglo-French forces in 1860—with the guns, supplies and wounded carried on junks. This plan was adopted. One by one the trains steamed slowly back to Yangtsun, where the bridge, though not demolished, was found to be impassable. Four junks were requisitioned.

But at Yangtsun, on 17 June, artillery fire was heard from the direction of Tientsin, with whose garrison the expedition had had no communication for four days; and on the 18th there was a still more sinister development. The German contingent under Captain von Usedom, who were still at Langfang, were heavily attacked by a force of 4000 regular Chinese troops, and their train, withdrawing after an action in which six Europeans were killed and nearly fifty wounded, was pursued for some distance by Imperial cavalry. Captured banners identified the Kansu warriors of General Tung Fu-hsiang, an ex-bandit who stood high in the Empress Dowager's favour.

It was clear that the gravest of foreseeable contingencies had come to pass: the Chinese armies had been ordered to make common cause with the Boxers. This ruled out all possibility of renewing the advance on Peking. Seymour prepared to withdraw down the river towards Tientsin, whence the mutter of distant gunfire was now continuous.

A great deal had happened since Seymour's departure on 10 June. The timely * arrival on the 13th of 1600 Russian troops brought the strength of the garrison available for the defence of the Foreign Settlements up to 2400; but the Settlements, which lay outside the suburbs of the native city, had a perimeter about five miles long, and on the night of the 15th a large part of the French Settlement was burnt by the Boxers.

The whole situation in North China had become a trap. Peking was sealed off; Seymour had lost touch with his base; the thirty-mile rail-link between Tientsin and the mouth of the Pei Ho would be cut at any moment; supplies and reinforcements could be seen moving into the Taku Forts, where torpedo-tubes were being mounted and mines (allegedly) laid in the channel. Once the trap was sprung by the closing of the Pei Ho, the naval squadrons riding twelve miles out to sea beyond the Taku Bar would be impotent.

The sailors took the bull by the horns. On the morning of the 16th it was decided at a conference on board the Russian flagship to 'occupy provisionally, by consent or by force, the Taku Forts,' and an ultimatum to this effect was conveyed to the

* Timely in a double sense. If the Russians (the only contingent of any Power's *army* then on the scene) had reached Tientsin before the 10th they would inevitably have been embodied, or would have embodied themselves, in Seymour's expedition; and in the days that followed Tientsin's defences would have been fatally under-manned.

Chinese authorities by the French consul at Tientsin, who was the senior member of the consular body. The ultimatum was to expire at 2 a.m. on the following day.

This was an exceedingly bold decision. Although they had been captured by attack from the landward in 1860, the Taku Forts had repelled with heavy losses an attempt made by British gunboats in the preceding year to force the mouth of the Pei Ho. There were four forts, two on each side of the river, which was only 200 yards wide. They appeared to be immensely strong. They had been rebuilt and modernised by German engineers, and their armament, though miscellaneous, included a number of heavy quick-firing guns made by Krupp. Under these guns, in a small naval yard, lay four brand-new destroyers (also made in Germany), each mounting six three-pounder quick-firing guns. To seaward of the Forts was a glutinous expanse of mud-flats, criss-crossed by lines of sharp stakes and wholly devoid of cover.

At the Taku Bar, twelve miles out to sea, the depth of the water varied between two and seventeen feet according to the state of the tide. The only fighting ships which could be brought across it to deal with the Forts were the following:

HMS *Algerine*, an old unarmoured sloop.

HMS *Fame* and *Whiting*, two modern destroyers.

The *Iltis* (German), a similar vessel to *Algerine*: also unarmoured.

The *Gilyak* (Russian), a modern gunboat.

The *Bobre* (Russian), an old steel gunboat whose armament was entirely muzzle-loading.

The *Koreetz* (Russian), a similar vessel to *Bobre*.

The *Lion* (French), the oldest gunboat in the flotilla.

The *Atago* (Japanese), an old iron gunboat with an obsolete armament.

Also present was the United States Navy's *Monocacy*, a turtle-shaped wooden paddle-steamer laid down in 1863 and possessing negligible fire-power. This ship (although hit by a stray

One of the captured Taku Forts

Austrian sailors in the assault

Boxers attack one of Seymour's trains at Lofa

Schönberg, the *Illustrated London News* artist whose work is represented elsewhere in these pages, was an eye-witness of the scenes he depicted

shell) stayed out of the fight. The instructions given by Washington to Admiral Kempff did not include authority to take part in hostilities against China, and it is possible that he had wind of a signal sent a few days earlier to the Navy Department from the Philippines by Admiral Remey, the senior commander on the Asiatic Station; this accused Kempff of 'cooperating foreign Powers to an extent incompatible interests American Government.' Kempff was criticised afterwards; 'at first,' one of his officers said, 'there was considerable feeling against him for standing out of an elegant fight when one was on hand.' But he was an enterprising officer whose hands were tied by his Government's policy, and he probably sympathised with the paddle-steamer's captain, Commander Wise, who wrote to him: 'I feel a natural regret, shared no doubt by the officers, that duty and orders prevented the old *Monocacy* from giving her ancient smooth-bores a last chance.'

An assault force of 900 officers and men was distributed among the nine little ships, which as night fell weighed anchor and took up their stations in line astern opposite the Forts on the northern bank, whence in the last of the light the Chinese artillerymen could be seen grinning cheerfully down at them through the embrasures. Outgunned at point-blank range, devoid of any central command, and with no room to manoeuvre, the thin-skinned flotilla was sustained rather by contempt for the foe than by any deep faith in tactics which were on paper suicidal. The sleepless men discussed with ribald unconcern the steadily receding prospects of a Chinese surrender.

At 12.50 a.m., with more than an hour to go before the ultimatum expired, the Forts suddenly opened fire with every weapon that could be brought to bear. Seven of the nine ships replied as hotly as they were able; but the destroyers *Whiting* and *Fame*, acting on a prearranged plan, glided unobtrusively upstream to the naval yard and brought off an exploit in the best G. A. Henty tradition. As they came abreast of the four German-built destroyers, the two British ships sheered in, each at the same time casting off a whaler manned by a boarding party. From the bows of *Whiting* and *Fame* men sprang, in the staccato flicker of the muzzle-flashes further downstream, on to the decks of No. 2 and No. 4 in the anchorage; the satellite assault-groups in the whalers took care of Nos. 1 and 3.

The Chinese destroyers had been prepared for action; their ammunition was on deck and their torpedo-tubes loaded. Yet in a matter of minutes all four ships (which if handled with only reasonable skill and resolution could have routed the puny bombarding force) were taken. The Chinese crews suffered few casualties, the British none. One of the captured ships was taken into service with the Royal Navy; the others were presented to Russia, Germany and France. Towards the officers and men who carried out a ticklish exploit with notable dash and precision the British authorities showed themselves less open-handed; the Admiralty refused them prize-money on the grounds that no state of war existed between China and Great Britain.*

The gun-battle between the Forts and the ships went on untidily for six hours. Soon after it began the Russian gunboat *Gilyak* switched on her searchlight—a new-fangled device of which she was no doubt justly proud—and as a result took a severe punishment from the Chinese batteries. But otherwise the gun-layers in the Forts made poor practice. Little damage was done to the intrusive flotilla, and at about three o'clock the landing force was put ashore and began to flounder through the deep mud towards the Forts. An hour later dawn broke. Now that the attackers could see their targets, their superior marksmanship began to tell. A shell (which each of five navies still claims the credit for firing) caused a devastating explosion

* Cecil Aspinall-Oglander: *Roger Keyes*. The lessons learnt in North China by Jellicoe and Beatty may not have had a direct influence on the Battle of Jutland; but in the raid on Zeebrugge (1918), and in his attempts to influence British strategy in the Second World War, it is easy (and perhaps permissible) to trace the effect upon the mind of Admiral of the Fleet Lord Keyes of the audacious enterprise in which, as a young lieutenant, he commanded HMS *Fame*.

in one of the Chinese magazines. The first fort was stormed at the point of the bayonet; resistance in the second disintegrated; and on the even larger forts on the south bank of the Pei Ho, another lucky shot having detonated an even larger magazine, no assault proved necessary. As a result of this explosion, which was visible to the international fleet, twelve miles away, 'the air was so thick with dust that the men belonging to the landing party could hardly see.' *

Thus, overnight, sea-power asserted once more its far-reaching, its almost magical influence over events on land. At the cost of 172 casualties, nine small and mainly obsolete ships captured the key to North China at the moment when it was being turned in the lock. If the assault on the Forts had been (as it should have been) repulsed, nothing could have saved the hostages to fortune which the Powers had disposed in all-but-defenceless coveys across the Chihli plain. The Legations, Seymour's relief expedition, the small garrison and the foreign community at Tientsin—all these would have been massacred piecemeal as their supplies ran out; and the consequences for the Manchu Empire would have been grave. Though it has a quaint air today, the night-action in the mouth of the Pei Ho was almost certainly a decisive battle in the history of twentieth-century China.

Because of the destruction of the telegraph lines, news of it was slow in reaching Peking; and because it was bad news, there was a further delay before the Empress Dowager was apprised of what had really happened. This short time-lag was of great importance.

On 19 June the Court received a Memorial which the circumspect Viceroy Yü Lu had despatched from Tientsin on the 17th. Although he wrote after the Forts had fallen, he reported only the delivery of the foreign Admirals' ultimatum on the previous day; and he followed this with a further Memorial (received in Peking on the 21st) which spoke of victories at

* Lieutenant C. C. Dix, R.N.: *The World's Navies in the Boxer Rebellion.* In 1860 the loss of the Forts had been ascribed by the Manchu general Sankolinson to 'the unfortunate explosion of a powder magazine.'

Taku and Tientsin, of gallant cooperation by the Boxers and of two enemy warships disabled, but which failed to mention that the vitally important Forts had been in foreign hands since the morning of the 17th.* It was on the basis of this Memorial (and in the light, therefore, of serious misapprehensions about the true situation) that an Imperial Edict was issued declaring war upon the world.

Before this Edict was written, however, measures of even more questionable wisdom had been put in hand. When the Court heard of the Allied ultimatum 'a new era began for the Boxers.' Rice and money were distributed, princes and grandees were placed in command of them. 'With these rewards and encouragements, the Boxers . . . became even more violent and reckless, making Peking a veritable pandemonium. . . . Each band had its own leader and each leader made his own laws. In fact, anyone wearing something red could claim to be a Boxer, and any Boxer seemed to be invested with authority to kill, burn and plunder at will. . . . As to how many of the lesser officials and the common people were pillaged, attacked and killed there are no statistics, but at one time the capital was so littered with dead bodies that the Imperial Court had to issue a Decree ordering the commanders of the Peking Field Force to have them removed from the city.' † Senior officials, scholars and other notable men were insulted and sometimes manhandled. Chaos reigned.

From the foreigners' point of view far the most serious aspect of these developments was not the impetus given to the Boxer movement, whose members were ill-led and poorly armed, but the fact that the Imperial troops were now ordered into the firing line.

Their impact was first felt at Tientsin. On 15 and 16 June

* Yü Lu strove always, and generally with success, to create a good impression. Mr Carles, the British Consul at Tientsin, asked on 16 June for authority to offer him asylum on board one of Her Majesty's ships 'in the event of his being in personal danger owing to his loyalty to the British.' Lord Salisbury telegraphed on the same day his instructions that this offer should be made.

† Tan.

the Boxers had made destructive inroads into the Foreign Settlements, where the garrison of 2400 men (including 1600 Russian soldiers) had the task of defending a five-mile perimeter which enclosed, among other things, several hundred women and children. On the 17th, after the Allied attack on the Forts thirty-five miles downstream, Chinese artillery opened fire on the Settlements; and on the following day a force estimated at 10,000 made a heavy attack on the defences, many of which were barricades improvised from bales of merchandise —wool, silk, cotton, sugar, rice and peanuts. Their construction was largely inspired and supervised by a young American mining engineer who later became President of the United States.*

Fierce fighting ensued. Communications with Taku had now been cut and the hard-pressed garrison was running short of ammunition. On 20 June a young English civilian, James Watts, volunteered to ride to Taku with news of their almost desperate situation; he was an excellent horseman and knew the country well. He set out at night, taking an escort of three Cossacks and one spare pony. They were twelve hours in the saddle. They charged at full gallop through villages and over the little hump-backed stone bridges where these danger-points could not be by-passed; Watts had one pony shot under him. They were favoured by a sea-mist as they approached the coast, and on the morning of 21 June Watts delivered to the naval authorities information in the light of which yet another relief expedition was mounted. For this exploit—again very much in the G. A. Henty style—Watts was created CMG.

A force of 440 Russian infantry with 140 United States Marines was already probing up the railway towards Tientsin, but had been repulsed near the outskirts of the city on the previous day (20 June). At this juncture there were barely a thousand men left at Taku; no more could be found from the warships, which had already been 'distressed' (in the Royal Navy's phrase) of every man who could be spared, and the four huge forts had to be garrisoned.

* Herbert Hoover: *Memoirs.*

Luckily there now arrived HMS *Terrible* from Hongkong and a Russian troopship from Port Arthur; the former had on board 300 men of the 2nd Battalion the Royal Welch Fusiliers and a small detachment of Royal Engineers. These, with 250 bluejackets and a tiny Italian contingent, left by rail on the 21st under the command of Commander Cradock, who had led the storming parties against the Forts.* They were preceded by another train carrying about 1000 Russians, 250 Germans and 150 Americans. Despite mishaps, including one derailment, the two trains got to within twelve miles of Tientsin, and were there reinforced by 150 men of the Weihaiwei Regiment, a newly-raised Chinese unit with British officers. The force's scanty artillery included one of *Monocacy*'s smoothbores, a twelve-pounder; with Washington's permission the United States Navy had abandoned the uncongenial role of a looker-on.

On 23 June the relief force deployed and advanced in the teeth of a blinding dust-storm. Prisoners reported that their way to the Settlements was barred by a body of Imperial troops which outnumbered them by ten to one; but although there was fierce fighting as village after village was cleared, the Allies made steady progress. 'Quarter was neither asked for nor given,' wrote a British midshipman, 'for in the Boxer proclamations were passages relating to European women and children which put them on a par with incarnate devils.' This was pure hearsay. Although unsupported, in retrospect, by documentary evidence, the existence of these proclamations was believed in by the fighting men. Truth, as ever, headed the casualty lists.

At last the Settlements were in view. Heartened by the sight of the Red Ensign still flying over the Town Hall, the tired men pressed on against weakening Chinese resistance, and after eight hours' dogged work joined hands with the defenders.

In hard fact all that had been achieved was to double the number of hostages to fortune in an extensive, unfortified,

* Cradock, by then a Rear-Admiral, commanded the British squadron in the Battle of Coronel (1914) and went down with his flagship, HMS *Good Hope*.

inflammable built-up area, hemmed in by large military and rebel forces well supplied with artillery, and wholly dependant for its communications on thirty miles of damaged railway which might be cut again at any moment. It was typical of the foreigners that they believed Tientsin to have been saved, not merely reinforced; and it was typical of the Chinese that they were right.

What, meanwhile, had happened to Seymour? Tientsin had had no news of him since 13 June; the reader last heard of him at Yangtsun, more than twenty miles north of Tientsin, on the 18th.

Before dawn on the following day the expedition which had set out to relieve Peking began its gruelling retreat down the river; the officers had buried their full-dress uniforms. Far ahead of them artillery pounded discouragingly on their destination. Every village had to be cleared at the point of the bayonet. Imperial cavalry harassed their left flank. They were shelled intermittently from the railway embankment, which dominated and ran parallel to the river. Between villages— between, that is, actions for which the troops had to halt and deploy—the column could move no faster than the four junks which it towed through the shallow water and which carried the wounded and the guns; these hulks continually ran aground. The heat was intense and the force on half-rations. At night picquets had to be mounted, mostly by the flank- and advance-guards who had borne the main burden of the day. After three days of this crawling fight Seymour had covered less than twenty miles and was still some ten miles from Tientsin, whence the guns continued to boom out their enigmatic, unhopeful message.

The column dragged itself down the river-bank like a wounded snake. At midnight on 21 June, after a hard fight in which Jellicoe, his chief of staff, had been to all appearances mortally wounded, 'even the Admiral, who had been the life and soul of the expedition, and also, by his bravery, unselfishness and courtesy, had made himself as popular with the foreigners as he already was with his own men, seemed a little despondent.' * But they carried another village, charging in column of fours without bothering to deploy, and struggled on. Soon they became aware of a tall, inexplicable, seemingly endless black mass, looming up in the night on the opposite bank of the narrow river. This was the Hsiku Arsenal, 'whose existence [Seymour recorded] was before unknown to us.'

A courteous challenge from this great stronghold (its walls enclosed nearly forty acres) was courteously answered, and was followed by a vicious hail of fire.

'We were caught in a sort of death-trap and for an instant all was confusion. . . . We seemed done for.' † The junks drifted on into the trap; the boat carrying most of the guns foundered, and five of the wounded in the others were killed. Luckily the Chinese fired high.‡ Some brave British bluejackets swam out and caught the tow-ropes of the errant junks. Two small storming-parties—one British, the other German—crossed the river above and below the Arsenal and took its outer defences from either flank; after confused fighting in the darkness the Chinese fled.

When dawn came Seymour found himself master of an immense square fort whose walls were 700 yards long. In the Arsenal was stored a great quantity of field-guns, machine-guns and rifles, with more than 7,000,000 rounds of small-arms ammunition; there were also fifteen tons of rice and an invaluable stock of bandages and other medical supplies. A well was dug and counter-attacks were beaten off; the charger of an officer who led one of them was cooked and eaten with relish.

The Arsenal was about six miles from the Foreign Settle-

---

* Bigham.

† *Ibid.*

‡ This was a common failing even among the Imperial troops. Captured rifles often had their sights elevated to the maximum, for it was widely believed among the Chinese that the figures on the hind-sights governed the muzzle-velocity of the bullet. It would be natural in a soldier suffering from this delusion to set his sights at (say) 1000 rather than at 100; and it would be inevitable, if he did so, that his bullets would pass over any target engaged at comparatively close range.

ments, and various unsuccessful attempts were made to communicate with the defenders of Tientsin. Finally, on 24 June,
Bigham's Chinese servant was sent off with a cipher message to
the British Consul, which he had to eat at an early stage of his
journey. He was arrested by the Boxers, by Imperial troops and
finally by a French outpost, but bluff and resource brought him
through and he delivered a verbal report at the British Con-
sulate. From Tientsin, the siege of which had been raised only
on the previous day, yet another relief expedition—the third to
be mounted by the Allies in a fortnight—was hastily organised.

The 24th was a severe day for the defenders of Hsiku. Again
a dust-storm raged; it was so violent that 'you could only bear
to look to leeward,' noted Seymour, who doubted whether the
Chinese could have been held if they had attacked downwind.
But next day the Chinese batteries to the southward fell silent.
Rifle-fire was heard in the middle distance, small bodies of
their assailants were seen withdrawing, and presently Cossack
pennons could be discerned fluttering above the tall crops of
millet on the plain. Almost unopposed, a column under the
Russian Colonel Shirinsky came into view, guided by Bigham's
resourceful servant.

Litters were improvised for the 232 wounded, and on 26 June
Seymour's expedition started for Tientsin under the protection
of its rescuers. The sailors were dead-tired; with four men to
each stretcher, they were finished as a fighting force.

Their casualties had been:

|  | Killed | Wounded |
|---|---|---|
| British | 27 | 97 |
| German | 12 | 62 |
| Russian | 10 | 27 |
| French | 1 | 12 |
| American | 4 | 28 |
| Japanese | 2 | 3 |
| Italian | 5 | 3 |
| Austrian | 1 | 0 |
|  | 62 | 232 |

# THE SIEGE AT PEKING

The column 'made a tremendous long line and would have been an easy one to attack,' wrote Beatty. In a private letter a few days earlier, with Tientsin still isolated and Seymour's whereabouts unknown, he had described the operations in North China as 'the maddest, wildest, damnedest, rottenest scheme that could emanate from the brain of any man.'

The epithets may stand; but 'scheme' is hardly the word for a series of impromptu, unrelated adventures, each blindly undertaken against great odds on grounds which were chivalrous or at least humanitarian rather than military. G. A. Henty, not Clausewitz, inspired Allied strategy (if such it can be called) on the plain of Chihli. The adventurers owed much to luck and more, perhaps, to their enemy's lack of resolution; they got off more lightly than they deserved. But between them they had done the only thing which would make it possible to avenge, if not to save, the Legations; they had kept the Pei Ho open and secured, however precariously, a base for an overland advance on the Chinese capital.

CHAPTER SEVEN

# The Murderers

*The foreign troops in the Legations still hold their position and wait for outside relief. It is requested that all the Wu Wei troops in the city be ordered speedily to dislodge them and kill them all, so that the mouths of the foreigners will be silenced. Later we can put the blame on the rebellious troops and rebellious people who went beyond our control.*

From a Memorial submitted to the Throne by a Censor on 5 July 1900.

OF the events described in the preceding chapter the Peking Legations knew virtually nothing.

Early on the morning of 11 June (the day after Prince Tuan's appointment to the Presidency of the Tsungli Yamen had been hailed as a good omen by Sir Robert Hart) carts were sent out to the railway station to meet the trains conveying Admiral Seymour's force. They were followed at a less unfashionable hour by several parties of Europeans on horseback. But no trains came, and in the heat of the day the reception committees rode back through the derisive ranks of Kansu soldiery, once more concentrated in the park-like grounds surrounding the Temples of Heaven and of Agriculture.

That afternoon the Chancellor of the Japanese Legation, Sugiyama, returned to the station. He went alone and unarmed, wearing a tail-coat and a bowler hat. Outside the Yung Ting Men he was dragged from his cart by the troops and hacked to pieces before an appreciative crowd. His mutilated corpse was left lying in the gutter; his heart was cut out and sent to General Tung Fu-hsiang, whose men had done the deed. Two days later a Decree was published in which the murder was attributed to bandits.

Partly perhaps because the Japanese Chancellor was an Asiatic, but mainly because his murder was only one of many alarming portents which beset them, this outrage seems not to have shocked the European diplomats as much as might have been expected. The atmosphere of crisis was now unmistakable. The streets round the Legations were deserted. Servants, grooms, chair-bearers, gardeners and interpreters were unobtrusively departing; in the eyes of the Boxers they were the *san mao-tzu*, the 'third-class coarse-haired ones,' and many of them, like the shopkeepers who dealt in foreign goods, were massacred with their families. Every hour brought fresh news of the destruction of missionary property, much of it within the walls of the capital.

By now all the missionaries within reach of Peking had sought asylum there; others, stationed farther afield, were attempting flight northwards towards Russian territory or were making for Treaty Ports on the Yangtse. Bishop Favier stood fast in the Peitang, one of the three great Roman Catholic cathedrals, where (although it was situated inside the walls of the Imperial City) several thousand converts had taken refuge; and a large but untenable Methodist compound near the American Legation was still occupied, on Mr Conger's insistence and against the advice of the American officers. But this was later abandoned, and the Legation Quarter, with nearly 400 guards to accommodate as well, faced an acute housing problem.

On 13 June great excitement was caused by the appearance of a Boxer in Legation Street—'a full-fledged Boxer with his hair tied up in red cloth, red ribbons round his wrists and ankles, and a flaming red girdle tightening his loose white tunic.' He was travelling in a Peking cart, and ostentatiously sharpened a knife on his boot as he sat in the usual position on the offside shaft.

The sight was too much for the German Minister. Baron von Ketteler was a man of strong views and impetuous courage;

'had we allowed the German Minister his head,' Sir Claude MacDonald had written to Admiral Seymour ten days earlier, 'the partition of China would now be a *fait accompli*.' * He attacked the arrogant intruder with his walking-stick. The Boxer dodged up an alley and made good his escape. But inside the cart † another Boxer was found, a boy who despite his youth was savagely beaten and made prisoner in the German Legation, where official demands for his release were rejected. 'So Boxers *are* in the city and quiet is still liable to be broken!' Hart wrote to the British Minister at noon.

Later the same day quiet was broken to an extent which not even the Inspector-General of the Maritime Customs could ignore. That afternoon a horde of Boxers irrupted into the Tartar City through the Ha Ta Men, immediately to the east of the Legation Quarter, slashing and stabbing indiscriminately as they pillaged the shops and houses. Terrified crowds swept past the Legations. 'Never,' wrote Putnam Weale, 'have I seen such fast galloping and driving in the Peking streets; never would I have believed that small-footed [i.e. Chinese] women, of whom there are a goodly number even in the large-footed Manchu city, could get so nimbly over the ground. Everybody was panic-stricken and distraught. . . . They went on running, running, running. Then the waves of men, women and animals disappeared as suddenly as they had come, and the streets became once again silent and deserted. Far away the din of the Boxers could still be heard, and flames shooting up to the skies now marked their track; but of the dreaded men themselves we had not seen a single one.'

Soon a great arc of flames, leaping up above the roofs and tree-tops which limited vision from the low buildings in the Legation compounds, seared the night sky to the east and northeast. The wind, which was from those quarters, brought to the anxious ears of the foreigners a loathsome medley of sounds. Above the roar of flames and the crash of rafters and masonry,

* M.P.

† The Peking cart was—and is—covered by a close-fitting hood of dark blue cloth, so that the occupants are invisible from outside.

above even the Boxers' orgiastic howls of '*Sha! Sha!*', could be heard the screams of fear and agony as the 'secondary devils,' the converts and their families, were speared, cut to pieces or burnt alive. Missionary property, Customs premises and the houses of the foreign teachers at the Imperial University were systematically fired. The great East Cathedral went up with a roar, the aged French priest in charge perishing with many of his converts in the flames. 'It was an appalling sight,' wrote Morrison.

Late at night many torches came bobbing down Customs Street towards the Austrian Legation, which—save for the out-lying Belgian Legation, occupied only by a small picquet of five men—was the nearest to the inferno. The Austrian machine-gunners allowed the Boxers to come within 150 yards, then opened fire. The angry chatter of the automatic weapon, amplified by the empty buildings on each side of the street, was music in the ears of the defenders. The torches vanished. But a reconnaissance party failed to find the expected pile of corpses, and next morning a tangle of severed telegraph wires farther up the street showed that the Austrians had fired high. The rebels' first brush with the Powers had seemingly confirmed their supernatural claims.

The same night a party of volunteers, led by a young French-man and accompanied by the brave Chamots, rode out to the South Cathedral and brought back to safety all the Catholic missionaries there, including five sisters of charity and twenty Chinese nuns. They had hardly left the Cathedral, which was nearly three hundred years old and contained a memorial tablet presented by the Emperor K'ang Hsi, when it was fired. It burnt for many hours, while in the surrounding streets—the centre of the Catholic community in Peking—hundreds, per-haps thousands, of Christians were butchered. Next day (15 June) patrols of American, Russian, British and German marines went out and brought in survivors, shooting any Boxers they met. Morrison, who went with them (and was indeed largely responsible for their going), witnessed 'awful sights . . . women and children hacked to pieces, men trussed like fowls, with noses and ears cut off and eyes gouged out.' Peking had become a charnel-house. Senior members of the Manchu Court were driving round at night in carts to watch, with evident satisfaction, the massacre of their fellow-countrymen.

On 13 June a telegraph line running northwards via Kiakhta to Russian territory, which had worked intermittently since the wires to Tientsin were pulled down on 10 June, was cut for the last time. Fulsome envoys from the Tsungli Yamen continued to seek interviews with the Ministers, to offer assurances that order was being restored and to deprecate the need for reinforcements from Tientsin. Otherwise the Legations were entirely cut off from the rest of the world.

Though they were not yet under attack, the American Minister estimated on 15 June that 'nearly 100 Boxers have already been killed by the various Legation guards.' This total almost certainly included a good many non-Boxers, for, as a missionary noted, 'most of the foreign troops were quite reckless in the way they fired upon the Chinese.' The total was increased on the 16th, when a strong British–American–Japanese patrol, searching for Christian refugees, surprised a gang of swordsmen who in a reek of incense and blood were performing human sacrifices in a small temple. The place was surrounded, forty-six Boxers were shot down in ten minutes and their surviving prisoners released. 'I myself killed at least six,' *The Times* Correspondent wrote in his diary.

At this stage the Imperial troops were still playing the role of passive onlookers, and Chinese soldiers manning the guard-posts on the Tartar Wall held amicable discourse with the few foreigners who visited them. They watched the converts being hunted down. They watched the firing of shops which sold foreign goods, and when the flames spread they watched the destruction of the whole commercial quarter—'the richest part of Peking, the pearl and jewel shops, the silk and fur, the satin and embroidery stores, the great curio shops, the melting houses, and nearly all that was of the highest value in the metropolis.' * The fire spread to the Chien Men, the huge central gate, crowned by a hundred-foot-high tower and opened only to permit the solemn egress of the Emperor on his ritual visits to the Temple of Heaven or the Temple of Agriculture. This landmark in the history of mankind was destroyed in a few hours. It was generally felt by the Chinese to presage the downfall of the Manchu dynasty; no reference was made to it in official Edicts.

These had begun to reflect the Court's alarm at the chaos for which its own policies were directly responsible. But though strict and detailed instructions were given for the restoration of order, the Boxers were scarcely mentioned, the blame being laid on 'brigands' and 'seditious characters.' On 17 June, Jung Lu (a childhood friend and lifelong associate of the Empress Dowager, who now commanded the five armies forming the Peking Field Force) was ordered—'Let there be no remissness!'—to take immediate and effective steps for the protection of the Legations. Several of the Ministers were asked for their views on what military dispositions would best achieve this end.

At noon on 16 June the Empress Dowager summoned an Imperial Council.† Its members needed to take two decisions. What was to be done about the Boxers in Peking? What was to be done about the foreign force advancing on Peking?

Several ministers of the milder sort urged that the Boxers should be driven out of the city; they were not patriots but rebels, and their claims to invulnerability were worthless. This proposal was received coldly by the Empress Dowager and with violent hostility by Prince Tuan. In the end it was vaguely resolved that the Boxers should be 'pacified.'

* Morrison (*The Times*, 13 October 1900).
† I have here followed Tan, whose study of contemporary vernacular sources, published by the Chinese Government in 1952, is of great value. There is no single authoritative account of the Imperial Council's deliberations; but (Tan writes) although 'the various versions are far from being the same . . . there is agreement on some important points.' This is as near the exact truth as anyone can now hope to get.

The Imperial Council seems to have had no clear idea of the difficulties which Seymour, although he was only thirty-odd miles from Peking, was encountering. Two of its members were ordered to go south, intercept him and dissuade him from entering the capital.* Meanwhile instructions were sent to the Viceroy Yü Lu and his generals to resist any further advance by foreign forces. Reinforcements from Manchuria were ordered to Peking.

A rather more decisive Council was held on the following afternoon, 17 June. The Empress Dowager had received a document in the form of an ultimatum. It purported to come —presumably via the Legations—from the Governments of the Powers; it had in fact been forged, probably by Prince Tuan. It demanded that the collection of revenues and the conduct of military affairs throughout the Empire should be placed in the hands of the foreign Ministers and that the Throne should be restored to the Emperor.

Nobody seems to have questioned the authenticity of this implausible document. Nobody asked which Powers were party to such an exigent *démarche* or suggested that (for instance) the Russian Minister, whose country was on paper China's ally, should be invited to explain what was behind it. The Empress Dowager reacted in the way that the authors of the document presumably hoped she would. 'Now,' she is reported to have exclaimed, 'the Powers have started the aggression, and the extinction of our nation is imminent. If we just fold our arms and yield to them, I would have no face to see our ancestors after death. If we must perish, why not fight to the death?' A Decree (which was widely ignored) went out to the provinces ordering them to send troops to Peking.

While this bogus ultimatum was being discussed in one of the great dark council-chambers of the Forbidden City, a real

* From a note which he wrote to Sir Claude MacDonald it is clear that the Russian Minister was approached by the Tsungli Yamen with a request that a member of his staff should accompany the two emissaries. This request was ignored, but de Giers commented: 'It gives me grounds to believe that the troops cannot be far away.' (M.P.)

ultimatum was being delivered by the French Consul to the Viceroy at Tientsin.

It was an uneasy time for the Legations, a twilit period of foreboding, of waiting from one hour to the next in the no-man's-land between peace and war.

Though the Boxers were regarded as obscene and hateful vermin, they were not greatly feared. Sir Robert Hart's daily letters to the British Minister bear witness to an ebbing courage. To Morrison he seemed 'painfully nervous and shaken;' Poole, the British Legation doctor, called him 'an awful old funk-stick.' But even he (who two days earlier had observed almost with incredulity that 'quiet is still liable to be broken') could write on 15 June: 'What a bit of luck for us that the Boxers have only swords, etc. Had they *guns*, they'd wipe us out in a night, they are so numerous!'

Tung Fu-hsiang's Moslem cavalry, flaunting banners of scarlet and black but armed with modern Mausers, were however treated with great respect. They had taken a leading part in anti-foreign incidents two years earlier, and when on 17 June, after a stone-throwing incident, a detachment of them was fired on by the Germans, Sir Claude MacDonald sent a tactful reproof to Baron von Ketteler, urging strict precautions against all acts of provocation; 'when our own troops arrive we may with safety assume a different tone, but it is hardly wise now.'

His note made no mention of another incident which Morrison had reported to him earlier that day. 'Ketteler and his merry men have just shot 7 Boxers from the top of the wall. 50 or 100 were drilling at a distance of 200 yards. 7 were killed and I suspect many wounded. . . . The stalking was excellently done.' The Boxers were regarded as fair game. Any prisoners taken were killed; one who was for a time kept captive in the British Legation caused, even though bound hand and foot behind locked doors, a sort of panic among the servants, who expected him at any moment to deploy his magic powers.

Most of the servants who stayed at their posts were Christians, who dared not leave the Legations. 'Good riddance!' Sergeant

Herring had been heard to say when the exodus of non-Christian retainers started; 'we don't want any skulkers round here.' * But in fact these defections were creating an exceedingly dangerous vacuum. Nobody then appreciated how dangerous it was, and it might not have been filled but for the humanitarian impulses and persuasive powers of Dr Morrison, abetted by some of the leading missionaries.

At first, one of these recorded, 'the Ministers seemed to display an almost cruel disregard for the massacre and sufferings of native Christians.' It was, as has been told, a volunteer rescue party of armed civilians who went out and saved the Catholic missionaries in the South Cathedral from certain death; and the subsequent despatch of patrols from the British and other Legations to bring in Chinese survivors of the slaughter was due largely to Morrison's insistence.†

The reluctance of the Ministers to offer asylum to the victims of a savage persecution is understandable on worldly grounds. The Legations were already overcrowded. To open their gates to those who were the immediate objects of the Boxers' wrath might invite reprisals from the Boxers. Undesirable elements might make their way in with the fugitives. Apart from the problem of feeding them, there were risks of panic and disease.

But to Morrison, as the screams came thinly through the smoke-laden air, these prudent arguments seemed contemptible. His crusade was successful. In all, some 2000 Roman Catholic Chinese (he himself gave a lower figure) were brought or found their way into the Legations; and this precedent gave the Methodists the excuse to ignore an official embargo and bring in their own converts when, a few days later, they had to evacuate their fortified compound near the Ha Ta Men.

* Sergeant Herring, known to the Chinese as 'the New Soldier' because twenty years earlier he had been the last to arrive of a guard detachment then stationed in the Legation, was a minor tyrant whose rule over the outdoor staff in the Legation compound was strengthened by his command of Chinese invective.

† See, among other sources, Nigel Oliphant: *A Diary of the Siege of the Legations in Peking*.

The effect of all this was to remedy a fatal and unsuspected weakness in the Legations' defences by providing them with a labour force. In the weeks that lay ahead the converts proved indispensable. They built a labyrinth of barricades, dug trenches, counter-mines and 'bomb-proofs,' demolished inflammable houses, milled corn, fought fires, cleared up débris, carried stretchers and performed under the blazing sun a vast amount of manual labour which the hard-pressed Europeans could not have tackled successfully without their aid. From a strictly military point of view the influx in these days of several hundred able-bodied Chinese and their dependants, then regarded by the Ministers as *bouches inutiles* if nothing worse, almost certainly saved the Legations.

The belief that they were about to be rescued, or at least reinforced, persisted. This fallacy usefully coloured the foreigners' outlook almost throughout the Siege. Just as small upper-class children of the period found it difficult to conceive of a dilemma from which their nanny would not, sooner or later, extricate them, so the Legations placed a tacit faith in their Governments. They had failed to foresee their predicament; they failed, not less signally, to understand the difficulties involved in extricating them from it.

Messages received on 15 June by the British and American Legations from the relief expedition at Langfang should have thrown doubt on its prospects of reaching, let alone fighting its way into, Peking. 'Please believe me,' wrote Seymour, after describing only a few of the obstacles to further progress along the railway, 'we are doing our utmost to get on'; should these obstacles prove insuperable, 'I will consider if we can *march* to your relief.' *

On the day this message came in Sir Robert Hart wrote: 'I wonder at the Relief Force spending so long in the train! After doing half of the journey that way, they could easily do the rest in two days across country.' † This attitude was general. Admiral Seymour was referred to as Admiral See-No-More,

* M.P.                    † *Ibid.*

the Russian Colonel Vogak as Colonel Go-Back. In the darken-
ing and disordered nursery, nanny's failure to make her awaited
appearance and set matters to rights evoked a sense of grievance.
Fortunately (as things turned out) the nursery went on for
several weeks expecting her to arrive at any moment.

The Legations had now been isolated for more than a week.
The days and nights passed slowly. Every aspect of the situation, every contingency which it might conceivably bring forth
had—or so it seemed to the foreigners—been thrashed out, over
and over again, in endless discussions. Yet the blow that fell on
19 June was wholly unexpected.

That afternoon twelve large scarlet envelopes were brought
into the Legations by minor functionaries of the Tsungli Yamen
and delivered to the eleven Ministers and to Sir Robert Hart.
They contained an ultimatum.

A despatch, the Yamen wrote, had been received from the
Viceroy of Chihli in which he reported that the Powers had
demanded the surrender of the Taku Forts by 2 a.m. on 17 June.
If this demand was not complied with, the Powers would occupy
the Forts by force.

'The receipt of this news,' the Yamen continued, 'has caused
us the greatest astonishment.' It showed on the part of the
Powers 'a deliberate intention to break the peace and to commit an act of hostility. The Boxer movement is now active in
the capital and there is much popular excitement. While Your
Excellency and the members of your family, etc., reside here the
Legations are in danger, and the Chinese Government is really
in a difficult position as regards affording efficient protection.
*The Yamen must, therefore, request that within twenty-four hours Your
Excellency will start, accompanied by the Legation guards, who must be
kept under proper control, and proceed to Tientsin in order to prevent
any unforeseen calamity.*' Troops, it was added, had been detailed
to furnish an escort for the journey. The time at which these
missives had been despatched—4 p.m.—was incorporated in
the text, so that there could be no doubt when the twenty-four
hours would be up.

The Spanish Minister, Señor Cologan,* was the doyen of the Corps Diplomatique, and in his Legation a meeting was hastily convened. Behind the gutted Telegraph Office a fireworks shop was burning; an intermittent series of explosions did nothing to increase the composure with which the Ministers discussed this grave development in a situation which was alarming enough already.

It must be remembered that they knew nothing whatever of the events which had made the capture of the Forts imperative. Shortly before communications were cut they had received vaguely disquieting reports about Tientsin from their consuls there; but they had no idea that the Settlements were under siege, and they still imagined Seymour—who was in fact towing his wounded at a foot's pace down the Pei Ho, fifty miles away —to be just outside the walls of Peking. Indeed, on the strength of a searchlight thought to have been seen from the British Legation on the previous night, he had been half-expected to arrive that very day.

Their first reaction was thus one of indignation against their compatriots at Tientsin and Taku, in whose precipitate action they saw only the wanton hazarding of their own lives. A letter written on 20 June (but apparently never despatched) by Sir Claude MacDonald to Mr Carles, the British Consul at Tientsin, conveys some of their angry perturbation. The senior consul at Tientsin, Sir Claude rather unreasonably observed, 'has much to answer for. . . . We wrote to the Yamen that the whole thing was incomprehensible,† *that we are Reps. of our Govts. as to acts of war and such a step as that taken by the Consular body was quite impossible, &c., &c.* . . . We are in absolute ignorance of where the relieving force is—*or whether there is any relieving force at all.*' The undercurrent of petulance is unmistakable; and the first of the two deleted passages gives a misleading account of the Ministers' reply to the Yamen, which was couched in accommodating terms and

* He is said to have been of Irish extraction.
† In the following passage the words in italics form part of the original text but were evidently deleted at a later date.

made no reference to acts of war or to the Consular body at Tientsin.*

The Corps Diplomatique sat far into the night, while rumours of the most disturbing kind buzzed round the Legation Quarter, most of whose occupants were convinced (as one of them put it) that 'if to stay meant probable massacre, to go meant certain destruction.'

In the Spanish Legation this realistic view was urged with vehemence by Baron von Ketteler; but a party of appeasement, led by the French and American Ministers, recommended acceptance of the ultimatum. As Morrison afterwards implied in *The Times*, it ill became M. Pichon, in his statutory position as Protecteur des Missions Catholiques en Chine, to advocate a course of action which, however favourably it might turn out for the foreigners, involved abandoning several thousand converts (to say nothing of Bishop Favier and the inmates of the Peitang) to a certain and unspeakable fate.

Nor is it easy to see how the arguments of the appeasers carried (as they eventually did) conviction to a majority of the Ministers. Just before the meeting Sir Claude MacDonald had received a note from Sir Robert Hart in which, after referring to 'feeling a bit upset occasionally,' he wrote: 'I am not at all in favour of *surrender*, but, when I think of the women and children, I wonder and wonder which course would ensure their safety most entirely.' It may well have been reasoning on these lines that prevailed over the fire-eating von Ketteler.

At any rate, shortly before midnight a compliant answer, signed by the doyen, was sent off through the moonlit, half-ruined streets to the Tsungli Yamen. After expressing astonishment at the Yamen's *démarche* and complete ignorance of what had passed at Taku, the note went on: 'The foreign Ministers can only accept the declaration and demand made by the

---

* But Sir Claude's letter makes it clear that he had not misread the ultimatum ('This I take it is a polite way of saying they are going to massacre us') and ends: 'I fully expect that shortly after 4 they will open fire upon us, when up goes the Union Jack and we nail the old rag to the Post . . . Please give Bearer 100 dollars if he gets this through.'

Yamen, and they are ready to leave Peking. It is, however, materially * impossible to organise their departure within the short space of twenty-four hours.' The Corps asked for particulars of the protection which would be given them en route, for means of transport and provisions to be made available, and for the company on their journey of 'some of the Ministers of the Tsungli Yamen.' They requested an interview with Prince Ch'ing and Prince Tuan at 9 a.m. on the following day.†

Most people had gone to bed when, after deliberating for six hours, the members of the Corps Diplomatique emerged from the Spanish Legation. In those who were still abroad the news of their decision, although foreshadowed by rumour, aroused consternation and disgust. The column of carts needed to move the foreign community out of Peking would be at least a mile long. If treachery was intended, how could the 500 guards and armed volunteers ensure its protection against its 'escort' of Imperial troops? If the Court wanted to keep its hands comparatively clean, it had only to instruct the escort-commander to adopt a policy of non-intervention when the Boxers attacked. A military expedition had failed to reach Peking from Tientsin; what prospects had a huge and almost defenceless caravan of completing the journey in the reverse direction? And what about the converts?

Moved by these and other considerations, committees of protest were organised, interviews with Ministers were insisted on and weighty letters were written in the small hours. In the crowded compound of the American Legation these activities were particularly rife. Mr Conger—'to his everlasting dishonour,' in Morrison's view—had ordered 100 carts to be assembled; the women 'were packing the tiny amount of hand-

---

* *Matériellement.* 'Physically' might have been a better rendering, but the translators had much on their minds.

† Since his appointment, ten days earlier, to the Presidency of the Yamen Prince Tuan had not called on the Legations, who thus—technically—had no cognisance of him. By the rules of diplomacy a small point was scored by putting his name after that of the man whom he had replaced; but the rules of diplomacy were no longer being observed in Peking, and it is doubtful if this shrewd thrust got home.

luggage we were to be allowed to take with us, wondering whether to fill the small bag with a warm coat, to protect us on this indefinite journey to the coast, or to take six fresh blouses. . . . It looked very much as if we were all to start out to our deaths the following morning.' *

In the more phlegmatic British Legation 'no packing was done, for it was there considered inconceivable that China would insist upon sending the Ministers their passports.' † One of his guests recorded in her diary that 'Sir Claude says he has no intention of moving a yard'; ‡ but Morrison, after remonstrating strongly with the British Minister, detected only a 'wavering' in his attitude towards departure. 'I went home,' wrote *The Times* Correspondent in his diary, 'and could not look my servant in the face.' Next morning Mr Conger asked him how he felt. 'I feel ashamed to be a white man,' replied Morrison hotly.

The Corps Diplomatique reassembled at an early hour. In his memoirs M. Pichon refers to the despatch at 7 a.m. of a note in which the Ministers asked to be put in touch with the Admirals who had captured the Forts; the idea seems to have been that the diplomats would use their good offices to have the Forts handed back to China as soon as the Relief Expedition arrived. This communication may have been drafted, translated, despatched and received; but the Corps did not meet until 9 a.m. and appear to have been collectively unaware of it.

They met at the French Legation, which for a no longer discoverable reason was deemed more convenient than the Spanish; and they waited until half past nine—eleven anxious, weary men, of whom one had barely an hour to live. They had asked to be received by the Yamen at nine o'clock. They had made their request only at midnight, and Chinese officialdom has never been nocturnal in its habits; but the ultimatum would expire in seven hours, the Ministers were impatient, and the

* Mary Hooker.
† Morrison (*The Times*, 13 October 1900).
‡ Diary of Mrs Tours.

non-arrival of a reply seemed to them 'an act of gross discourtesy.'

What were they to do? The fullest account of what they did do is contained in a confidential letter written on 4 September by Sir Claude MacDonald to Mr Bertie, the Permanent Under-Secretary of State at the Foreign Office.

'As no answer had come by 9.30, it was suggested by the majority of the Ministers that we should wait until one did come, as it would be undignified to go to the Yamen and sit there waiting for the Princes. Thereupon von Ketteler, who is, or rather was, a very passionate and excitable man, banged his fist on the table and said "I will go and sit there till they do come, if I have to sit there all night." '

At this (perhaps because an instinctive objection to unilateral action by any of its members was deeply rooted in the Corps Diplomatique) the Russian Minister proposed that they should all go to the Yamen together, with an armed escort.

'Von Ketteler replied: "There is no danger; yesterday and the day before I sent my Dragoman, and he was in no way molested." ' (His 'Dragoman' was the Chinese Secretary of the German Legation, a sinologue named Cordes.)

'Then why not send him now?' de Giers suggested.

'A good idea,' said von Ketteler. 'I think I will.' The meeting broke up. But the German Minister changed his mind.

The fire-scarred streets round the Legations were silent and deserted when Baron von Ketteler and Herr Cordes set out for the Tsungli Yamen, whose unimposing offices were about a mile away. They travelled in sedan-chairs with hoods of scarlet and green denoting their official status, and were accompanied by two liveried outriders on ponies. The German Minister was smoking a cigar and had provided himself with a book to beguile the inevitable *longueurs* of the ante-chamber; he had seen much service in China. An escort of five heavily armed sailors was standing by, but von Ketteler dismissed them. He looked, someone remarked, 'as if he were going on a picnic.'

A quarter of an hour passed. Then there was a sudden clatter of hoofs. Belabouring his pony and yelling unintelligibly, one of the outriders swept down Legation Street, through the flimsy barricades and into the German Legation compound. His grim news spread like wildfire; von Ketteler had been murdered.

Half an hour later Herr Cordes dragged himself into the American Methodist Mission near the Ha Ta Men, fainting as he crossed the threshold. He had been shot through both thighs but had somehow eluded his pursuers. To Morrison immediately afterwards he gave his account of what happened.

'We were close to the police-station on the left [of the Ha Ta Men Street]. I was watching a cart with some lance-bearers passing before the Minister's chair, when suddenly I saw a sight that made my heart stand still. The Minister's chair was three paces in front of me. I saw a banner soldier, apparently a Manchu, in full uniform with a mandarin's hat and a button and blue feather, step forward, present his rifle within a yard of the chair window, level it at the Minister's head and fire. I shouted in terror "Halt!" At the same moment the shot rang out, the chairs were thrown down. I sprang to my feet. A shot struck me in the lower part of the body. Others were fired at me. I saw the Minister's chair standing, but there was no movement.' After describing his escape he concluded: 'I affirm that the assassination of the German Minister was a deliberately planned, premeditated murder, done in obedience to the orders of high Government officials by an Imperial bannerman.' *

Certain evidence suggests that, somewhere in the devious counsels of the Court, von Ketteler's doom had been sealed several days earlier. On 14 June the *North China Daily News* published an unconfirmed report from Chinese sources that one of the foreign Ministers had been murdered, and two days later the Press of several European capitals carried a similar story, this time specifying the German Minister as the victim.† There

* *The Times*, 13 October 1900.

† *The Times*, 17 June 1900. 'It is not often,' Smith pointed out afterwards, 'that a crime of this extraordinary character is telegraphed around the world four days in advance of its occurrence, and yet when it actually happens remains for some time unknown.' The report caused a flurry of diplomatic activity in Europe.

is no doubt that, as Smith wrote, 'his imperative manner was at that time particularly obnoxious to the Chinese'; and the fact that the German Legation, according to Cordes, had in its possession documents implicating the commandant of the Peking gendarmerie in anti-foreign activities may have had something to do with the crime.

Six months later von Ketteler's murderer was arrested and decapitated by German troops on the spot where he had done the deed. He was a man called En Hai, a lance-corporal in the Peking Field Force, and it is impossible not to feel that he was rather unlucky. An officious censor, who had pleaded in a Memorial to the Throne that 'his name should not be allowed to fall into oblivion,' facilitated the work of the avengers; and a watch belonging to his victim provided a Japanese spy in the pawnbroking world with a further clue.

En Hai made a speech to a small but sympathetic crowd before his pigtail was seized and his neck stretched out by the executioner's assistant. 'I merely obeyed the orders of my superior officers,' he said; 'otherwise why should a small person like myself venture to take the life of so exalted a personage as the German Minister? My officers offered a reward of 70 taels and promotion to anyone who would shoot the Minister, and I agreed to do so. My part of the contract was carried out, but I only received 40 dollars and no promotion, and thanks to my waiting in Peking for promotion I have been arrested.' He was still muttering abuse of 'stupid princes' when the sword fell.

An expiatory monument, in the form of an arch of white marble, was erected by the Chinese Government on the scene of the murder, but was demolished in 1917 when China entered the First World War against Germany. 'Even before it was taken down,' wrote a close student of the Peking scene, 'and passers-by might still read (in Chinese, German and Latin) how Baron von Ketteler had been traitorously done to death, the actual value of this monument as an object-lesson was doubtful. If one asked one's rickshaw coolie, for instance, to whom that monument had been erected, he was almost sure to

answer that the arch had been set up to honour the memory of
the Chinaman who had killed the German Minister.' *

Although everyone was deeply shocked by the news of von
Ketteler's death, it clarified the issues for his colleagues. All
thoughts of departure were, to the general relief, abandoned.
In due course a gleefully disingenuous despatch from the
Tsungli Yamen, which made no mention of the murder,
regretted that it would be unsafe for the Ministers to go there
for the interview they had requested; the actual words used
were 'It is to be feared that the foreign Representatives might
have cause for alarm on their way to the Yamen from the
Legations, which would be a subject of regret to the Princes and
Ministers.' The need for adequate preparations for their journey to Tientsin was accepted; 'the time,' it was vaguely said,
'can be extended so as to allow further consultations.'

Later an even more cynical despatch reached the German
Legation (whence a patrol of fifteen sailors had gone out to
recover the Minister's body but had been driven back). This
stated that two Germans in chairs had fired into a crowd near
the Tsungli Yamen; the crowd had retaliated and killed one of
them. The Princes and Ministers wished to be informed of the
identity of this man. No answer was sent.

When the murder became known a bare five hours remained
before the expiry of the ultimatum at four o'clock. A wave of
feverish and in some respects belated activity now swept
through the Legation Quarter. An escort of United States
Marines supervised the evacuation of the isolated premises of
the Methodist Mission, whence seventy-six American mis-

---

* Varè: *The Last of the Empresses*. Of several execrable poems inspired by
the Siege, the following lines by an anonymous resident of Shanghai offer a
fair example:

> Make haste! Make haste! Cold is our colleague's brow;
> He whom we loved lies bleeding, butchered, low;
> While round our walls his murderers scream and yell,
> Drunk with the blood they shed when Ketteler fell!

sionaries and their children, with a train of converts which included 126 schoolgirls, were brought in with such personal belongings and supplies as they were able to carry. So large an addition to the cramped community was not easily or quickly absorbed; it was in a fretful mood that the missionaries eventually took up their quarters in the small chapel of the British Legation.

This Legation was the largest and, because it was not dominated by the Tartar Wall and commanded in general good fields of fire, the least immediately exposed to attack. In the plan of defence, such as it was, it had been allotted the role of a central redoubt, in which non-combatants and supplies would be concentrated and on which the garrisons of the other Legations would fall back if dislodged from their positions.

On the afternoon of 20 June it was thronged by a cosmopolitan gathering of men, women and children which numbered about 900; except for the Chamots, who remained in their hotel, the whole of the foreign community in Peking, swollen by many missionaries from outside, was assembled in a compound roughly three acres in extent, which also contained a large number of ponies and mules, a small flock of sheep and a cow. Its normal population was about sixty.

Smith gives a sketch of the scene as the hot afternoon wore on towards the hour of destiny: 'Uncounted carts loaded with every variety of household furniture continually arrived. Swarms of coolies struggled through the broad passages, the stream of those endeavouring to enter becoming constantly entangled with the equally strong stream of those trying to get out again in order to go back and reload. The whole Legation had been turned inside out, recharted, and its separate buildings assigned to different nationalities. This was the Russian house, that the French, and a third was devoted to the use of the staff of the Imperial Customs. The spacious front pavilions began to be covered with the most miscellaneous luggage, especially cases of provisions and wines, as this was the headquarters of the numerous Belgian, French and others in the employ of the ruined Lu-Han railway. The stable-house was full of Norwegians. The rear pavilion was 'Reserved' and was divided into several messes. In one corner two men represented what was left of the Hongkong & Shanghai Banking Corporation, in another corner several military officers had such headquarters as were possible, while *The Times* Correspondent was content with a mattress on the floor-tiles, near which was stacked up in a huge pile his library, happily rescued just before his house was destroyed.'

'The place,' another missionary wrote, 'resembled nothing so much as the deck of an ocean liner just going out of dock, only that it was on a much larger scale, and that order had to be reduced out of chaos not by a band of well-trained sailors who knew exactly where everything was to go, but by the passengers each for himself.'

In the other Legations the picquets were strengthening make-shift barricades, replenishing fire-buckets or scanning the roof-tops with field-glasses. To the harsh blare of trumpets a squadron of Tung Fu-hsiang's cavalry, black-turbanned, banners waving, galloped past the Austrian Legation in a cloud of dust, headed for the Imperial City. From the American and German outposts on the Tartar Wall minor military activity was reported round the great pagoda crowning the Ha Ta Men. But there were no unmistakable portents of war.

As four o'clock approached a group of men gathered on the lawn in front of the British Minister's house, where the student interpreters had laid out a clock-golf-course in preparation for a period of enforced confinement. They held their watches in their hands. Five minutes more . . . four minutes more (it reminded one of them of Eights Week at Oxford) . . . three minutes . . . two minutes . . .

Heavy firing broke out to the east, in the direction of the Austrian Legation. It was immediately replied to.

Captain Strouts, commanding the Legation guard of Royal Marine Light Infantry, was among those on the lawn. A sergeant marched up to him and saluted.

'Firing,' he announced, raising his voice to make himself heard above the rattle of musketry, 'has commenced, sir.'

Captain Strouts acknowledged his salute.

'Thank you, Sergeant Murphy,' he said.

The Siege had begun. Everyone felt suddenly more cheerful.

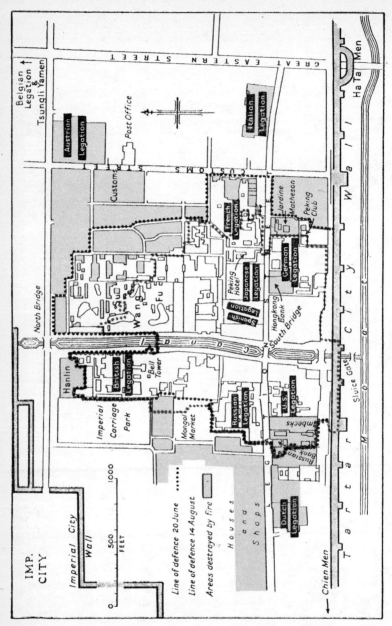

The Defences of the Legation Quarter

# CHAPTER EIGHT

# *Trapped*

*The foreigners are like fish in the stew-pan.*
The Empress Dowager to Prince Tuan, 21 June 1900.

THE first volleys had hardly been exchanged when the Austrian Legation, at which most of them were directed, was evacuated by its garrison, who fell back on the French barricades. Hard things were said, not unreasonably, about this withdrawal, which rendered the Customs houses on the opposite side of the street untenable and thus left the entire north-eastern sector of the defences in Chinese hands; but, as will be seen from the map opposite, the Austrian position was an isolated one and might in the long run have cost more to hold than it was worth.

Its loss was followed, as dusk fell, by a nightmare incident at the bridge over the canal immediately to the north of the British Legation. To the east of the canal, enclosed by a high wall, lay an ornamental park in which stood the Fu (or palace) of Prince Su; in this were now quartered most of the 2000 Catholic refugees. Permission for them to seek shelter there had been obtained from the owner by a man called Huberty James, an eccentric but warm-hearted professor at the Imperial University who had been one of Morrison's chief helpers in the rescue-work.

James 'seemed,' as Morrison put it, 'to have a blind faith in the Chinese.' Watchers from the British Legation were horrified to see him emerge from the Fu and run up to the bridge, which was in Chinese hands. He was fired on at close range, appeared to be hit and was then cut down and dragged away by three cavalrymen. It was believed that he had been killed more or less outright; but according to a Chinese source he was only wounded and after being tortured was not decapitated until three days later.* His head was exhibited on one of the city gates; 'the face has a most horrible expression,' Ching-Shan recorded.

These were unhopeful beginnings; and but for their illusions about Seymour—still 'almost hourly expected'—the trapped foreigners might well have despaired as they took stock of their resources.

The total strength of the Legation guards was 20 officers and 389 men. These were of eight nationalities, the contingents being made up as follows:

|  | Officers | Men |
| --- | --- | --- |
| British | 3 | 79 |
| Russians | 2 | 79† |
| Americans | 3 | 53 |
| Germans | 1 | 51 |
| French | 2 | 45§ |
| Austrian | 7‡ | 30 |
| Italians | 1 | 28§ |
| Japanese | 1 | 24 |

There were in addition two categories of armed volunteers. The first—numbering seventy-five, of whom thirty-two were

* *The Diary of His Excellency Ching-Shan.* Translated by J. J. L. Duyvendak. Extensively relied on by Bland and Backhouse (*China Under the Empress Dowager*), this source is now regarded as suspect. But although its author— whoever he may have been—is an unreliable guide to Court intrigues at the highest level, there seems no reason to doubt the authenticity of incidental details which are partly corroborated elsewhere.

† Including seven Legation cossacks.　　‡ Including two midshipmen.

§ The French and Italians had detached, respectively, one officer and thirty ratings and one officer and eleven ratings for the defence of the Peitang.

Japanese—was composed of ex-soldiers or ex-sailors, who between them mustered a wide experience of war. The second was a more irregular force with a strength of fifty. They did garrison duties in the British Legation and were known as the 'Carving Knife Brigade,' from their habit of lashing cutlery of this type to weapons varying from 'an elephant rifle to the *fusil de chasse* with a picture of the Grand Prix. . . . The most experienced of them [Morrison went on] was he who had once witnessed the trooping of the colour in St James's Park. They were formidable alike to friend and foe.'

Among the sailors and marines, who had disembarked and entrained for Peking at short notice, there was a serious shortage of ammunition. The Japanese had only 100 rounds per man; the best-provided contingent had 300. Since every nationality used a different make of rifle, no common reserve of ammunition could be created.

The garrison possessed four pieces of light artillery. They had started out with five, but the heaviest, a Russian field-gun, had been inadvertently left behind in the Tientsin railway station, only the ammunition being brought. The best of these weapons was an Italian one-pounder, with 120 shells. The Americans had a Colt heavy machine-gun with 25,000 rounds, the Austrians a Maxim, and the British a five-barrelled Nordenfelt, thirteen years old and incapable of firing more than four shots without jamming. Tools, fire-fighting equipment and medical supplies were all scarce.

In some other essential respects, however, the Legations were surprisingly well off. Within the British compound there were five wells of sweet water and two of brackish; although water was theoretically rationed until the drought broke, there was never serious anxiety on this score. An abandoned grain-shop on Legation Street yielded nearly 200 tons of wheat and much rice, maize and other provender. The spring race-meeting had been held early in May, and the stables were still full of ponies; these, numbering about 150, together with a few mules ensured a supply of fresh meat. Fodder for the animals was discovered in sufficient quantities among the Chinese houses within the perimeter.

The diplomats had made no preparations for a situation which they had failed to foresee. It was almost miraculous—the missionaries indeed claimed it as a miracle—that when the need arose to feed more than 3000 people for an indefinite period no major difficulties were encountered, at least for several weeks.

Two outlying Legations—the Belgian and the Dutch—were abandoned on the first day of the Siege and were burnt by the Chinese. But their attacks on the main positions, though frequent and vicious, were not pressed home. There was general agreement among the besieged that, if they had been, the defences would have been overrun, for in these early days such barricades as existed consisted mainly of up-turned Peking carts. There were few loopholes, no sandbags, no trenches—none of that network of strongpoints and revetments and burrows in the masonry which gradually came into being and formed a sort of carapace round the vulnerable compounds. Of the numerous committees set up on 21 June (mostly under the chairmanship of energetic American missionaries, 'to whose powers of organisation,' Sir Claude MacDonald wrote, 'the comfort and comparative safety of the British Legation were mainly due') far the most important was the Fortifications Committee. Mr Gamewell, the head of it, had been an engineer before he became a missionary; there was probably no single individual to whom the besieged became more deeply indebted.

Somehow they rode out the first full day and the long, noisy nights on either side of it. In the teeming British Legation the non-combatants were settling down, adapting themselves to cramped quarters, unfamiliar neighbours, inadequate sanitary arrangements, the zing of bullets overhead, the smell of fear. Then, suddenly, at nine o'clock on the morning of 22 June, there was a panic. The detachments of Italy, Austria, France, Germany, Japan, Russia and America abandoned their positions and fell back in haste and confusion on the British Legation. 'It was a veritable stampede,' wrote Morrison. Three-quarters of the defences were left unmanned.

The man responsible was the captain of the Austrian cruiser *Zenta*, von Thomann. Although in Peking only as a sightseer, he found himself the senior officer in the besieged Legations and as such had on the previous day assumed supreme command of the garrison. Shortly before nine o'clock he had been told—'by an irresponsible American', according to Morrison—that the United States Legation had been evacuated. Without attempting to verify this baseless report, he ordered all the detachments east of Canal Street to withdraw to the British Legation. The Americans, seeing this movement in progress from the Tartar Wall, joined in the retreat and carried the Russians with them. No firing was going on, and the Chinese, though they burned down the Italian Legation and occupied one abandoned barricade in Customs Street, unaccountably failed to exploit their golden opportunity.

The detachments were immediately ordered back to their posts by their respective Ministers, most of whom were now quartered in the British Legation, and the positions were re-occupied. Captain von Thomann was relieved of his command (he was later killed) and at the request of the Russian, French and Italian Ministers—with which those of America and Japan afterwards associated themselves—Sir Claude MacDonald took over responsibility for the direction of the defence. As a young man he had served in the Highland Light Infantry and had fought in several minor African campaigns.

A commander-in-chief was badly needed; everybody had been saying so since the crisis began. As early as 7 June the commander of the French contingent, Captain Darcy, had come away disgusted from a polyglot council of war at which many essential matters had been left undecided 'in spite of the efforts of Captain Strouts, who is a model of tact, and of Herr von Below [the German Chargé d'Affaires], who speaks four languages fluently and who tried hard to get everyone to stick to the point.'

Now that the fighting had started, some central authority was urgently necessary. Already the committees and the commanders of contingents were at loggerheads; 'I forbid you to use a drop of that water,' the head of the amateur fire brigade was sharply told by the chairman of the committee in charge of water-supplies.* There was uncontrolled competition for tools, bricks, timber and coolies. In the firing-line few officers knew where the sector of front for which they were responsible began or ended, or where their neighbours' posts were sited. There was much muddle and duplication of effort.

Seldom can a commander-in-chief have exercised his powers by stranger methods than those which protocol imposed upon Sir Claude. His *de jure* position, in so far as he had one, rested on the fact that, although not the doyen of the Corps, he was the senior of the Ministers whose nations' armed forces were represented in Peking. He had however no direct jurisdiction over those forces, and could convey orders to their officers only in the form of written requests addressed to the Ministers concerned.

Some of these, and the answers to them, survive. The scrawled writing on grimy scraps of paper contrasts with the formal, flowery French. Moments of truth are here and there recaptured. It is easy, for instance, to deduce that things were critical for the Germans on 13 July. Von Below's notes are in a firm, clear hand; his requests are reasonable and precise; even when urgently made, they always end '*Veuillez agréer, M. le Ministre, l'assurance de ma très-haute considération.*' Of all Sir Claude's battle-correspondents he gives the impression of being the coolest, the best attuned to war.†

* Morrison Diary.

† Von Below was one of the only two diplomats who preferred to stay with their own fighting men and did not seek shelter in the British Legation. The other was von Rosthorn, the Austrian Chargé d'Affaires, who with his wife lived in the Chamots' hotel next to the French Legation, which was partly defended by Austrian sailors. Whether or not, as one or two sources hint, the von Rosthorns moved out of the British Legation after a quarrel with a British diplomat, they bore themselves gallantly throughout the Siege. Madame von Rosthorn was badly burnt about the face and hands.

But at some anxious moment on 13 July he could find no time for niceties. He even wrote—in pencil—on a visiting card:

## Chevalier de Below

*Gentilhomme de la Chambre*
*de S. M. le Roi de Prusse*

*1ᵉʳ Sécrétaire de la Légation Impériale*
*de l'Allemagne en Chine*

And his message was only four words long: '*Renforts vite. Très attaqués.*'

Once battle has been joined, a commander-in-chief can normally influence its outcome only by the use of his reserves. Sir Claude had no reserves; but he was constantly called upon to act as a sort of broker who borrowed men in penny packets and sent them to the aid of the hardest-pressed Legation. It was a difficult, invidious and extremely important task—how difficult can be judged from an exchange of notes on 27 June.

> The Russian Minister asks, twice, that the British should remove a sandbag barricade which is blocking his withdrawal-route to the British Legation.
>
> Sir Claude replies that he is being heavily attacked from the north and can spare no men for this duty. Indeed, 'I *may have* to call upon you and Mr Conger to help to repulse this attack—so please have some men ready.'
>
> Mr Conger's comment is: 'We are having the heaviest attack we have ever had here and every man is engaged.'
>
> At 2.30 p.m. Sir Claude writes again: 'It is absolutely essential that the Fu should be held at all hazards. I hope therefore you will order over as many of your men as possible.'
>
> The Russian Minister complies: 'I am sending you my last ten men, but I must have them back as soon as you no longer need them.'

In general it seems clear that his colleagues had confidence in Sir Claude MacDonald's judgment, and that he exercised his precarious authority with skill and good sense. Hewlett, the young student interpreter who acted as his A.D.C. throughout the Siege, wrote one night in his diary that the British Minister possessed 'tact, cheerfulness, and *a sense of what posts were in truth most threatened.* This no other man could accomplish.' Though allowance must be made for the writer's personal loyalty, this favourable verdict (of which I have italicised the most important part) is borne out by other evidence.

It would not have been humanly possible to avoid all friction. An undated note from M. de Giers recalls some forgotten storm in the military tea-cup, and reminds us what a very small tea-cup it was:

> M. le Ministre—
> I regret that I am unable to share your view that by giving a nursing orderly a rifle you transform him into a soldier, or that a cavalryman with a cavalry carbine is worth two sailors with bayonets who have been trained in infantry fighting. Be that as it may, I shall be most obliged if you will send me the 15 men whom you were kind enough to promise me, together with coolies and whatever is necessary for burning down the Chinese houses. . . . They have just brought in a sailor wounded in the head; this leaves me with 57.
> With best wishes,<br>Giers.

> Another man has been wounded; this leaves 56.

Neither side expected the Siege to last long. The foreigners had got it firmly into their heads that rescue was on the way and might arrive at any moment. The Chinese knew better but failed, reasonably enough, to see how the contemptible barbarians could hold out for more than a day or two against overwhelming odds and greatly superior fire-power. On 23

June the Empress Dowager issued the following Decree to the Imperial Council:

'The work now undertaken by Tung Fu-hsiang should be completed as soon as possible, so that troops can be spared and sent to Tientsin for defence.'

The character (*shih*) here used for 'work' was unusually vague and imprecise. In ordinary circumstances, Tan points out, a Decree 'would at least name specifically the matter in question, if it did not spend a few words to explain its nature.'

Had all gone according to plan the foreign community in Peking would have been wiped out. The fact of the massacre could not be kept secret indefinitely, but there was no reason why the full circumstances should ever be known. The grim euphemism used in this Decree betrays a prudent anxiety not to leave documentary evidence of the Court's complicity in the attack on the Legations.

This day (23 June) was one of great danger for the besieged. On the previous evening the Chinese had set fire to a huddle of native houses abutting on the south-east corner of the British Legation compound. A scene of wild confusion followed. The larger of two small and ancient fire-engines broke down. Most of the leather buckets leaked or had lost their handles. From roof-tops in the Mongol Market the Chinese directed heavy but random volleys into the fringes of the conflagration. Only with the greatest difficulty was the fire brought under control.

Immediately to the north of the British Legation stood the Hanlin Yuan, whose great halls and courtyards had for centuries enshrined the quintessence of Chinese scholarship. Little more than an arm's length separated its outer walls from those of the Legation, over which in some places its ornate wooden eaves projected. If the Chinese meant to burn their victims out, this was far the most favourable sector in which to start the operation. Among the diplomats, however, this danger was scouted; it was felt that the Chinese veneration for learning, for tradition and for architectural beauty would deter them from doing anything to imperil a building which housed among other things the oldest and richest library in the world.

Next morning the wind was blowing strongly from the north and diplomatic judgment was once more proved at fault. The Chinese set fire to the Hanlin, working systematically from one courtyard to the next. The old buildings burned like tinder with a roar which drowned the steady rattle of musketry as Tung Fu-hsiang's Moslems fired wildly through the smoke from upper windows.

The British had taken the precaution of burrowing a hole through their own wall which gave them access to the nearest of the Hanlin cloisters. Royal Marines poured through, followed by amateur fire-fighters, behind whom in a long human chain Ministers' wives and missionaries, children and Chinese converts kept up an erratic water-supply with the help of receptacles ranging from soup-tureens to *pots de chambre*.

Some of the incendiaries were shot down, but the buildings were an inferno and the old trees standing round them blazed like torches. It seemed as if nothing could save the British Legation, on whose security the whole defence depended. But at the last minute the wind veered to the north-west and the worst of the danger was over.

The fire-fighters had already demolished the nearest of the Hanlin halls. The next one was the library. No complete record of its irreplaceable contents survives, but they included the Yung Lo Ta Tien, an encyclopaedia commissioned by the second Emperor of the Ming Dynasty. Completed by a team of over 2000 scholars in 1407, this astonishing work embodied 'the substance of all the classical, historical, philosophical and literary works hitherto published, embracing astronomy, geography, the occult sciences, medicine, Buddhism, Taoism and the arts.' It comprised more than 23,000 books. The Yung Lo Ta Tien had never been printed, and the only other copy had been destroyed in a fire in the sixteenth century.

A few undamaged books and manuscripts were salvaged more or less at random by sinologues. Some of the hand-carved wooden blocks on which works of great antiquity were preserved found their way into the British Legation; they were used by the Marines for shuttering up loopholes and by the children, among whom 'Boxers' was now the only fashionable game, for constructing miniature barricades.

Otherwise the Hanlin and its treasures, laboriously accumulated down the centuries, perished in a few hours. Vandalism so wanton and so decisive would have been hard to forgive if it had been committed in a conquered city as an act of retribution. History affords no comparable example of cultural *felo de se*.

Attempts to burn out the other Legations were made at this time; all were frustrated. This method of attack was subject to the law of diminishing returns; before long all the buildings round the besieged perimeter had been reduced to ashes, and thereafter, although small fires were sometimes started by torches and incendiary missiles, the danger of a wholesale conflagration receded.

More serious, and less ephemeral, was the menace of artillery. On 22 June two nine-pounder Krupp guns began (in the parlance of the day) to 'play' on the American and Russian Legations from the burnt-out tower over the Chien Men; the range was about 1000 yards, and the fire was accurate. This was an ominous development. Save for the little Italian cannon, with its 120 rounds, the defenders had no weapon with which they could even attempt to silence the Chinese battery. There was no telling how many more guns the enemy might bring into action; and all those with experience of war realised that, if the Chinese deployed even a small part of their ample artillery, the makeshift barricades must in time be battered down and the Legations rendered untenable.

Efforts to strengthen the fortifications were redoubled. 'Bomb-proofs' were dug for the non-combatants—dank trenches roofed with beams and earth which, after a short time, even the timorous shunned. But the most urgent need was for sand-bags, and sewing machines whirred as the ladies went to work. They used very diverse materials—Lady MacDonald's best curtains, the exquisite silks and satins of Prince Su's concubines, the legs of old trousers—and the barricades grew in beauty as well as strength. Some military pundit ruled that the sandbags must be made inconspicuous, but after abortive experiments the ladies, deeply shocked already to find themselves converting fabrics worth up to twelve dollars a yard into billets for bullets, jibbed at the idea of smearing the pretty things with coal-dust, and the breastworks retained their incongruous affinity with the boudoir. Many thousands of sandbags were made; the rate of production by the best workers was one every four minutes.

In the event the sparing use of artillery by the Chinese provided one of the many enigmas of the Siege; these will be discussed in a later chapter.

24 June was a day of fierce attacks, often accompanied by fire-raising. Casualties among the defenders were mounting, but their organisation was improving and useful captures of rifles and ammunition were being made. In the course of the day three gallant sorties were launched. A small force of Germans and Americans charged with great dash along the Tartar Wall, driving the enemy before them almost as far as the Chien Men; this enabled the Americans, with the help of a gang of converts under a missionary, to erect a barricade on top of the Wall. The Germans built a complementary barricade on their sector of the Wall, and these two positions, denying the Chinese a commanding lodgement from which they could almost spit on the nearest defenders, became a vital bastion.

The second sortie was made by Royal Marines into a labyrinth of burning houses to relieve acute pressure on the British defences. Its leader, Captain Halliday, was severely wounded, but the foray was successful, thirty-four Chinese being killed in one house alone. For his bravery in this action Halliday was awarded the Victoria Cross. In a third sortie a mixed force under the Japanese Military Attaché, Colonel Shiba, mastered a critical situation in the sector known as the Fu.

On the following day a strange thing happened. Fighting was continuous and severe until four o'clock, when a horn sounded from the Imperial City. It was answered from all sides by other horns and bugles. The volley-firing ceased instantly. A few stray shots spattered on here and there, then died away. Silence fell. Chinese soldiers picked themselves up from behind their barricades and ambled off in the sunlight. Among the besieged a frenzy of speculation broke out.

A post on the roof of the British Minister's stables reported unusual activity on the North Bridge, the place where Huberty James had been cut down on the first day; it looked as if some sort of placard was being exhibited. A cosmopolitan crowd hurried to the viewpoint, and soon sinologues with the aid of field-glasses were translating eighteen characters painted in black on a huge white board.

They formed an Imperial Edict. It ran:

> *In accordance with the Imperial commands to protect the Ministers, firing will cease immediately. A despatch will be delivered at the Imperial Canal Bridge.*

A notice-board was quickly found, and a message painted on it saying that the Edict had been understood and the despatch would be received. A Chinese volunteered to bear it. An official hat was put on his head, a small white flag in his hand, and he set out with hesitant steps, watched eagerly by men who tried in vain to persuade themselves that this was some sort of trick, that it did not mean that they had been reprieved.

As the herald approached the bridge the soldiers on it shouted: 'Here he is! He's come!' It was a jocular shout, but it was also loud. The poor messenger lost his nerve, dropped his notice-board face-down and scurried back to the British Legation. Nothing would persuade him to sally forth again.

Although there was a parade of scepticism, and advantage was taken of the lull to strengthen the barricades, almost everybody believed in his or her heart that the Siege was over. It was generally supposed that the sudden cease-fire must be due to the imminent arrival of the Relief Force; the Legations did not know that Seymour was now trapped in the Hsiku Arsenal, seventy miles away. There was intense excitement, and the arrival of the despatch at the North Bridge was eagerly awaited.

Meanwhile some of the defenders made cautious sightseeing excursions into the enemy lines. From the ruins of the Hanlin one of them gazed towards the pink walls, capped with yellow tiles, of the Imperial City, only a hundred yards away.

'The sun's slanting rays now struck the Imperial City. Just outside the Palace gates were crowds of Manchu and Chinese soldiery—infantry, cavalry and gunners grouped all together in one vast mass of colour. Never in my life have I seen such a wonderful panorama—such a brilliant blaze in such rude and barbaric surroundings. There were jackets and tunics of every colour; trouserings of blood-red embroidered with black dragons; great two-handed swords in some hands; men armed with bows and arrows mixing with Tung Fu-hsiang's Kansu horsemen, who had the most modern carbines slung across their backs. There were blue banners, yellow banners embroidered with black, white and red flags, both triangular and square, all presented in a jumble to our wondering eyes. The Kansu soldiery of Tung Fu-hsiang's command were easy to pick out from amongst the milder-looking Peking Banner troops. Tanned almost to a colour of chocolate by years of campaigning in the sun, of sturdy and muscular physique, these men who desired to be our butchers showed by their aspect what little pity we should meet with if they were allowed to break in on us. Men from all the Peking Banners seemed to be there with their plain and bordered jackets showing their divisions; but of Boxers there was not a sign.' *

Dusk fell. From the stable-roof the outline of the North Bridge grew indistinct, then disappeared. The despatch had not come.

But in the Legations hopes were still high. The Japanese reported that they saw rockets in the distance; on the previous night someone in the British Legation had thought he heard artillery in action somewhere to the west. Many people were

* Putnam Weale.

still deep in argument and speculation when at midnight furious firing broke out on all sides.

The attempt at massacre had been resumed.

Why had it been interrupted? Some of the besieged took the brief lull to be a ruse, intended to throw them off their guard and improve the prospects for a concerted night-attack; others rejected this explanation, arguing that so feeble a gambit was well below Chinese standards of chicanery. All saw in the incident clear evidence that the besieging forces were subject to an effective central control and could have been called off at any moment.

Ching-Shan gives a circumstantial account of events in the Imperial City which led up to the sudden truce. Early that morning, while the Emperor and Empress Dowager were still abed, Prince Tuan and other notables, at the head of a Boxer rabble, burst into the Palace of Peaceful Longevity, making a clamour and denouncing the Emperor as a friend of foreigners. Highly incensed, the Empress Dowager emerged. Glaring down on the mob from the head of a flight of steps, she rebuked them in scathing terms, mulcted the Princes of a year's allowances, and ordered their Boxer associates to be decapitated on the spot. So great was her revulsion against the rebels that she authorised Jung Lu, the Commander-in-Chief, to order a cease-fire and open parleys with the besieged; 'for three hours,' Ching-Shan wrote in his diary at 9 p.m., 'not a shot has been fired.' But later that evening despatches from Tientsin reported (falsely) signal victories over the barbarians. The Empress Dowager changed her mind and renewed her determination to 'eat the flesh and sleep on the skins' of the foreigners; and thus it was that the fighting flared up again.

This story may not be the whole truth, but there is no particular reason to reject it out of hand. Certainly something happened that day to give Jung Lu the opportunity to interrupt a course of action of which he deeply disapproved.* He himself referred to the incident a fortnight later in a telegram to

* Jung Lu's attitude to the Siege is analysed in Chapter Fifteen.

the Southern Viceroys; but he did not say what quirk of Imperial policy made the cease-fire possible, and he attributed its brevity to the fact that the besieged 'not only paid no attention but opened fire.'

Thus, as so often when consulting Chinese sources, the historian is left with two divergent accounts of the same incident, in which the only verifiable statement of fact is palpably untrue.

The German
Minister:
Baron von Ketteler

The American
Minister:
Mr Edwin Conger

Admiral Sir Edward Seymour

CHAPTER NINE

# Make Haste!

*We are writing a page of history.*
Morrison Diary, 27 June 1900.

THROUGHOUT the world an intense curiosity prevailed about the events in North China.

During the first two weeks in June the diplomatic telegrams from Peking made it clear that something odd and ominous was afoot. For months the Ministers had been grumbling about Chinese intransigence, reporting anti-missionary outbreaks at obscure places with unpronounceable names, and forwarding copies of long, circumlocutory Edicts which they described as highly significant, but which, after spending two months in the mails, threw no very vivid light on the situation. None of the Ministers can be said to have prepared his Government's mind for an extraordinary crisis; and it is a tribute to Queen Victoria's perspicuity that on 6 June, after studying two far from alarmist messages from Sir Claude MacDonald, she sent from Balmoral a cypher telegram to Lord Salisbury: 'Situation looks very serious. Trust at all events we shall display no apathy.' *

Premonitions of catastrophe had hardly focused attention on Peking when the last telegraphic link with the Chinese capital was cut on 13 June. Three days earlier Seymour had informed the Admiralty that in response to an urgent appeal from the

---

* A similar telegram three days later elicited from Salisbury the observation that 'Russia, not China, seems to me the greatest danger at the moment.'

I

British Minister 'I am landing at once with all available men;' and for a week thereafter his progress up-country was charted by brief messages transmitted through Mr Carles, the British Consul at Tientsin. Then he too, like the Legations, vanished from ken; and immediately afterwards Tientsin was cut off. On 21 June Admiral Bruce was signalling to the Admiralty from the Taku Bar: 'No communication from Commander-in-Chief [Seymour] for seven days or with Tientsin for five days.' Later that day, after Watts's night-ride to the coast had brought first-hand information from Tientsin, he reported in another signal: 'Reinforcements most urgently required. Casualties have been heavy. Supplies of ammunition insufficient. . . . There are no reinforcements to send.'

By this time the Taku Forts had been stormed, and the Powers were exchanging informal, rather pedantic inquiries as to whether a state of war with China existed. The consensus of opinion was that it did not, since although the Forts had fired first they were understood to have done so without orders from higher authority.*

The Chinese for their part issued a manifesto rather than a formal declaration of war on 21 June; but their envoys accredited to the Governments of the hostile Powers were ordered to remain at their posts, and the language of subsequent Edicts fluctuated unpredictably between defiance and conciliation. One dated 29 June, for instance, included this passage: 'Even supposing China was not conscious of her true [i.e. weak] position, how could she take such a step as to engage in war with all the Powers simultaneously, and how could she, relying upon the support of an anarchistic populace, go into war with the Powers?'

In any community the disappearance of an individual excites curiosity and gives rise to speculation. Now that eleven diplomatic missions and an international force of 2000 men had in the course of a week been mysteriously lost to view, it was

---

* This was a misapprehension. The local commander had been ordered from Peking on 13 June to offer resistance to a show of force.

natural that keen interest and anxiety should be felt throughout the world. Affairs in North China ousted the Boer War from its hallowed position in the leading news column of *The Times* and were given a similar prominence by the Press of other countries.

Rumours abounded. At first they tended to be hopeful. On 20 and 21 June there were persistent reports that Seymour had reached Peking. A week later a telegram from the German Admiral was alleged to have been received in Berlin with news of von Ketteler's arrival at Tientsin. A rumour which constantly recurred (and which somehow managed to be current in the Legations) spoke of massive Russian forces marching on Peking from the north.

But as time went on, and Peking still remained shrouded in mystery, the rumours grew steadily gloomier. 'Prepare to hear the worst,' advised a Reuter report from Shanghai on 7 July, and on the previous day news of a general massacre in Peking had, according to *The Times* Correspondent in Rome, induced a 'painful stupor' throughout Italy.

At the end of June the recovery of Seymour's mauled expedition from the Hsiku Arsenal, following immediately on the relief of Tientsin, made the picture clearer but not, as far as Peking was concerned, more hopeful. Seymour's experiences had proved, to put it mildly, that the days in which you took your full-dress uniform on active service in China were over. From underestimating the military prowess of the Chinese the Allies swung to the other extreme and tended to overestimate the forces needed for the task which Seymour had failed to accomplish.

It has been generally assumed that Seymour led a forlorn hope whose failure was inevitable. In fact there seems no reason why he could not have reached Peking if he had not made himself the prisoner of his trains. His chances of success would have been greatly improved if the diplomats had invoked his aid earlier, instead of wasting valuable days on projects for a joint audience with the Empress Dowager and other fripperies.

But even starting, as he did, on 10 June he could, using either junks or carts or both for transport, have covered the eighty miles to Peking in a week; this would have got him there before the seizure of the Taku Forts made the intervention of Imperial troops inevitable. He would indeed have risked an awkward battle with Tung Fu-hsiang's army, or with some other part of the Field Force, outside Peking; but he risked that in any case by using the railway.

The Boxers did not stop Seymour; they stopped his trains. Although they had no high explosive, this was a simple thing to do; and it was because the expedition was tethered to its rolling stock that, after covering thirty miles on the first day, it was slowed down, halted and turned back without making very much further progress. The Boxers were not a serious obstacle to the advance of a disciplined and self-contained force of infantry, as even the Imperial troops had proved whenever they were allowed to. It was not because he had only 2000 men that Seymour's task proved impossible, but because, lacking any other means of transport, he chose the first to hand. He cannot be blamed for doing so. The sailors' business in Peking was urgent. Even if they had disposed of ponies, waggons, harness, pack-saddles, junks and coolies (and they lacked all these essentials for an overland campaign), they would still have used the railway. It should have carried them to Peking in a matter of hours. They could not foresee that it would become a *cul de sac*, blocked at both ends.*

On 29 June the first, and for a long time the last, authentic communications from the Legations reached the outside world. They were brought to Tientsin by a Chinese courier. One was from Sir Robert Hart and had been despatched on 24 June. It read: '*Foreign community besieged in the Legations. Situation desperate. MAKE HASTE! !*' The second, dated the 25th, was

---

* There is a close analogy between the immobilisation of Seymour's trains and the methods used by the Chinese to neutralise the British frigates *Imogene* and *Andromache* after they had forced the Bogue Forts near the mouth of the Pearl River in 1834. Blockships, stakes and cables closed the channel above and below them, so that 'the ships had been rendered harmless. They could neither go on nor go back; nor could their crews fight their way to Canton.' (Maurice Collis: *Foreign Mud.*)

from a missionary, and reported among other things the murder of the German Minister, so often and so oddly foreshadowed by rumour.

It was all very well for Sir Robert to write—to (as he supposed) the commander of a force just outside the walls of Peking—'Make haste.' Among the Allies * a sense of impotence prevailed. Troops, guns and warlike stores (but very few horses) were reaching Tientsin in driblets; but the Foreign Settlements there were still under a loose but dangerous kind of siege. The women and the wounded had been sent down to Taku, and things were easier than they had been. But even when the enemy's strongpoints had been cleared and his batteries silenced, there remained the old or 'native' city of Tientsin to be dealt with. It lay immediately to the north-west of the Settlements, and no advance towards Peking could be contemplated until its strong walls had been stormed.

Admiral Alexeiev, the Governor-General of Port Arthur, arrived at the end of June. The following extract from a signal to the Admiralty, despatched on 1 July by Admiral Bruce after a 'long conversation' with the distinguished newcomer, throws some light on Allied military thinking in North China: 'He [Alexeiev] agrees with me that, with all reinforcements expected, Russian and Japanese, it will only bring total to about 20,000 men, which would enable us to hold the base . . . but impossible to advance beyond Tientsin.' 'Tiger-like' had ceased to be an appropriate epithet for the Powers.

They were all mounting expeditions at home, but North China was a long way away; the prospect of sufficient forces arriving in time to save the Legations appeared remote. In these circumstances the British Government, after securing Russia's approval for their action, approached the Japanese Government with an offer to bear financial responsibility for the speedy despatch of a strong relief force. The Japanese, who

* The Powers acting more or less in concert in China were not allies in the technical sense. I use the term to denote the eight nations whose regular forces took part in the defence and the relief of the Legations, and to avoid the need to deploy a stage-army of cumbrous synonyms.

were newcomers on the international stage, expressed a cautious preference for joint action and, although they maintained a steady flow of reinforcements, failed to throw an army of liberation swiftly on to the mainland.

Meanwhile the Chinese envoys in foreign capitals delivered from time to time assurances that the Legations were being afforded every protection, normally receiving in return condign threats of the vengeance which would be meted out to the Peking authorities if the foreigners came to any harm. An ingenious method of bringing pressure to bear on the Manchu Court was unanimously proposed by the Consular body at Tientsin on 29 June; its members recommended that 'the Chinese Government should be informed that in case the persons of the foreign Ministers are touched, the Mausolea of the dynasty will be destroyed by the European troops.'

This suggestion commended itself strongly to the Kaiser, but was coolly received by the Foreign Office, who pointed out that to the best of their belief the Mausolea were at Mukden in Manchuria. Their destruction could be effected only by a strong expedition after an overland advance of 200 miles; moreover, 'the threat appears, at first sight, very unlikely to have any effect upon mutinous soldiery or a riotous mob.'

Throughout the first half of July the world's Press carried a succession of alarming but unconfirmed stories, mostly from Chinese sources in Shanghai, about the fate of the Legations; but the newspapers also published, though less prominently, reassuring statements from Chinese officials and an appeal addressed, nominally by the Emperor, to Queen Victoria, the Tsar and the Emperor of Japan asking for their good offices in bringing about a settlement of China's troubles. This appeal, dated 3 July, did not mention the Legations, which on that day were subjected to a particularly ferocious attack.

It was not until 16 July that the last rays of hope were finally extinguished by a despatch from the *Daily Mail*'s Special Correspondent in Shanghai. Headed 'The Peking Massacre,' this message confirmed and amplified the substance of the most horrific rumours already current. Authoritative Chinese sources were quoted and the story, soberly told, was buttressed with a mass of circumstantial detail. It was accepted, with rage, grief and horror, as the truth.

The journalist described how, on the night of 6–7 July, the Chinese brought up artillery and proceeded methodically to destroy the defences behind which, until then, the heroic garrison had been conducting a successful resistance. Desperate fighting went on all night. Time and again the waves of attackers were hurled back. But at length the Europeans began to run out of ammunition. Early on the morning of the 7th they rallied for a last stand in the British Legation and were over-whelmed. Everyone left alive was 'put to the sword in a most atrocious manner.'

This account was accepted as the authorised version of what had happened. To the *Daily Mail*'s harrowing picture some other newspaper added a grim postscript; it came to be believed all over the world that the men had shot the women and children before succumbing themselves.*

The whole story held the stage until the end of July. 'It would be foolish and unmanly,' wrote *The Times* on the day after it appeared, 'to affect to doubt the awful truth.' The world howled for vengeance. The Kaiser, reviewing a contingent of the German expeditionary force before it embarked at Bremerhaven, exhorted the men to give no quarter. 'Just as the Huns a thousand years ago, under the leadership of Attila, gained a reputation by virtue of which they still live in historical tradition, so may the name of Germany become known in such

* This gloss was almost certainly an echo of newspaper stories about the siege of Tientsin, where 'men had been appointed to shoot the women and children when it should come to the final stand' (Brown *et al.*). Whether any such arrangements were made there is no means of telling. They seem never to have been contemplated in the many mission stations whose de-fenceless occupants met, and knew that they would meet, a cruel and often lingering death. The legend that European women were outraged before being killed is supported by no evidence and is inherently unlikely; to the sexual appetite of the Chinese male the female barbarians—large-footed, long-nosed and white-skinned—made a negligible appeal.

a manner in China, that no Chinese will ever again dare to look askance at a German.' Europe did not forget this characteristic speech; the Germans have their last Emperor to thank for encouraging their enemies or critics to call them Huns.

In London a memorial service for the victims of the massacre was arranged in St Paul's Cathedral. 'In the selection of the psalms,' one newspaper reported, 'special care has been taken to avoid those which seem to breathe a spirit of revenge.' But by 23 July, when the service was due to be held, doubts had begun to arise about the veracity of the *Daily Mail* story. Their chief cause was the receipt by the State Department of a short cipher telegram from Mr Conger; it read '*For one month we have been besieged in British Legation. Quick relief only can prevent general massacre.*' Its authenticity was not entirely beyond dispute, and there was uncertainty as to the exact date of despatch; but it was regarded in Washington as genuine. The service in St Paul's was cancelled at the last moment.

---

### St. Paul's Cathedral.

*MONDAY, July 23rd, 1900, at 11.30 a.m.*

---

ADMIT BEARER TO

## MEMORIAL SERVICE

**For the Europeans Massacred in Peking.**

---

### SEAT IN CHOIR.

Enter by S.E. Gate, facing Watling Street.

Doors Open at 10.45.          ROBT. GREGORY, *Dean.*

---

Newspaper editors are human. It was natural that they should handle with reserve reports indicating that an event, which they had described in graphic detail and fulminated about at great length, had probably not taken place at all. They had, as it were, a vested interest in the tragedy and were not prepared to give good news the benefit of the doubt. When at the beginning of August the arrival in several capitals of telegrams from their Ministers in Peking made it clear that the besieged had not in fact been butchered, it was with a slightly mortified astonishment that the newspapers passed on the glad tidings to their readers. 'Europe has been greatly surprised this week,' wrote the *Spectator*: adding rather perfunctorily 'and also relieved.'

The *Daily Mail*'s anonymous Special Correspondent was much reviled for what was assumed to be a deliberately misleading despatch. 'We do not know,' wrote Cordier, 'the name of the ghoulish practical joker (*sinistre farceur*) who plunged Europe and America into despair by the wealth of shocking details with which he embellished his fabrication.' But as a matter of fact his message was singularly free from 'shocking details.' The story it tells is merely an amplified and allegedly authoritative version of earlier accounts from Chinese sources which several correspondents had telegraphed without vouching for their authenticity. Ten days before it was written Lord Salisbury had told Queen Victoria that it was 'impossible to exaggerate the horror' of the news from Peking and there was no reason to disbelieve it.

Although wholly imaginary, the *Daily Mail*'s account of what had happened to the Legations was far more probable than what actually did happen to them. It was not a 'fabrication' but a rehash of a story already widely current. And it was sensational only in that it promoted an ugly rumour to the inescapable truth. When protests were made afterwards, the editor of the *Daily Mail* submitted a dossier of textual evidence to *The Times*, whose editor concluded that the documents 'are conclusive as to the good faith of the *Daily Mail* in publishing the story.' *

The archives of the *Daily Mail* throw no clear light on the

* *The Times*, 20 August 1900.

identity of their Special Correspondent in Shanghai. In a letter written from Peking on 20 October 1900 to Moberley Bell, the manager of *The Times*,\* Morrison gave a summary of his career which is worth reproducing in full; the portrait of a rascal is a reminder that some at least of China's visitors gave ample warrant for her xenophobia.

'I see that *The Times* whitewashed the *Daily Mail* and bore witness to the good faith with which they had published that disgraceful telegram from Shanghai which caused misery to so many families. The man who sent the telegram was I understand F. W. Sutterlee. This man was manager of the firm of Keen Sutterlee and Co. of Philadelphia who in January 1896, after the failure of the firm, sold thrice over by means of forged warehouse certificates the same stock of wool and then skipped with the proceeds to Tientsin under the name of W. F. Sylvester. In Tientsin he went into partnership with Louis Spitzel, an Austrian Jew naturalised British, who had been in trouble with the police in England for being in possession of goods knowing them to have been stolen. These two men carried on business in Tientsin under the name of Taylor & Co. and with them was a man Baker, alias Parker, alias Taylor, who had been the warehouse clerk whose forgery of certificates enabled Sutterlee to effect his swindle in January 1896.

'At the outbreak of the war between the United States and Spain the two rascals, joining with them a third man, a Jew named Louis Leonard Etzel, probably a brother of Louis Spitzel, went down to Hongkong and Manila and engaged in a lucrative trade selling arms to the Philippine insurgents. On one occasion the firm loaded a vessel with firearms in Canton and shipped them to the Philippine Islands. They made a sworn declaration that the arms were for Singapore and they entered into bail of 15,000 dollars with Mr Drew, the Commissioner of Customs at Canton, that they would produce within six weeks a certificate from the American Consul in Singapore that the goods had been landed in Singapore or their bail would be forfeit. The Consul in Singapore—Pratt—was in their

\* *The Times* archives.

pay, engaged in the smuggling of arms to rebels at war with his own Government. This treachery was just at this juncture discovered and he was removed from his post. Sylvester was never able to produce the certificate that the goods had been landed at Singapore and he was called upon to forfeit his bail. He had the impudence to contest the case "Drew *v*. Sylvester." He admitted that he had signed the undertaking with Mr Drew but he contended that the contract was void *ab initio*. He lost his case and since has been living as Sutterlee in Shanghai at the Astor House and acting as the trusted Correspondent of the *Daily Mail*. . . . You will see that the *Daily Mail* did not exercise a very wise choice in the appointment of their Correspondent.'

The credence given to this rogue's despatch of 16 July was, as we shall see, to have an influence on Allied strategy in North China during the fortnight following its publication.

CHAPTER TEN

# *The Ordeal*

*All the children are seedy and looking dreadfully white. . . . Daisy also got hit this evening, but not seriously. She was walking in the compound when a shell burst over-head, a piece striking her on the ankle-bone and causing a good deal of pain. . . . The bullets positively rained upon the walls of our room, like heavy hailstones or a game of fives.*

From the Diary of Mrs B. G. Tours.

A SIEGE is a testing experience. In the Legations the atmosphere was unusually claustrophobic and oppressive. From the walls of a city or the ramparts of a fortress the beleaguered can at least scan the horizon, gaze into freedom and draw comfort from the sight of distant hills and fields. Their prison cell has a window. As they look downwards on their enemies, they can daydream of a morning when the besieging army will be seen to have struck its tents and to be marching, for inscrutable reasons, away across the plain.

These small but important compensations were denied the Legations. The great grey city which enclosed them would never march away. Save from the posts on the Tartar Wall, they could not see out of their cell. On all sides roofs and tree-tops restricted their vision to little more, and often to less, than a hundred yards; to the north and south their positions were enclosed and dominated by forty-foot-high walls. No sortie could hope to penetrate more than a few yards into the laby-rinth of narrow lanes and small houses that hemmed them in; there was not even a no-man's-land, and reconnaissance is not once mentioned in the annals of the Siege, for the good reason that it was physically impossible. It was a situation which offered little sustenance to the human spirit.

After the brief, unaccountable cease-fire on 25 June the fury and weight of the Chinese attacks increased; on one night alone it was estimated that their riflemen had fired 200,000 rounds into the Legations. The defenders' casualties mounted steadily; by 3 July the naval detachments had lost in two weeks of fighting thirty-eight killed and fifty-five seriously wounded—nearly a quarter of their total strength. Five of the twenty officers were dead or in hospital. All ranks were terribly tired.

Of the Legations still standing the French was the most exposed. But the two crucial sectors of the perimeter were the Tartar Wall behind the German and American Legations, and the Fu, a rambling fourteen-acre park dotted with palaces, pagodas, stables, servants' quarters, gardens and ornamental knolls. This was a long, awkward bit of front to hold; a breach in it would admit the enemy into the heart of the defended area and cut the British Legation off from the others.

The Tartar Wall was as wide as a road—'wide enough,' as someone put it, 'for four carriages to be driven abreast at full speed.' From the Legations it could be reached only by two curving ramps, exposed to fire and devoid of cover. To the east rose the towering pagoda surmounting the Ha Ta Men, to the west the charred ruins of its counterpart over the Chien Men. The German and American positions were breastworks built across the width of the wall; the nearest Chinese barricades confronted them at a range of a few yards. These posts, which could normally be relieved only at night, combined the inconveniences of trench warfare with the perils of fighting on a sky-line.

The men hated them. In the first days of the Siege there was a disposition among the Americans to regard their barricade, which was badly sited, as untenable. On 25 June Mr Conger submitted to Sir Claude MacDonald that it would have to be given up. Sir Claude dissuaded him; to allow the Chinese unrestricted use of the Wall would be fatal, for it would enable a plunging fire to be poured into the defences from above. The

German and American posts (the Russians helped to man the latter) were reinforced by Royal Marines from the British Legation; but duty on the Wall continued to be unpopular. A shaky pencil note, undated, from Captain Myers, commanding the United States contingent, to Mr Conger reported that 'It is slow *sure* death to remain here. . . . The men all feel that they are in a trap and simply await the hour of execution.' *

On 1 July the German post was surprised and the men who held it driven from the Wall; the Americans, seeing their rear threatened, withdrew precipitately. After an anxious council of war in the British Legation, Captain Myers, with fourteen Americans, ten Russians and ten British, returned to the Wall and reoccupied the American barricade, against which the Chinese had unaccountably made no move.

The German post was never recovered, but on 3 July a dashing sortie, proposed by Mr Conger and Mr Squiers, captured a bastion held by the Chinese, thus extending and greatly strengthening the garrison's precarious hold on the Wall.

The sortie was led by Captain Myers, who in the course of it tripped over a spear and was badly wounded in the leg. Fifteen Americans, fifteen Russians and twenty-six British assembled in the darkness behind the American barricade. According to a young ex-officer of the Scots Greys who distinguished himself in the action, it began in a pessimistic atmosphere. 'Captain Myers made a speech, which was interesting because it was so utterly unlike what a British officer would have said under similar circumstances. He began by saying that we were about

* M.P. Cf. Morrison Diary for 10 July. 'Today on the Wall there were 13 men under Captain Hall. He is never put on the Wall, his men having no confidence in his judgment. He has no control over his men who get blind drunk and insult their NCO with impunity. One man [was] brought down mad drunk from his post where he had tried to kill a Russian NCO. . . . What punishment will he get? I asked. The Captain says when he gets him back to his ship he will give him a mighty rough time. But for striking the NCO? That he said is more serious. He would probably have his chew of tobacco stopped.' After the Siege Captain Newt Hall's conduct was, at his own request, the subject of a naval court of enquiry. It found that the evidence against him did not warrant a court martial but can hardly be said to have cleared his name.

to embark on a desperate enterprise, that he himself had advised against it, but that orders had been given, and we must do it or lose every man in the attempt. . . . He ended up by saying that if there was anyone whose heart was not in the business he had better say so and clear out. One man said he had a sore arm and went down—not one of ours, I am glad to say.' *

A few moments later they scrambled over the barricade and charged. After confused fighting in darkness and a deluge of rain the bastion was taken, twenty or thirty Chinese were killed and many rifles and bandoliers of ammunition were collected. This was the most important offensive operation carried out by the garrison during the Siege—'a struggle which more than any other was the pivot of our destiny,' as a missionary put it.

In the Fu, the other vital sector, the Japanese were the backbone and the brains of the defence. They were supported, not very reliably, by the Italians and were reinforced by young volunteers—mostly Customs employees or student interpreters —from the British Legation.

Theirs was the smallest of the contingents from Tientsin, comprising only one officer and twenty-four sailors; it had the unusual distinction of suffering over a hundred-per-cent casualties, since several of the men were wounded more than once. Besides the sailors, there were thirty-two armed volunteers, mostly ex-servicemen; a number of the able-bodied Chinese converts in the Fu were given captured rifles and, by acting as sentries during quiet interludes, enabled the increasingly exhausted garrison to get a little rest. But all in all it was a very small force with which to hold a long and vulnerable front.

The Japanese were commanded by their Military Attaché, Colonel Shiba, the ablest and most experienced officer of any nationality present. He was universally liked and respected, and the Japanese, with whom in those days few Europeans or Americans had had very much to do, emerged from Peking as

* N. Oliphant.

paragons; everyone admired their courage, their dependability and their cheerfulness, and they are the only nationality of whom no criticism, veiled or otherwise, is to be found in the copious records of the Siege.*

On the Tartar Wall men tended to look over their shoulders. The atmosphere was jumpy, insecure and unhappy; it was a place which panic had visited and to which panic might return. The equally dangerous Fu exuded confidence, almost serenity. Early in the proceedings, on 27 June, Sir Claude received this note from Colonel Shiba:

> Dear Sir,
>
> They are nearing to break down the Fu's wall. I want to crush them when they come in. Will you please send some reinforcements to me with the bearer?

The wall was breached. Tung Fu-hsiang's Moslems surged through into an inner courtyard, where many were mown down before they could surge out again. There was a professional touch about Colonel Shiba.

He had, nevertheless, to give ground as time went on, falling back from one intricate line of defence to the next, manning each with fewer riflemen as his casualties increased. By 13 July, after twenty-three days' fighting, three-quarters of the Fu was in Chinese hands; yet such was the *mystique* created by the resource of Shiba and the tenacity of his men that the situation in this sector, however menacing, was always felt to be under control.

Within the beleaguered perimeter living conditions grew steadily worse. The men manning the outer defences in and around the Russian, French, German, Japanese and American Legations envied the relative security of the British compound, where the women and children were concentrated; but its three

* The Japanese, wrote a lady who served throughout the Siege as a nurse in the ill-found, overcrowded hospital, were 'the only nationality of whose conduct one could predict anything with almost absolute certainty.' (Jessie Ransome: *The Story of the Siege Hospital in Peking.*)

Dr G. E. Morrison with his
servants and grooms

Sir Robert Hart

Herbert Squiers

Polly Condit Smith

acres, into which 500 Europeans, 350 Chinese and some 200 ungulates were crammed, exhibited few of the guilty splendours which the front line automatically associates with the base.

There was serious overcrowding. The Dutch Minister slept in a cupboard in the small house allotted to the Russian Minister and the fifty-one members of his family and staff. The Spanish doyen of the Corps Diplomatique spread his mattress across the threshold of a similar building occupied by the personnel of the French Legation. Forty people sat down to every meal in Lady MacDonald's dining-room. Missionaries, Royal Marines, Belgian railway engineers, Customs officials, professors, lady's-maids, valets and an entire Chinese girls' school—all had to be fitted in somewhere and fed somehow. Cooking was a problem whose difficulties were increased by the irregular hours kept by all those engaged on active duties. Kitchens had to be improvised. 'The ornamental rockwork in front of the theatre in the Legation grounds is hollowed out in many places for the reception of large kettles wherein the horse-meat is boiled, superintended by a company of [Chinese] cooks with aprons made of chintz.'

Pony-meat and rice were the staple diet, washed down by champagne, of which there was a copious supply in the two stores, Imbeck's and Kierulff's. These also yielded plenty of tobacco; Polly Condit Smith noted that 'even some of the women, principally Italians and Russians, find relief in the constant smoking of cigarettes.'

They smoked for the sake of their nostrils rather than their nerves. At the best of times Peking was a malodorous city, especially in summer. Inside the Legations the problems of sanitation and sewage-disposal were now insoluble. Outside them, in the ruins, the corpses of their assailants putrefied. At night, when the firing died down, dogs and sometimes pigs could be heard worrying them. The stench was appalling. Many people possessed only the clothes they stood up in. The fighting men hardly ever took theirs off. While the drought lasted nobody had a bath.

It broke on the last day of June. Torrential rain flooded the trenches and shelters, burst the fabric of the flimsier sandbags, and cascaded through the bullet-riddled tiles. The rain saddened the defenders, who reckoned that it would impede the advance of the putative relief force. After the rains the heat, already great, increased; the temperature went up to 110° in the shade. The children pined and sickened. M. Pokotilov, who as head of the Russo-Chinese Bank had in happier times cut a potent, enigmatic figure as the arbiter of Oriental destinies, was now in charge of a cow, the only cow; but she got little grazing and gave little milk. There was an increasingly forlorn air about the squadron of perambulators grouped under shady trees in a corner theoretically immune from bullets. Six European children died. One of the babies born was christened Siege.

Personalities began to define themselves. The activists and the shirkers, the grumblers and the optimists, the brave men and the cowards—at such close quarters and under so severe a stress no one could dissemble his true nature. The Ministers were criticised because, although for the most part able-bodied and comparatively young, none of them except Sir Claude MacDonald took an active part in the defence; people felt that, since their vacillation and lack of foresight had contributed largely to the mess everyone was in, the Ministers might at least have filled a sandbag or two. Polly Condit Smith, whom a fellow-American described as 'ever calm and always sociable' and who was a tolerant, generous-minded witness, gives this sketch of Ministerial attitudes:

'The Italian Minister * sits chatting with his wife, a very beautiful woman, in a *chaise longue* most of the time. M. Pichon, the French Minister, nervously and ceaselessly walks about, telling everyone who speaks to him: "*La situation est excessivement grave; nous allons tous mourir ce soir.*" M. de Giers, the Russian Minister, walks eternally between his Legation and the British compound, and looks every inch a Minister. Mr

* The Marchese di Salvago Raggi. He was the only man in the Legations who continued to dress for dinner. He was thirty-six.

Conger, the American Minister, walks about. Poor Señor Cologan, the Spanish Minister, is very ill. M. Knobel, the Dutch Minister, offered his services as a sentry, but stated at the same time that he did not know how to shoot and was very shortsighted. Sir Claude MacDonald, the British Minister, is now the Commander-in-Chief and he tries sincerely to do his duty as such. His path is a thorny one, however; most of the Legations are so jealous of his compound being the centre and best stronghold *par excellence* that they are outrageously inconsiderate of all orders issued.'

It is of M. Pichon that we get the clearest picture, and the least flattering. Although known in his own country (of which he was afterwards thrice Foreign Minister) as *'le héros de Pékin,'* there is abundant evidence that he was a poltroon. Morrison, who implied this clearly in *The Times,* was more forthright in private correspondence; 'a craven-hearted cur' was the expression he used to Moberley Bell. In his diary he quoted the verdict of one of M. Pichon's compatriots: *'il ne fait que pisser dans ses caleçons.'* The French Minister was constantly making dramatic, alarmist and unfounded statements: *'On recule de la Légation de France!'* *'Il y a quelque chose qui brûle! Nous sommes perdus!'* One young Englishman described him in a letter as 'the laughing-stock of the whole place,' another in his diary as 'a horrible coward.' In his own published diary of the Siege he tells of his daily visits to the French Legation 'under a hail of bullets'; but he seems seldom to have been there at a critical moment of its heroic defence and, when he was, he invariably hastened back to the British Legation to see about reinforcements. Perhaps his chief contribution to the Siege was the provision of comic relief.

In the American Legation the outstanding figure was the First Secretary, Herbert Squiers. 'Had Mr Squiers been Minister,' one American missionary considered, 'we would never have been in our present terrible situation.' A man of energy and resource, Squiers became chief of staff to Sir Claude MacDonald when Captain Strouts, of the Royal Marine Light Infantry, was killed; he had seen fifteen years' service as a regular officer in the United States Cavalry before entering the diplomatic service.

Squiers was, however, unpopular with the American Marines. They would have accepted, though with a bad grace, control by a civilian, whether he exercised it in Mr Conger's name or in Sir Claude's or both; but they resented—for the feud between the Marine Corps and the Army was an old one—control by an ex-cavalryman who did not encourage their officers to forget that, had he soldiered on, he would have been their senior. There were no doubt faults on both sides; but though there was coolness, there was no serious friction, and Squiers, whose wife and fifteen-year-old son also did yeoman service, emerges with credit from the Siege.

So, in a rather negative way, does Mr Edwin Conger, an unimaginative Civil War veteran who, if he only 'walked about,' at least kept his head. Mrs Conger makes a more positive impression. One day a bullet entered a room full of women and children and passed through a baby's cot within an inch of its head. Its mother, who had five other small children, picked it up and the company moved to a room on the opposite side of the house. Mrs Conger was present, 'conspicuous for her concise manner and an open follower of Mrs Eddy. She earnestly assured us that it was ourselves, and not the times, that were troublous and out of tune, and insisted that, while there was an appearance of war-like hostilities, it was really in our own brains. Going further, she assured us that there was no bullet entering the room; it was again but our receptive minds which falsely led us to believe such to be the case.' *

On another occasion, during a particularly heavy night attack, she found Polly Condit Smith 'lying on my mattress on the floor, not even beginning to dress for what I suppose half the women in the compound believed to be the beginning of the final fight. In a more than tragic manner she said: 'Do you wish to be found undressed when the end comes?' It flashed through my mind that it made very little difference whether I was massacred in a pink silk dressing-gown, that I had hanging

* Mary Hooker.

over the back of a chair, or whether I was in a golf skirt and shirt waist. So I told her that in the light of experience I had come to the conclusion that, as it was absolutely of no benefit to anyone my being dressed during these attacks, I was going to stay in bed unless something terrible happened, when I should don my dressing-gown and, with a pink bow of ribbon at my throat, await my massacre.'

Throughout the Siege almost all the ladies behaved admirably; even a French governess who thought that she was being poisoned did her best to be reasonable: '*Madame, je ne demande que peu, simplement qu'on me fait rentrer toute de suite en France.*' One suspects that Mrs Conger's idiosyncrasies helped them, however indirectly, to maintain a staunch and cheerful demeanour.

To most denizens in the fortress-slum of the British Legation their Chinese assailants were familiar only as the producers of uncouth 'noises off.' At a rough guess, ninety per cent of the foreigners in Peking never saw a Boxer with their own eyes; and in the first four weeks of the Siege only the marines, sailors and volunteers manning the outer defences set eyes on members of the Imperial forces which took over from the Boxers the duty of annihilation.

It was much the same on the other side of the barricades. The besieged thought of the Chinese as fiends in human shape —rather feeble and slightly ridiculous fiends, it is true, who should have known better how to use their artillery, how to aim their rifles, and how to co-ordinate and press home their attacks. But fiends nevertheless: a cruel, cunning and innumerable horde.

But the fiends were in hard fact young, simple, ignorant, reluctant soldiers, underpaid, ill-trained and poorly led. They did not need to be convinced that foreigners were hateful and worthy of extirpation. It took little to induce them to shout 'Kill! Kill!', to set fire to other people's property, and to discharge their rifles in the general direction of the barbarians (or even at the tutelary spirits presumed to be hovering in the

night-air over their dwellings) until the barrels became too hot
to hold. But hardly any of them had ever seen one of their
disgusting though formidable enemies; and curiosity is a leading Chinese characteristic.

So is cupidity. There was a price on foreigners' heads. There
had been in 1860. On 6 September of that year an Edict,
said to have been inspired by the concubine who four decades
later was the effective ruler of China, offered: 'For the head of
a black barbarian, 50 taels [Indian troops were included in the
Anglo-French expedition], and for the head of a white barbarian, 100 taels.' The rates ruling in 1900 were 50 taels for a
male foreigner, 40 for a female and 30 for a child; this time they
were to be taken alive, but documents captured at Tientsin
show that the authorities paid generously for the heads of dead
barbarians. A Chinese newspaper report (which should be
accepted with extreme reserve, but is a reminder of the importance of such incentives) stated that: 'As foreigners are not
easy to obtain, all Chinese having high noses and deep eyes
have been beheaded by the Boxers.' The report went on to
suggest that so many heads had been brought in that the offer
of blood-money had been withdrawn.*

When a young Russian, crazed with liquor looted from one
of the stores, broke out of the perimeter, went lurching up to a
Chinese barricade, and was shot down at point-blank range,
there was keen competition to recover his body. In attempts to
do so eleven Chinese were picked off by snipers. The Russian's
corpse, which was eventually dragged inside the enemy barricade under cover of darkness, was the third and last to fall
into Chinese hands during the Siege.

Of the minor characters who flit elusively across an overcrowded stage perhaps the most tiresome was a Norwegian
missionary called Nostegarde, who went out of his mind.† When
the marines were assembling at three o'clock in the morning of
3 July for their desperate sortie along the Tartar Wall, this

---

* *North China Daily News*, 27 July 1900.

† Some sources describe him as a Swede, and there is no unanimity about
the spelling of his name.

lunatic appeared in their midst wearing a long black cassock and a top hat and 'with many gesticulations began to cry for justice. Someone, he said, had been speaking ill of him and taking away his good name. The more men tried to pacify him the more excited he got. He shouted, he howled, he appealed to King Oscar and the whole of the Norwegian royal family to right his wrongs. Nothing would quiet him; at last he was gagged and taken away struggling and stifling.' It was a bizarre prelude to an important military operation.

Nostegarde was immured in the stables, where he continued at intervals to howl. Then one day he escaped and made his way into the Chinese lines. The Chinese stand in awe of madmen, and the missionary was treated with consideration. He was taken to Jung Lu's headquarters, where his personal papers were examined; they included a letter to the Russian Minister in which Nostegarde apologised for indecently exposing his person to Madame de Giers. When he was sent back to the Legations four days later he admitted to answering freely the numerous questions he had been asked. Not only had he told the besiegers all he knew about the strength of the garrison, the state of the fortifications and the damage done by shellfire, but he had impressed on them the need for their riflemen to aim low, as most of the bullets passed harmlessly overhead. Everyone immediately noticed (or thought they noticed) an improvement in the standard of Chinese marksmanship, and there were heated demands that Nostegarde should be shot as a traitor; but cooler counsels prevailed, and the crazy evangelist was put back in the stables for the duration of the Siege.

The International Hospital was housed in the chancery of the British Legation. Through it in the course of the Siege passed 125 severely wounded men (of whom seventeen died), one severely wounded woman and forty cases of sickness— mostly enteric and dysentry—of whom two died.

It was a grim place. Fortunately Dr Velde, a German surgeon, and Dr Poole, the British Legation's resident physician, were skilful as well as devoted. They were ably seconded by a sick-bay attendant from HMS *Orlando* and an amateur nursing staff, to which the handsome Madame de Giers was an unexpectedly valuable recruit; Madame Pichon, on the other hand, Dr Poole found 'a great nuisance.'

Their resources were pitifully inadequate. The hospital had only four small iron bedsteads and seven camp-beds; most of the patients, whose numbers after the first two or three weeks never fell below sixty, lay on the floor, on mattresses stuffed with the straw in which wine-bottles had been packed. Antiseptics were scarce, there were hardly any anaesthetics and no X-ray apparatus. In the end only one thermometer (it belonged to the widowed Baroness von Ketteler) was left unbroken. Bags of sawdust and powdered peat were used as dressings.

The windows were sandbagged, and as the sun beat down on the low, overcrowded building the wounded suffered severely from the heat. There were no proper mosquito-nets and the flies were a torment. They were bolder and more ubiquitous (it struck one patient) than the flies round a sweetmeat stall in an Indian bazaar, and every time a heavy gun was fired at night they rose from their roosting-places with so deafening a buzz that it woke the patients. The diet of pony-meat, varied with scraggy mutton until the sheep ran out, was monotonous and unsuitable for sick men; but the Chinese cooks showed as much versatility as their materials allowed, and 'game,' which consisted of magpies and sparrows, was esteemed a special delicacy.

Although some of the non-combatants had plenty of leisure, the besieged had few recreations. After Kierulff's store was looted (by permission of its proprietor, who thought it was going to fall into Chinese hands) a number of gramophones and musical boxes added to the almost perpetual din. In the evenings the American missionaries gathered outside the door of the chapel in which some eighty of them were quartered and sang 'Marching through Georgia,' 'Nearer, My God, to Thee,' 'De Ringtailed Coon' and other melodies. Sometimes a Russian lady of striking beauty, who had been a professional opera-singer, obliged with an *aria* as the nocturnal volleys whistled overhead. The well-stocked library of Mr Cockburn, the First

Secretary, provided some with solace. It included several books dealing with the Indian Mutiny, and accounts of the Relief of Lucknow were in keen demand; the fate of Cawnpore was less closely studied.

Life behind the firing-line, though it could hardly be called dull, was monotonous. It was rumours, more than anything else, that kept hope alive and helped to pass the time. It is impossible to over-estimate the value of these rumours, not one of which had the slightest foundation in fact, to the morale of the besieged. They built up a dream-world outside the enclosing walls, a world across which avenging columns marched irresistibly towards Peking while the Manchu Court prepared for a hurried flight. Inside the walls they provided the agenda for endless absorbing debates, during which contingencies and precedents were expertly canvassed and nobody troubled to point out that only three days ago they had been over exactly the same ground with an entirely different set of premises. Intellectually and emotionally, the Legations may be said to have lived on rumours.

Distant gunfire, rockets and searchlights inspired many of them. Reports of these phenomena were often so convincing that Sir Claude MacDonald put up notices about them on the Bell Tower. Erected in honour of Queen Victoria's Jubilee in 1887, this tower stood—and indeed still stands—in an open space near the main gate of the British Legation. On it were posted orders, announcements, lost and found notices, advertisements offering to buy or sell things, and translations of the *Peking Gazette*. The Bell Tower was a sort of alfresco Agony Column and, in addition to being the appointed rallying-place when the bell sounded a 'general alarm,' became in quieter times a social centre, a sort of parish pump towards which people drifted to exchange gossip and discuss the events of the day.

Here was read with elation, on 2 July, a notice in Sir Claude MacDonald's handwriting about a searchlight seen twenty-five or thirty miles to the south-east. Nothing came of the searchlight, although several people saw it several times; its hopeful rays were probably due to the opening and shutting of the doors of a Chinese blast-furnace. But five days later a similar notice recorded 'heavy cannonading to the south-west,' and the crowd round the Bell Tower forgot their troubles as they pieced together circumstantial reasons for relief coming from this somewhat unexpected quarter. The Siege lasted fifty-five days; scarcely one of them passed without rumour providing plausible grounds for supposing that rescue was, if not imminent, well on the way. Yet for the first forty-five of those days no operations to relieve the Legations were in hand. Rumour, and the illusions it created, kept up their spirits. The truth would have plunged them in despair.

## LOOPHOLES.

Loop holes should never be left open except when being used for looking through or fired through. A small brick placed at the narrowest part, is quite sufficient to prevent the enemy from firing through and hitting people passing.

*ClaudeMacDonald*

After a time they grew sceptical of the stock rumours—the searchlights and the signal-rockets, the carrier pigeons seen hovering overhead, the tales of disaffection and internecine quarrels among their enemies. But they were saved from the dejection into which they might otherwise have fallen by a Chinese spy, who said he was a member of Jung Lu's bodyguard and sold military secrets to the Japanese.

This able fellow went on the principle that the customer is always right. His customer wanted a relief force to advance rapidly from Tientsin; he accordingly arranged for this to happen as far as it lay within his power to do so. For a whole week

—from 26 July to 2 August—he made it possible for daily bulletins, illustrated by maps, to be posted on the Bell Tower announcing the approach of a large foreign army.

Victory succeeded victory with gratifying regularity, and before long the Allied spearheads were within twenty miles of Peking. On 30 July another Chinese agent, who reported that no foreign troops had yet left Tientsin, came under grave suspicion and was locked up. The Legations expected to hear bugles or even bagpipes at any moment; the original spy was given urgent letters to the commander of the advancing forces and promised even greater rewards if he brought back an answer.

For several excellent reasons he was not able to do this. On 31 July the relief force suffered a reverse, losing sixty killed. Nor was this a temporary setback. On the following day the Chinese rallied strongly and drove the foreigners still farther away from Peking, killing seventy of them; and in next to no time they had withdrawn under heavy pressure all the way back to Tientsin. The shock of this news would have been hard to bear had it not coincided with the receipt of authentic reports foretelling the early departure of a real relief force. People were very angry with the spy; but when account is taken of all the confident hope and sustained, pleasurable excitement he had aroused, it is difficult to feel that his considerable gains were wholly ill-gotten.

The spy and his fairy-tales belong to the closing stages of the Siege. We are still in the first half of July, when the position was daily becoming more desperate.

Three main causes justified a growing alarm. The garrison was wasting away, and so was its stock of ammunition.* A skeleton force was not only losing more officers and men than it could afford, but it was in general losing its best officers and men. The fighting, though static, was of a kind which set a premium on an individual's personal qualities and skill at arms. The best leaders, the best shots, the keenest and the boldest men

---

* When, on 11 July, the French captured fifteen prisoners they were bayonetted to death to save cartridges.

were dropping; warlike attributes were less evenly spread among the survivors. Despite miscellaneous captures, ammunition was running low, and by 7 July only fourteen shells remained for the little Italian one-pounder, which was indispensable for dealing with enemy guns firing over open sights from behind barricades or embrasures.

The second great danger was the Chinese artillery. So far only nine or ten guns, not all of them modern, had been brought into action. They had caused strangely few casualties, but they were slowly reducing the buildings inside the perimeter to rubble, while in some sectors, and especially in the Fu, they were being used at point-blank range against the outer defences with excellent effect. Attempts to capture individual guns were made, mostly by the Japanese; all failed. Everyone realised that at any moment the Chinese might deploy more and better artillery; and even the guns already being served were seriously eroding the defences.

The third menace was the Chinese barricades. The Chinese had no stomach for frontal attacks, to which despite their numbers they never resorted during the Siege; but they were adept at extending their siege-works under cover of darkness, when the garrison held their fire so as not to waste ammunition. As the constricting maze of barricades pressed in ever closer on their outposts and gradually made them untenable, the besieged felt that they were being buried alive under brickwork. The crashing waves of Chinese rifle-fire were so much sound and fury, scarcely more lethal than the blare of their war-trumpets; but the breastworks and redoubts inching forward every night till their occupants could compel the evacuation of a barricade by lobbing stones over it—these exerted a pressure which must in the long run prove fatal. Upon the foreign enclave in the Chinese capital masonry was slowly closing in, like flesh closing over a wound.

These three main perils—the mounting casualties, the unanswerable cannon and the encroaching siege-works—were inexorable. There was no remedy, no riposte, no escape. The garrison did however slightly improve their ability to deal with the last two by constructing quite a large piece of ordnance.

In a foundry within the lines the rusty but rifled muzzle of an old gun was discovered on 7 July. It was believed to be a relic of the Anglo-French expedition of 1860. Sergeant Mitchell of the American detachment took charge of it. The rust was chipped off and the muzzle mounted on a spare set of wheels belonging to the Italian gun. The ammunition for the Russian nine-pounder (left by an oversight at Tientsin) had been dropped down a well during the panic on the second day. It was fished up, and the shells, after having their damp charges renewed, were found more or less to fit the breech.

The original discovery having been made by Chinese converts under a British missionary, the gunner being American, the carriage Italian, the ammunition Russian and the muzzle quite possibly French, the diplomats called their new engine of war the 'International.' The marines knew it as 'Betsey' or 'the Empress Dowager.' Its performance surprised everybody, not least the Chinese. It had no sights and was too inaccurate for long-range work; but on barricades and emplacements thirty yards or so away it was capable of inflicting heavy damage, which it often followed up by a discharge of grapeshot in the form of old nails and bits of scrap-iron. Its chief drawback was that it emitted a dense cloud of smoke, and thus drew fire; but it was a definite asset, and the besieged felt proud of their ingenuity.

'Betsey,' however, could not turn the tide of war, which ran ever more strongly against the besieged.

Friday the 13th of July was, according to the British Minister, 'the most harassing day for the defence during the whole Siege.' It was also the first day of the Eton and Harrow match, and a young Harrovian wrote in the diary which he kept for his parents: 'Am wondering if you will go to Lord's today. We are gradually being closed in upon, and unless relief comes soon we shall be in an awful fix.' M. Pichon took the grave step of burning his archives in a corner of the compound; it should have been a solemn, dramatic moment, but a breeze sprang up and 'Madame Pichon rushed about stamping on bits that blew away and burnt them again.'

Heavy firing, which had gone on all night from every side, continued throughout the 13th. In the Fu the Japanese were dislodged from the seventh of their nine defence-lines. The Germans in their sector saved a critical situation by a bayonet charge. The Americans had fierce fighting on the Wall. The British Legation was hard pressed. At four o'clock in the afternoon the tocsin was sounded from the Bell Tower to denote a grave emergency.

Shortly afterwards, as dusk was falling, the whole Legation Quarter was shaken by two terrible explosions. Mines had been detonated under the French Legation, and the Chinese swept howling into the chaos they had created, setting fire to buildings left partially intact.

Two French sailors were buried in the débris or blown to bits. Several other men, including the Austrian Chargé d'Affaires, von Rosthorn, were wounded. The French fought back magnificently among the ruins and succeeded in holding a strong bridgehead in their compound. But the mines had made an ugly dent in the defences, and their use in one sector suggested that others were threatened by this new peril. The sound of underground picks was detected near one of the main British positions and a counter-mine was started.

It had been a bad day, with five men killed and twice that number wounded; this rate of casualties was insupportable. '*C'est le massacre final qui se prépare*,' wrote M. Pichon in his diary. '*Quatre cent cinquante coups de canon.*' He had not been to the French Legation, but he was conscientious about keeping a tally of the enemy's shells.

On the following day (14 July) there was an extraordinary development. Attempts were continually being made by the besieged to despatch couriers to Tientsin. So far none of them had been heard of again, but now an elderly Roman Catholic convert, sent out four days earlier, re-entered the lines. He said that he had been captured and beaten; his letter was taken from him and he was brought to Jung Lu's headquarters. Here he was kindly treated for three days, then given a letter to Sir Claude MacDonald and told to bring back a speedy reply.

The letter was signed 'Prince Ch'ing and Colleagues,' * but was couched in a far less graceful and lapidary style than that normally employed in even the most disobliging pronouncements of the Tsungli Yamen.

'For the last ten days [it began] the soldiers and militia have been fighting, and there has been no communication between us, to our great anxiety.' The Yamen had just learnt from a captured convert that the foreign Ministers were in good health, 'which caused us very great satisfaction.' Because of the Boxers, however, the Yamen's original idea of escorting the diplomats to Tientsin was no longer practicable; 'we should be very apprehensive of misadventure.'

In these circumstances the Ministers were requested to proceed, in detachments, to the Tsungli Yamen; 'but at the time of leaving the Legations there must on no account whatever be taken any single armed foreign soldier, in order to prevent doubt and fear on the part of the troops and people, leading to untoward incidents.' After asking for a reply by noon on the following day, this singular communication ended: 'This is the only way of preserving relations that we have been able to devise in the face of innumerable difficulties. If no reply is received by the time fixed, even our affection will not enable us to help you. Compliments.'

After consulting his colleagues (whose relief at once more having diplomatic business, of however unusual a kind, to transact may be imagined) Sir Claude returned a dignified reply. Among civilised states, he pointed out, the persons of foreign envoys had always been regarded as sacrosanct, even in time of war. The troops of the Chinese Government had been firing on the Legations with rifles and artillery since 20 June.

* Prince Ch'ing, it will be remembered, had been replaced as President of the Tsungli Yamen by Prince Tuan early in June.

If harm came to the diplomats there would be 'grave probability of personal reprisals against all those in official positions in the city.' The Legations would continue to defend themselves, and the Ministers saw no merit in the proposal that they should remove to the Yamen.

The old convert departed with this missive. Few seriously expected him to return with a reply.

On the morning of the next day the garrison suffered a grievous blow. Captain Strouts and Dr Morrison were returning from the Fu, where they had been superintending the relief of the night-picquets. A hail of fire caught them as they were crossing an exposed bit of ground. Strouts fell mortally wounded, Morrison was hit in the thigh; a bullet passed through the tunic of Colonel Shiba, who was coming to meet them. Strouts's death, three hours later, cast a gloom over the little community. He was a fine officer, trusted and liked by all the detachments, with whom as Sir Claude's chief of staff he had frequent contacts.

Morrison's wound (he characteristically did not mention it in the long account of the Siege which he wrote for *The Times*) made a gap in the ranks which was equally regretted. 'Although not a military man,' wrote Smith, 'he had proved himself one of the most important members of the garrison, being always in motion and cognizant of what was going on everywhere, and by far the best informed person within the Legation quadrangle. To this must be added a cool judgment, total disregard of danger and a perpetual sense of responsibility to help everyone to do his best.' Earlier in the Siege Polly Condit Smith had called him 'the most attractive at our impromptu mess—as dirty, happy and healthy a hero as one could find anywhere.'

A popular young student interpreter called Warren had been killed on the previous evening; towards dusk he and Strouts were buried in the same shallow grave. 'The scene in the little cemetery behind the First Secretary's house was a very striking one. The whole world turned out to follow these two to the grave—Ministers, officers, marines, missionaries, ladies, children, all who were not on duty were there. There was a furious attack going on; bullets were whistling through the trees and three or four shells burst overhead.'

This sad moment was to be a turning-point in the history of the Siege. During the ceremony the British outposts reported that the convert who had been used by the Chinese as an intermediary was again approaching the main gate of the Legation. He was a frail old man and made slow progress. He had been given a white flag, but lacked the wit to wave it; shells from a Krupp gun exploded round him, endangering an eager reception committee who were trying to establish his pacific status by waving their white handkerchiefs outside the main gate.

At length he tottered in. He carried two messages. Their import was baffling, but their significance great.

One was for Mr Conger. It was written, on a telegraph form, in a State Department cypher to which he, alone of the members of the American Legation, held the key. It read: '*Communicate tidings bearer.*' It was the first message which had reached the besieged from the outside world since their ordeal began.

The second missive was addressed, by Prince Ch'ing and his shadowy colleagues, to Sir Claude MacDonald. Its tone was more accommodating, and its style more polished, than the earlier communication from this source. It almost apologised for suggesting that the Ministers should move to the Yamen, and undertook that the Chinese Government would 'continue to exert all its efforts to keep order and give protection.'

The pundits, though intrigued by the marked improvement in literary style, spent much of the night in exposing these assurances as worthless. But the guns became silent, the rifle-fire slowly died away, and next morning the fiends in human shape, grinning affably over their barricades, were doing their best to fraternise with the weary garrison.

An armed truce was unaccountably in force.

CHAPTER ELEVEN

# The Truce

*A decree was yesterday verbally received to the effect that, the weather being now hot, the Legations probably required fruit and vegetables, which were to be at once forwarded to them.*

The Tsungli Yamen to Sir Claude MacDonald, 20 July 1900.

THE actions of the Chinese Government so far described in this narrative have been impulsive, arbitrary and headstrong. They have not been easy to justify in terms of China's own interests, or indeed to explain at all. The curious *démarches* which began in Peking on 14 July and brought about a sort of unofficial armistice three days later appeared to the besieged as bewildering and enigmatic as any of the developments which preceded them. But this sudden switch in the policy of the Manchu Court was, for once, a rational reaction to the pressure of outside events. To understand it we must go back to Tientsin.

Here, it will be remembered, the Foreign Settlements had been relieved and Seymour's column extricated from the Hsiku Arsenal at the end of June. But although the large Chinese forces about Tientsin had been brushed aside, they had not been defeated. Accurate and increasingly heavy artillery-fire began to pour into the Settlements, and the Chinese made several determined frontal attacks, notably on the railway station where the Russians fought with admirable tenacity. Although communications with Taku were kept open, Tientsin was still invested; 'we were just as much besieged as ever,' wrote Beatty on 11 July.

After a fortnight of bitter but rather aimless fighting—the

162

Allied forces, numbering by the end of June some 14,000 men, had no central command and no agreed plan of operations—an action of decisive importance was undertaken. This was the capture of the old walled city of Tientsin; it lay immediately to the north-west of the Settlements, had a population of about a million and was defended by an estimated 12,000 Imperial troops with 10,000 Boxer auxiliaries. The walls were immensely strong and pierced only by four tunnel-like entrances barred by massive gates.

It was upon the South Gate that the main Allied assault was directed. This was led by the Japanese, supported by the Americans, French and British. The Russians and Germans were operating against Chinese positions on the north bank of the river and thus threatened the city from the rear. The total Allied strength seems to have been about 5000, though estimates vary.

In contrast to Chinese architecture, Chinese fortifications conformed for centuries to a pattern of austere but effective simplicity. The old city of Tientsin, the second most important and much the richest in North China, was a rectangular box with one hole in the middle of each of its sides. Each hole, or gate, was approached by a causeway running in a straight line across open country laced for half a mile or more with canals, lagoons, marshes and irrigation channels. The only way of entering the city was through the gate, and the only way to reach the gate was along the causeway.

The Allied operations against the South Gate were directed by the senior British officer present, Brigadier-General Dorward. As a commander he does not seem to have inspired much confidence; Seymour's departure to Taku, Beatty wrote, 'left Dorward to work his wicked will.' Considering that he must have had adequate information about the ground over which he had to advance—much of it impassable owing to water-obstacles and all of it swept by fire from the dominating city-wall—his tactics appear injudicious.

The wall was impervious to rifle-fire and too thick for artillery to make much impression on. By deploying his infantry in extended order and advancing against the wall as though, like a trench or a zareba, it was equally vulnerable to attack throughout its whole length, Dorward merely exposed his line of battle to the fire of an enemy upon whom—save by the gunners—no damage could be inflicted until the South Gate had been forced. His total of over 700 casualties in one day was far the heaviest sustained by the Allies in any action during the campaign in North China.

The Japanese, who led the attack along the causeway, lost more men than any other nationality, but at least they lost them in a worthwhile cause. The 9th United States Infantry, fresh from the fighting in the Philippines, were handled almost as roughly in a role which gave them no chance to do anything except provide the Chinese with target practice. They were on the right flank. Their line of advance was enfiladed at close range by Chinese batteries on the north bank of the river. In an attempt to avoid the fire from these, or at least to lessen its effects, the Americans edged in towards the centre of the line and came under more heavy fire from the wall. They lost their colonel and four other officers and were soon pinned down in an exposed position from which further advance was impossible. 'The shelling was far more terrific than any I experienced during the Civil War, and I served under General Sherman,' recorded the American Consul, Mr Ragsdale, who was present. Small parties of the Naval Brigade and of the Weihaiwei Regiment brought the Americans what succour was possible, and they eventually withdrew under cover of darkness. It is difficult not to feel that they underwent a severe ordeal to no purpose.*

When night fell after a day of scorching heat the Allies had little to show for the day's work and seemed as far from capturing the city as when the operation had started. But everyone

* 'I blame myself,' Dorward wrote on 15 July to the officer commanding the United States forces, 'for the mistake made in the taking up of their position by the 9th Regiment, not remembering that troops wholly fresh to the scene of action and hurried forward in the excitement of attack were likely to lose their way.'

had faith in the Japanese who, as a British midshipman wrote, 'broke their engagements to none and showed their backs to nothing.' The force's spearhead went silently and doggedly about its business in the darkness, and at 3 a.m. on 14 July a shattering explosion was heard from the South Gate. The supporting troops, who included the 2nd Battalion the Royal Welch Fusiliers, pounded down the causeway and through the breach. Chinese resistance melted away. By sunrise alien flags were flying from the walls, and Tientsin, large parts of which were in flames, was being indiscriminately looted.

That afternoon Prince Ch'ing and his collaborators despatched the first of many letters to Sir Claude MacDonald.

The loss of Tientsin was not the first or by any means the last development which strengthened the hands of the more moderate-minded members of the Manchu Court and offered some hope that China might at the eleventh hour abandon her wild, suicidal purpose of defying the world and butchering its envoys.

Like a djinn conjured effortlessly from a bottle, the Boxer movement was to have saved China by providing a magical bulwark against her foes. But something had gone wrong. The spirit hordes, the invincible legions from the caves and the mountains and the upper air, had not taken the field; and although the Boxers had rallied to the Imperial standards, they had proved unable to redeem their pledge to protect the Dynasty and exterminate the foreigners. It is true that in many parts of the country they had hacked missionaries to pieces, decapitated their children and driven carts over the half-naked bodies of young female evangelists till life became extinct. But these actions, though meritorious, were not difficult to perform, and in open combat with the barbarians the Boxers had proved a broken reed.

They had ceased to take an effective part in the Siege of the Legations. A Memorial by a censor, submitted on 7 July, is typical of the criticisms which for some time had been reaching the Court from officials and commanders:

When the Boxers first came, they claimed that they had supernatural powers, that they were invulnerable to guns and swords, and that they were capable of burning the foreign houses and exterminating the foreigners as easily as turning over a hand. Now they are different: first they evade by artifice, then they retreat and make no advance. Only the army of Tung Fu-hsiang has attacked with all effort day and night.

As for protecting the Dynasty, the Boxers had put it in a far worse predicament than it was in before they appeared on the scene; for the outrages either committed by or officially ascribed to them had achieved the almost impossible by uniting the Powers in one common purpose. They had sunk their differences. For once, the barbarians all wanted to do the same thing: march on Peking. And when they marched, they would march in an ugly mood.

These things were obvious to influential Chinese throughout the Empire. Since the beginning of June the Viceroys and Governors in the southern and eastern provinces had been making representations—or, more commonly, exhorting each other to make representations—to Peking counselling prudence and urging the suppression of the Boxers. It was difficult for them to ignore, let alone disobey, the Edict which on 21 June declared war on the Powers after the capture of the Taku Forts; but Li Hung-chang, who was then Viceroy at Canton, decided to take the line that the Edict must have been issued without the full authority of the Throne, and this convenient formula was adopted by all his fellow-Viceroys except the foul Yü Hsien, who in the inaccessible province of Shansi continued to murder every missionary he could lay hands on.

The response to the Empress Dowager's appeal for reinforcements was languid. The Governor of Kiangsu, summoned to Peking, took with him 1500 men; when the foreign Consuls at Shanghai (with whom the Viceroys in the Yangtse Valley were in continuous and amicable contact) protested, he said,

reasonably enough, that he needed the troops for his own protection on the journey. Chang Chih-tung, the Hankow Viceroy, sent 5000 men, but made it clear that he expected the
troubles to be over before they reached Peking. His attitude was
so accommodating that at the end of July the British Consul at
Shanghai recommended that he should be given, on the
security of some cotton-mills, a large loan with which to pay his
troops; Her Majesty's Government would do well, Mr Warren
telegraphed, to 'take this opportunity of confirming the
Yangtse Viceroys' assurances of support and of strengthening
their power.' On 14 August the Foreign Office agreed to oblige
Chang Chih-tung with a loan of £75,000, and expressed the
pious hope that the Viceroy would forward receipts from his
generals to show that the troops really had been paid.

It is unlikely that the Empress Dowager was aware of this
transaction; but she and the extremists who dominated her
counsels could not disregard the steadily accumulating evidence
that the Empire was not answering the helm. On 14 July, the
day Tientsin was lost, a Memorial reached the Court from
thirteen southern Viceroys and Governors, urging that foreigners
should be protected and compensated for damage done to their
property, that the rebels in the north should be suppressed, and
that an apology for von Ketteler's murder should be sent to
Berlin.

Two days later a further Memorial from the same signatories
respectfully called attention to the folly of an Edict ordering
them to stop the payment of interest on foreign loans. If this
were done, they pointed out, 'the bond-holders would be
frightened and would press their Governments to occupy our
Customs and disturb the provinces along the Yangtse and the
coast.' Turmoil and bankruptcy would result and this, it was
disingenuously submitted, 'would seriously affect the defence
preparations of the provinces outside Peking.'

To these unmistakable symptoms of internal disunity was
added a growing volume of threats from outside. On 5 July
the British Government notified the Chinese authorities,
through their Minister in London, that they would be 'held

personally guilty if the members of the European Legations and other foreigners in Peking suffer injury;' and three days later a similar warning was received from Paris. Germany bellowed for vengeance against von Ketteler's assassins. On 11 July the Chinese Minister at St Petersburg was informed that the Russian Government was moving troops into Manchuria to suppress the disturbances which were imperilling its interests there. From all over the world troopships were converging on Taku. The outbursts of almost hysterical indignation which followed the publication on 16 July of the 'massacre' story showed the enormity in foreign eyes of the crime which only her military ineptitude had prevented China—as yet—from committing.

It was not a change of heart, a sudden access of wisdom or humanity, which on 16 July silenced the rattle of musketry and the roar of cannon round the Legations; it was a belated recognition by the Manchu Court that almost the only way in which they could make China's position more calamitous than it was already would be by killing the envoys.

On the first day of the truce, the 17th, the besieged found the silence uncanny, even disconcerting. The Chinese soldiers in their garish uniforms sat sunning themselves on top of their barricades and, except to the north and west of the perimeter where Tung Fu-hsiang's Moslems maintained a scowling reserve, a certain amount of fraternisation took place. The adversaries inspected each other's barricades, and the foreigners for the first time fully realised the strength and intricacy of the fortifications which hemmed them in.

An illicit trade in eggs sprang up, and the Japanese even managed to purchase several of their enemies' rifles. Two Chinese soldiers sought, and after being blindfolded were granted, admission to the perimeter. One of them was a trumpeter, formerly a valued member of Sir Robert Hart's band. His officer, irritated by some musical lapse, had struck him on the head with his sword, half severing one ear, and the soldier had come to be patched up by Dr Poole.

# THE TRUCE

It was a strange day. 'The community lived in a state of amazed suspense. Every hour saw a new marvel.' One of the marvels was the bold exploit of M. Claude Pelliot, a young member of the French Legation who was in later life to win renown as an orientalist. Saying that he was going to pay some visits, he climbed over the Chinese barricades and disappeared, many thought for ever. He returned safely that evening. He had been conducted to Jung Lu's headquarters, where he was given an excellent meal and closely questioned by the Commander-in-Chief about conditions in the Legations. Pelliot said that these left nothing to be desired, except that the besieged had no fresh fruit. When he was escorted back to what was left of the French Legation his pockets bulged with the finest peaches.

Though broken once or twice by unexplained nocturnal volleys, the demi-official cease-fire continued in force until the end of the month. The British played cricket. Sailors rowed up and down the canal on improvised rafts. People found the flies and mosquitoes more irksome than they had when danger was abroad. On two occasions, by command of the Empress Dowager, carts laden with gifts of melons, vegetables, ice and flour entered the perimeter. The sterner moralists were for sending these back; but to forgo the delicacies for the sake of striking an attitude would have been not only silly but dangerous. Melon clubs were formed, and after each fruit had been cooled in a well, cut up, and seasoned with claret, mock-pompous discussions of its merits and elaborate tasting ceremonies, to which members of other clubs were invited, helped to pass the long, hot, fly-blown hours. It was a month, as Pelliot had told Jung Lu, since they had had any fresh fruit. The flour, which the Chinese converts felt certain was poisoned, was kept in reserve against an hour of imperious need. It was eventually issued to troops of the Relief Force, who at first were entirely dependent for rations on the theoretically starving garrison; and was eaten without ill effect.

Throughout the truce a correspondence unique in the history of diplomacy passed between Sir Claude MacDonald and the

Chinese authorities; it was not interrupted when hostilities were resumed, and the last letters were exchanged when the Allied forces were at the gates of Peking.

It was never clear, and is still uncertain, from whom the Chinese missives came. 'Some of the letters,' Sir Claude reported to the Foreign Office, 'were in the usual Tsungli Yamen form, and were accompanied by the cards of all the Yamen Ministers, but these were the more formal communications. The important part of the correspondence . . . purported to come from "Prince Ch'ing and others" or "Prince Ch'ing and colleagues," and to Prince Ch'ing accordingly were addressed my replies; but there is no ground for supposing him to have been especially responsible for the letters we received. Differences of style and tone suggested the possibility that they came from different sets of persons. . . . On the whole it must be assumed that we were really in direct correspondence with the Heads of the Chinese Government, the changes in tone being due to the effect produced by events at Tientsin, and possibly to fluctuations in the influence of different advisers of that Government.'

The Corps Diplomatique repressed a strong and natural impulse to vent the full force of their indignation on their correspondents. 'A certain reserve and reluctance to give free expression to one's feelings cannot [wrote Sir Claude] be described as an unusual feature of diplomatic correspondence, but such reserve can rarely have been so irksome, and at the same time imposed by such cogent motives, as in our case.' The diplomats' object was at all costs to prolong the Alice-in-Wonderland negotiations. To show anger or exigence, or to treat with the contempt they deserved the preposterous suggestions and threadbare excuses which formed the main content of the Chinese letters, would have been to play into the hands of the extremists. Reliable news had reached the Japanese Legation on 18 July that Tientsin had been captured and an attempt to relieve the Legations was being prepared. There was everything to gain by temporising, everything to lose by exacerbating the Chinese and thus in all probability bringing the truce to an end. The fact that the Imperial troops were hard at work improving their fortifications suggested that the lull was regarded as a temporary state of affairs.

On 15 July, in response to a suggestion made by Sir Claude to Jung Lu, an emissary from the Yamen presented himself at the main gate of the British Legation, where he was received by the Corps Diplomatique with what many felt to be an unbecoming show of affability. Back numbers of the *Peking Gazette*, which came to hand shortly afterwards, revealed that in June this man, Wen Jui, had been appointed by Imperial Decree a leading light in the Boxer organisation, and his choice as an envoy was—particularly since nothing whatever came of his mission—seen in retrospect as a deliberate insult.

'It is possible,' ruminated Prince Ch'ing and his colleagues on the following day, 'that the foreign Envoys do not fully realize the keen desire of our Court to protect the Legations, and we feel bound to give a detailed explanation.' No explanation, detailed or otherwise, followed; but after references to 'a general ferment, absolutely beyond our control,' which nothing but the destruction of the Legations could satisfy, the project for a move to Tientsin was revived, and was backed by veiled threats of an 'unforeseen disaster' if the diplomats stayed where they were. The letter, which was confused in style, omitted the formal courtesies which normally rounded off communications from the Yamen.

The Chinese attitude seemed to be hardening, and on 20 July Sir Claude returned a circumspect reply, setting forth the disadvantages and dangers of a removal to Tientsin without actually refusing to entertain the idea.

On the 25th the Chinese renewed their request for the diplomats' departure and asked them to fix a day for it 'in order that we may make ready boats and provisions.' Two other messages on the same day earnestly invited the Ministers to send telegrams home *en clair* 'stating that all is well, without touching on military affairs.'

Sir Claude delayed his replies until the 27th. He declined the invitation to telegraph *en clair* and asked for more details about the arrangements for transport to Tientsin. Prince Ch'ing had said nothing about the carts and chairs in which the party would have to travel as far as the river. If he would be a little more explicit, the diplomats would be in a position to study the project seriously.

Next came a suggestion that the numerous converts in the Legations should be 'sent out and directed to quietly pursue their avocations'; their presence must be causing 'much inconvenience in this hot weather.' This was followed by more requests to the diplomats to fix the date of departure.

By now Sir Claude's answers were laced with complaints about violations of the truce, which was clearly coming to an end. There was intermittent firing at night, guns were being moved into position, and stones thrown over the barricades caused injuries to the garrison.

But still the strange correspondence continued. The firing of which Sir Claude complained, wrote Prince Ch'ing, had been due to a mutual misunderstanding; 'it was more or less on the same footing as the sounding of the evening drum and the morning bell—an everyday matter—and is really hardly worth a smile.' This phrase (probably an abbreviation of the classic saw, 'hardly worth a smile from a wise man') gave much offence in the Legations, which had been under severe attack on the night in question.

Bullets were now pouring into the perimeter as furiously as ever. Yet some of the normal amenities of diplomatic intercourse had been restored. On 3 August the Tsungli Yamen granted the Ministers the right to communicate with their Governments in cypher and undertook to send messages 'by 600 *li* couriers' (they were supposed to, and possibly sometimes did, ride in relays 200 miles in a day) to the nearest intact telegraph office at Tsinanfu. The Italian Minister was informed, with deep regret, of the assassination of the King of Italy, and a similar message told Sir Claude MacDonald that the Chinese Minister in London had been instructed to convey to Queen Victoria the condolences of the Imperial Court on the lamented demise of HRH the Duke of Saxe-Coburg-Gotha.

'I should be astonished,' replied Sir Claude on 8 August, 'to learn that while the Chinese Minister in London was preparing his communication his Legation was under a constant fire from British troops, yet it is in a situation analogous to this that the Foreign Representatives at Peking find themselves placed.'

By this time there was a serious shortage of food. The last ponies were being killed. 'Went to say goodbye to poor old Memory. He was wretchedly thin. Very sad,' wrote a young diarist who had hoped that the Siege would be over before Memory's turn came. The foreigners still had enough to live on, but the converts who did not or could not earn the extra rations given to men who worked on the barricades or otherwise helped in the defence were in a state of near-starvation. Many of their small children had died and more were seriously ill. The trees in their corner of the Fu had been stripped of bark and leaves for food. On 7 August nine stray dogs were killed for their benefit. Despite orders to conserve ammunition, sharpshooters shot crows for them when they got the chance.

Since the earliest days of the Siege numerous attempts had been made to get messages out to Tientsin. Of the brave Chinese who volunteered to carry them many had been captured and killed, and only one or two (including the bearer of Sir Robert Hart's *cri de coeur*) had reached their destination. None had succeeded in completing the return journey until, on 18 July, a convert sent out by the Japanese on 30 June re-entered their lines.

The contents of the written message which he delivered to the Japanese Minister, Baron Nishi,* were sparse and, as it later turned out, misleading. They were posted on the Bell Tower:

* The Baron, Morrison wrote in his diary, had 'a most curious resemblance to an anthropoid ape.' He was unable to speak any foreign language except Russian, and the conclaves of the Corps Diplomatique (which were conducted in French) were prolonged while M. de Giers, his rival, acted as his interpreter. His gifts as a diplomat were unremarkable.

# THE SIEGE AT PEKING

A mixed division consisting of 2400 Japanese, 4000 Russians, 1200 British, 1500 Americans, 1500 French and 300 Germans leaves Tientsin on or about 20 July for the relief of Peking. The foreign Settlement has not been taken by the enemy.

This bulletin caused joy and excitement. The high though illusory hopes it raised (the Relief Force did not in fact leave Tientsin until the beginning of August) were soon being nourished by the heart-warming fabrications of the Chinese spy which were described in Chapter Ten. The truce, and the curious vacillations of policy revealed in the letters from 'Prince Ch'ing and others,' lent colour to the belief that the Allies were advancing on Peking. Everyone waited with painful eagerness for reliable news from the south.

It arrived on 28 July. On that day a boy of fifteen, who had slipped out of the perimeter on 4 July carrying in a mendicant's bowl of rice a letter from Sir Claude MacDonald to Mr Carles, the British Consul at Tientsin, returned after many adventures and escapes with an answer sewn in the collar of his coat. The glad news spread swiftly, and excited crowds were already surging round the Bell Tower when a copy of the message was affixed to it.

Poor Mr Carles! Seldom can a hundred words written neatly on a tiny piece of paper have earned for their author an unpopularity so instantaneous and so extreme. 'Men moved away,' wrote Morrison, 'to express their feelings beyond hearing of the ladies.' It was possibly the unhappiest moment of the Siege. 'Had not the arrival of the messenger been witnessed by numbers of people,' the British Minister recorded, 'it is more than probable that no notice of the contents of the letter would have been posted on the Bell Tower.'

The message was dated 22 July 1900. The versions reproduced in Sir Claude MacDonald's despatch to the Foreign Office, in Morrison's articles in *The Times* and in the numerous published accounts of the Siege are incomplete. I here quote

the original in full, italicising the passages omitted from the
hitherto authorised version, which it seems safe to assume was
that exhibited on the Bell Tower:

> Your letter of 4 July. There are now 24,000 troops
> landed and 19,000 troops here. General Gaselee is ex-
> pected at Taku. *When he comes I hope to see more activity.* The
> Russians are at Peitsang. Tientsin city is under foreign
> government and the Boxers' power here is exploded. *Do
> try and keep me informed of yourselves.* There are plenty of
> troops on the way if you can keep yourselves in food for a
> time, *all ought yet to come out well. The Consulate is mended to
> be ready for you when you come.* Almost all the ladies have left
> Tientsin. *Kindest remembrances to all in the Legation.*
>
> W. R. CARLES.

The cuts were presumably made by the British Minister
before the substance of the message was posted on the Bell
Tower, but it does not seem that history, working until now
on the expurgated text, has done serious injustice to the
memory of Mr Carles, who emerges from both versions as a
silly man with small grasp of essentials.

Even in its shortened form, without the ominous sentence
'When he comes I hope to see more activity,' this message razed
with a brutal finality the cloud-capped towers and glittering
palaces of hope which the besieged had built on the misleading
intelligence brought in during the last ten days. Stunned,
angry and bewildered, they vented their indignation on Mr
Carles.

'It was amusing,' wrote Morrison, 'to witness the petulance
with which the British were forced to admit that this somewhat
incoherent production was really written by a Consul still in
the British service. From this document it was impossible to
know whether the troops were on the way to Peking from
Tientsin, or to Tientsin from Europe, who were the troops, and
how many, or whether the number landed was 24,000 in all or
43,000, while the observation that the troops were coming if

our provisions held out seemed to imply that if our provisions failed the troops would return to Tientsin.' *

It relieved everyone's feelings to berate Mr Carles, but it soon dawned on them that behind the irritating conundrums posed by his ambiguities and omissions lay a deeper, more important mystery. What was going on at Tientsin? On 22 July there had been 24,000 Allied troops (or possibly almost twice that number) within 100 miles of the Legations. What were they doing? Their commanders must know, if only from Sir Claude's letter to Mr Carles, the full gravity of the situation in Peking. The British Consul appeared to be an unusually vague man, but if, when he wrote, an expedition had been on the point of marching, surely even he would have alluded to the fact?

A siege does not diminish the self-importance of those who undergo it. Cooped up in their predicament, engrossed in their specialised fate, dreaming continually of rescue, they are quick to suspect lethargy or even callousness in the outside world as the days pass and the liberating armies tarry. It was in a disgruntled, captious mood that, as night fell and the volleys crashed about them, the besieged drank their champagne and discussed over and over again the implications of the British Consul's ineffable communication.

What *was* happening at Tientsin?

* Two days later, fortunately for the prestige of Her Majesty's Consular Service, an equally jejune communication arrived for Mr Conger from Mr Ragsdale, the American Consul at Tientsin. It began 'I had a dream about you last night,' contained almost no news of any kind, and ended 'It is my earnest wish that you may all be spared.'

M. Pichon (*left*) with Captain Darcy in the French Legation

The Fu after the Siege

'Betsey,' the home-made gun

CHAPTER TWELVE

# Operation Babel

*General Frey's plan was accepted with enthusiasm and gratitude by soldiers who, reduced by circumstances beyond their control to a static role which they found wearisome and uncongenial, suddenly saw before their eyes the unexpected opportunity of associating the nations which they represented in an important international action upon whose most trivial developments the anxious attention of the whole world was focussed, and whose auspicious outcome would provoke in every country a veritable outburst of joy.*

Général H. Frey: *Français et Alliés au Pé-tchili.* The author is describing his efforts to ensure that token detachments of the armies of France, Germany, Italy and Austria, who had failed to keep up with the advance and returned to Tientsin, would be in at the kill.

AFTER the capture of Tientsin City on 14 July 'a strange lethargy,' one of the abler war-correspondents noted, 'seemed to take possession of everyone, with an utter disbelief in the possibility of saving the Legations.' This disbelief was strengthened two days later, when the *Daily Mail*'s story of a total massacre echoed round the world. It was weakened when, as time went on, messages began intermittently to reach Tientsin from the besieged; but it was never dispelled, for the messages took several days in transit and gave varying accounts of the garrison's prospects in a situation which all described as critical. A British brigadier-general, for instance, reaching Tientsin on 28 July, wrote: 'The latest news from Peking is that they can hold out till 4 August.' Other sources record similar calculations. None was encouraging.*

Thus the atmosphere of boot-and-saddle urgency in which Seymour and his men had piled into their trains more than a

---

* Cf. Letter from Sir Claude MacDonald brought in on 29 July: 'We have provisions for about two weeks. . . . If Chinese do not press their attack we can hold out for some days—say ten.'

month earlier was lacking. Moreover, both in Tientsin and in the capitals of the eight nations whose armed forces were to take part in the relief operations, a feeling of caution was abroad. Great emphasis was laid on the need to build up a strong and well-found expedition before embarking on a campaign which appeared, in the light of Seymour's experiences, to be fraught with difficulties and dangers.

Estimates of the total force required for the capture of Peking became larger and larger as time went on. Those who made them may not always have been thinking exclusively in terms of pure strategy. Seymour, who told the Admiralty on 2 July that 'quite 40,000 troops' were needed, would have been less than human if he had not tended to exaggerate the difficulties of a task in which he himself had failed. The Japanese Foreign Minister, who put the figure at 70,000, was unlikely to minimise the warlike qualities of the Chinese and thus to cheapen the Japanese victories of five years ago. Admiral Kempff signalled to Washington that a force of 60,000 would be needed, with a further 20,000 men to guard the lines of communication.

The bigger the force, the longer the delay before it could move against Peking. But to some of the Powers delay was not wholly objectionable. Because of von Ketteler's murder Germany claimed a certain priority in the crusade against Chinese barbarism. The Kaiser already held strong views on the Yellow Peril. 'I will not rest,' he told a detachment of his specially equipped expeditionary force, whose enormous straw hats were to excite the mirth of their comrades-in-arms, 'until the German flags, united with those of the other Powers, float victoriously over China and, planted on the walls of Peking, dictate the terms of peace.'

But the men to whom he addressed these words on 2 July would not reach North China until late in August, and meanwhile there would be none of his soldiers available to carry the German flags to Peking.* The news of the relief of the Legations was

---

* In the event a small German naval detachment of 108 officers and men took part in the relief operations. They entered Peking four days after its capture by the much larger contingents of Japan, Russia, America and Great Britain.

'naturally at first a great disappointment for the Kaiser.' * The
G. A. Henty tradition was no longer paramount in North China.

Although none of them said so in as many words, all the
Powers were haunted by a vague fear that the International
Relief Force might, after accomplishing its primary task, be
obliged, or tempted, to accept wider responsibilities. If Peking
fell and the central authority in China disintegrated, no one
could forecast the pattern of events; but it was obvious that in
such a contingency those nations with the strongest forces on
the spot might reap far greater advantages than those whose
flags were meanly represented or whose troopships were still at
sea. On 20 July a Russian reference to the 'ulterior military
measures which the Powers may have to undertake in China'
caused a *frisson* of alarm in London. 'What is the meaning of
these phrases?' Lord Salisbury telegraphed urgently to the
British Ambassador in St Petersburg.

Partly as a result of this inquiry, the vexed problem of a
Supreme Commander was mooted. Here the Kaiser got his
way. He lobbied the Tsar into proposing and the Japanese into
seconding his nominee, Field-Marshal Count von Waldersee.
The French withheld their approval for as long as they reasonably could (von Waldersee had been prominent among their
conquerors in 1870), but at last grudgingly announced that
their own Commander-in-Chief 'would not fail to place his
relations with the Marshal upon a proper footing.'

On 18 August, mastering his chagrin at the news that the
International Relief Force had accomplished its object four
days earlier, the Kaiser 'handed me' (von Waldersee recorded)
'the Field-Marshal's baton with a somewhat too vivacious
address which unfortunately got into the newspapers.' Two
men of the Imperial Bodyguard were attached to the departing
knight errant (who, to be fair, had small stomach for these
theatricals); the Kaiser 'told them that they would be held
personally responsible for my life and that they must never let
me out of their sight. To Sergeant Major Nasser he allotted the
duty of holding me back should I ever ride too much to the front

* Alfred, Count von Waldersee: *A Field-Marshal's Memoirs.*

in battle.' Six weeks later the Supreme Commander arrived in North China. He never took part in anything that could be dignified by the name of a battle, but he saw plenty of bloodshed; 'in all the countless executions I have witnessed,' he wrote, 'I have never seen a Chinaman betray any sign of fear or emotion.'

By the end of July a force of some 25,000 men had been mustered at Taku and Tientsin, and many more were on the way. Several of the leading Powers had prior military commitments which restricted the scale of their intervention in North China. The United States Army was deeply involved in the Philippines; in Manchuria the Boxer ferment had led to widespread fighting and imposed on Russia's Far Eastern garrisons a major diversion of effort; the French were preoccupied with problems of internal security in Indo-China; Britain was hamstrung by the Boer War. Only Japan and Germany had no battles to fight; Germany was a long way away and lacked experience in the mounting of overseas expeditions.

Nevertheless the wheels of war were turning. From a *Journal of the Principal Events Connected with China*, compiled by the Intelligence Division of the War Office in 1901, we get a glimpse of the Victorian Empire girding up its loins for a distant campaign in a climate which, though unbearably hot in the summer, would soon be bitterly cold.

From India came oxen and ambulance tongas, lambswool drawers, puttoo gloves and poshteens (an outbreak of cholera in Afghanistan curtailed the supply of these). Goat's-hair socks, as worn by the Norwegian Army, were purchased from Scandinavia. Two thousand tons of firewood, a rare commodity in North China, were providently shipped from Australia. On 28 July a balloon section was embarked at Southampton; its horses would sail from Calcutta.*

* French aviation was also represented in North China. General Frey asked Paris for a balloon, and a '*section d'aérostatiers*' eventually landed at Taku. 'Their services,' the General recorded, 'were far from useless,' but he did not say what those services were. One cannot help feeling that, if any of the Allies had been airborne in China, the ascent would not have gone unrecorded.

# OPERATION BABEL

It was not until General Gaselee, the British Commander-in-Chief, reached Tientsin on 27 July that the need for urgent action was seriously considered by the Allied council of war. At that date the accepted policy was to wait until overwhelming strength had been built up and everybody who mattered was ready to start. A fortnight later, when the Relief Force was half-way to Peking, the British Ambassador in St Petersburg was telegraphing that the Russian Government had 'received no official news of any engagement or of an advance on Peking. The latest telegram from Admiral Alexeiev says, on the contrary, that it was agreed by all the commanders that it was quite impossible to advance on Peking before the middle of August.'

It was the old-fashioned, kind-hearted General Gaselee— 'apparently easy-going,' von Waldersee found him—who persuaded the commanders on the spot to put first things first, to take the bit between their teeth, and to make at least 'an early forward movement' in the hope of relaxing pressure on the besieged.

At first the idea did not meet with favour. The Russian Commander-in-Chief, General Lineivitch, who arrived on 1 August, was for waiting, and his American colleague, General Chaffee, was reluctant to start without his artillery. Gaselee had been ordered to detach one of his two brigades for the defence of Shanghai, and therefore arrived at Tientsin comparatively empty-handed. But he was a likeable man. He collected, by informal contacts, individual partisans of his enterprising strategy (one of them was the colonel of the 14th United States Infantry),* and he talked the Japanese round. Before long the competitive instinct began to assert itself. The advocates of prudence had unanswerable arguments; but if the British and their friends were going to start in despite of them, it ill became anyone to be left behind.

General Gaselee was not to be deterred. His orders were to relieve the Legations; he was going to do his best to carry those orders out. Though not a guileful man, he put everybody else in

* Brigadier General A. S. Daggett: *America in the China Relief Expedition.*

an impossible position. The eyes of the whole world were on North China. If the British marched, alone, to disaster, the courage of their allies would be called in question; if the British were by any chance victorious, their allies would look fools as well as cowards.

The opposition melted away, the cogent reasons for delay were forgotten. After a five-hour conference on the morning of 3 August it was resolved to start on the 5th; and so completely had they shaken off their lethargy that the leading files of the International Relief Force marched out of Tientsin, past the Temperance Hall, at dawn on 4 August, twenty-four hours ahead of time.

The expedition was made up, in round numbers, as follows:

| | |
|---|---:|
| Japanese | 10,000 |
| Russians | 4,000 |
| British | 3,000 |
| Americans | 2,000 |
| French | 800 |
| Germans | 100 |
| Austrians and Italians | 100 |
| | 20,000 * |

The force was adequately equipped with artillery, but it was hampered by its lack of cavalry for reconnaissance and pursuit.† The Japanese had one cavalry regiment, but its lightweight chargers were of poor quality and, partly owing to the severe

* These totals, from British official sources, are almost certainly exaggerated. Most accounts give a figure of 16,000 to 17,000 for the whole force.

† 'Our cavalry was of the utmost use to us throughout the whole campaign,' wrote a member of the Anglo-French expedition to Peking in 1860. In this much smaller force the British element included two and a half regiments of cavalry; the French, who had only the few spahis of Montauban's bodyguard, were often at a disadvantage from this cause. (Lt.-Col. G. J. Wolseley: *Narrative of the War with China in 1860*; Robert Swinhoe: *Narrative of the North China Campaign of 1860*.)

heat and partly to bad horse-management, only sixty out of 400 animals completed the march to Peking. The 6th United States Cavalry had landed at Taku but their horses were still unfit after the voyage and the regiment had to be left behind. Apart from a few Cossacks, the Bengal Lancers, who did useful work, were the only other unit of this arm to serve in the campaign.

The route followed was that taken by the expedition of 1860, along the banks of the Pei Ho. A train of junks and sampans six miles long was poled or towed up the shallow river with many delays and mishaps; but the troops' immediate needs were carried in or on various forms of animal transport. The Americans had brought their own mules and handled them with a skill and assurance which were much admired, as were the big Studebaker waggons which they pulled. Many of the Japanese pack-horses were stallions, which led to endless trouble. The French had only a few tiny Annamite ponies, the size of small donkeys, and the Germans, Italians and Austrians had virtually no transport at all. Requisitioned ponies and mules were unsatisfactory to begin with, and took unkindly to pack-saddles and other harness which fitted them in unaccustomed places. The roads—normally there was only one—were narrow gullies eaten into the loess by hoofs and wheels down the centuries. The rains converted them into rivers of mud. Many animals, especially among the trace-horses of the artillery, succumbed to the terrible heat.

Nevertheless the Relief Force started off with great dash and after thirty-six hours were at Yangtsun, with twenty-five miles and two victories behind them.

The short campaign is unique in military history, and its conduct is of fascinating interest to the student of warfare, of international relations or indeed of human nature at large. But it cannot be claimed that the actions fought in the course of it demand, or would repay, reconstruction in detail. Until the last, when Peking itself was assaulted, all conform to the same pattern: an approach march in column, a perfunctory and inadequate reconnaissance, a hurried redeployment in accordance with a vaguely agreed plan, a haphazard artillery bombardment, a frontal advance against a strongly entrenched position, and a Chinese rout which for lack of cavalry could not be effectively exploited.

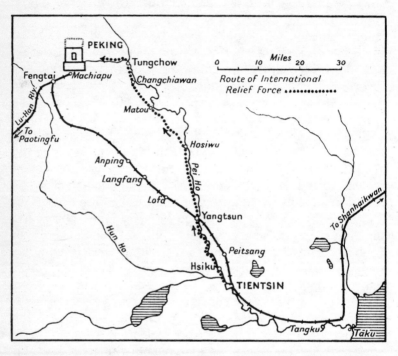

The first battle was really decisive, for although the Chinese disengaged with light losses and got most of their guns away, it gave them a shock from which their morale never recovered. It was fought at Peitsang, a few miles north of the Hsiku Arsenal, on the morning of 5 August. The Japanese (wearing, like the Russians, white tunics) bore the brunt, advancing in their usual suicidally close formation against strong entrenchments with unflinching steadiness. The British artillery, which included two naval twelve-pounders, veterans of the relief of Ladysmith, was in support, and their infantry had some fighting; but it was a Japanese victory, and a very useful one.

Much emboldened, the Allies pressed forward, and on the next day fought again at Yangtsun, ten miles nearer Peking. Once more they had to deal with an elaborate system of trenches and earthworks, strongly held and well furnished with artillery. This time the British and Americans led the attack, with the Russians and French in support and the Japanese in reserve. It was a day of appalling heat, which was at its worst when the battle started in the early afternoon.

Half-mad with thirst, blinded by sweat, the infantry stumbled forward. Nobody had any very clear idea what he or anybody else was doing, but somehow the Chinese positions were stormed one after another. In the middle of the action an Allied battery began to shell a company of the 14th United States Infantry. Four men were killed outright and eleven more wounded, most of them mortally. An American officer, sent back to apprise the gunners of their tragic mistake, collapsed with heat-stroke.

Nobody knows whether a Russian or a British battery was responsible. One account speaks of Russian guns unlimbering alongside the Royal Artillery and asking for the range; they were given it but were not warned, or failed to realise, that it was in yards, not metres. Whether this is true or not, it is typical of the sort of thing which happened throughout an impromptu campaign by a polyglot force whose sub-units marched and fought (as the ultra-professional General Frey put it) 'rather as bands of partisans than as regular troops taking part in a planned operation.'

Luckily the badly-led Chinese had little stomach for a fight and by the evening of 6 August Yangtsun had fallen. When the Relief Force left Tientsin less than two days earlier, the plan— in so far as a plan existed, or was understood, or was agreed to— had been to go no farther than Yangtsun until strong reinforcements arrived. But the unexpected weakness of the enemy's resistance had transformed laggards into thrusters. The generals smelt glory, the troops smelt loot. The expedition spent the 7th at Yangtsun, resting, sorting itself out, and waiting for the junks to catch up; but at a commander-in-chiefs' conference that morning it was resolved to push straight on to Peking with a force of 14,000.

When the leading troops moved off soon after dawn on the 8th they were engaged not so much in a military campaign as in a cross-country marathon.

By now the field had been thinned out; of the eight starters, only the Americans, British, Japanese and Russians were standing. The small German, Italian and Austrian detachments, unable to solve their transport and commissariat problems, had returned to Tientsin without firing a shot in anger. The French contingent was, though only in a numerical sense, much stronger, and its Commander-in-Chief addressed himself with frantic determination to the task of keeping the Tricolor in the race. He recorded his efforts in a massive volume of stately prose; and his narrative, written in the third person singular, throws so revealing a light on the political atmosphere of the expedition that the fortunes of the French, although of scant military significance, are worth following in some detail.

From his account of the North China operations Frey emerges as an imaginative strategist, for he was always proposing outflanking movements and diversions in which his own troops would play a leading part. It is perhaps unworthy to suggest that in doing so he was influenced by the hope that his plan, if adopted, might enable the French with the help of their Russian allies to establish a lead over the other nationalities; and it is only fair to an experienced soldier to point out that the plans always envisaged a short delay until French reinforcements arrived. He had temporary hallucinations rather than basic illusions about the troops actually under his command; he admitted that they lacked the stamina for a long campaign, 'although readily capable of a supreme effort demanding energy, audacity and a firm resolve to succeed.'

This estimate of their martial qualities was, fortunately, never tested in action. France's armies were ill represented in North China. In the numerous accounts of the expedition every contingent criticises some things about some of the other contingents; the French are the only troops whom everybody criticises for everything. 'The scum of the French army and quite disgraceful' (Roger Keyes), 'we all knew France could make a better show than that' (H. S. Landor), 'the French are in universal disrepute—even the Russians do not want to have anything to do with them' (von Waldersee)—there is not one dissentient voice. Even the narrative of their Commander-in-Chief only manages to invest them with, at best, a certain pathos.

Originally about 1000 strong, the French contingent comprised two battalions of Infanterie de la Marine and two batteries of mountain and one of field artillery. The troops were Tonkinese—tiny little men who were dwarfed even by the Chinese soldiers of the Weihaiwei Regiment; *'ils n'aiment pas être tués,'* one of their officers confided to an ally. There was a serious shortage of officers, and only one—by name Captain Bobo—could be spared to provide General Frey with the nucleus of a staff. The units had done a long, enervating tour of duty in Indo-China and were in wretched physical condition. Their blue uniforms, which Frey described as 'lamentable rags,' were indistinguishable at a distance from the clothes of Chinese peasants. To lessen the risk of their allies taking them for Boxers, they were ordered to adjust the blue covers of their large white sun-helmets so that these showed up half-white and half-blue. This prudent measure was misconstrued by some of the war-correspondents, whose despatches (Frey complained in words which would only lose in translation) attributed the odd appearance of his men's headgear to *'un inconcevable laissez-faire, ou bien un amour excessif de la fantaisie.'* The French transport consisted largely of rickshaws and wheelbarrows.

At Yangtsun on 6 August General Frey received a letter, dated the previous evening, from Colonel de Pélacot; the writer was still at Peitsang with the French infantry, who had taken no part in the fighting and had marched only ten miles since leaving Tientsin.

'The men [de Pélacot reported] are exhausted and, according

to the doctors, incapable of doing a full day's march to-morrow. 14 men of the 1st Battalion and 19 men of the 2nd Battalion are absent. I await your orders for tomorrow. If I receive none, I shall go back to Tientsin.'

It must have been with a heavy heart and a troubled mind that General Frey attended the commander-in-chiefs' conference outside General Lineivitch's tent on the morning of 7 August. Fame beckoned imperiously. It now seemed highly probable that only a succession of easy victories lay between the Relief Force and Peking; but to take part in a walkover one must be able, at least, to walk, and of this the French contingent was for the time being incapable. Frey had to admit that he was no longer mobile. He would, he said, return to Tientsin (where he privately hoped that fresh French troops would by now have arrived), reorganise his force and catch up with the Allied vanguard as soon as possible.

Meanwhile he would detach 200 troops for the essential duty of garrisoning Yangtsun. He was warmly thanked by his colleagues, but his offer was prompted less by the spirit of inter-allied solidarity than by the fact that for the men concerned to retreat was just as much out of the question as to advance. They could no more march back to Tientsin than they could march on to Peking. A 'screen' of fifteen Cossacks to look after the foundered Tonkinese was accepted with gratitude.

It is impossible not to admire the daemonic, single-minded energy with which this elderly man, working almost unaided under arduous conditions, now proceeded to ensure that French arms would be represented before the walls of Peking. He hurried back to Tientsin. No French reinforcements had arrived. He sought out the Germans, the Austrians, the Italians. 'Impelled by a sense of military confraternity forming almost an international Order of Chivalry,' he offered to facilitate their advance by every means at his disposal. At all costs the French must arrive in time to share the glory and the spoils of victory; the more poor relations they could bring with them, the less danger there would be of the first-comers reaping disproportionate rewards.

The three smallest detachments—the junior members of
Frey's Order of Chivalry—consisted of sailors who had been
with Seymour and had had more than enough of the North
China plain for one summer. But they bestirred themselves and
set off northward at a leisurely pace. General Frey resolved to
*'pousser en avant le plus rapidement possible tous les éléments du Corps
français susceptibles encore de marcher'*; some of the men who were
not *susceptibles de marcher* were embarked in junks; and on
10 August the little straggling crusade limped apathetically off
on the path to glory.

Meanwhile the main body was marching doggedly and painfully towards Peking. Brushing aside trifling opposition, they
captured Hosiwu early on 9 August, Matou at dawn on the
10th and Changchiawan on the 11th. This was the place
where in 1860 the Allied envoys and their escort were made
prisoner while negotiating under a flag of truce. Of thirty-
nine men—English, French and Indian—only nineteen survived the cruelties to which they were subjected. It was as
a reprisal for their treatment that the British burnt down
the Summer Palace, which had already been looted by the
French.

The walled city of Tungchow, fourteen miles from Peking,
was now the only major obstacle between the Relief Force
and the besieged Legations. Their progress had been steady
and their losses slight. The Japanese, who led the advance,
had done virtually all the fighting; they had lost—since
Yangtsun—only two killed. But the march had been a testing
ordeal.

The British had the worst of it, for they brought up the rear
and could not move off—for the whole force used the same
narrow, churned-up track—until the sun was already high.
They consisted of the Royal Welch Fusiliers (known to General
Frey as *'le Royal Irlandais'*), the 1st Sikhs, 7th Rajputs and 24th
Punjab Infantry, the Weihaiwei Regiment, the 12th Regiment
Royal Field Artillery, the Hongkong Artillery and a small
detachment of Royal Engineers; the naval siege-guns travelled

by junk, and the Bengal Lancers were normally up with the advance-guard.

Legend has it that General Gaselee accepted the invidious role of rearguard to allay Russian suspicions of the British and the Japanese. So strong were General Lineivitch's fears that his rivals would steal a march on him and reach Peking first that at one stage the expedition threatened to lose such precarious cohesion as it had and degenerate into a devil-take-the-hind-most scramble. Whether this legend has any foundation in fact it is impossible to say; but it is quoted in many British sources and, though not referred to in Gaselee's laconic despatches, is in keeping with his solid, sensible character.

Much of the plain was covered with crops of *kaoliang*, a form of millet which grows to a height of ten feet or more; this made reconnaissance very difficult and should have made ambushes very easy (they were in fact seldom attempted). Drinking water was scarce. The wells were no longer believed to be poisoned, but they had often been emptied by the time the rearguard arrived, and watering men and horses at them was a slow, tantalising business.

The worst hardship, for all the contingents, was the heat. The Russians and Japanese stood it best, but everyone suffered. 'We marched through an American detachment,' wrote the commanding officer of the 7th Rajputs. 'The men were marching slowly along at about two miles an hour, with heads bent and eyes half closed, and though utterly knocked up by the heat determined to stick it. I do not think they even noticed us as we passed them.' Lieutenant Smedley Butler of the United States Marines recalled that: 'Nearly fifty per cent of our men fell behind during the day. . . . In the cool of the night they would catch up with us and start on again next morning.' *

The pitiless sun caused fatal casualties to men and horses. There were virtually no trees outside the villages, and the tail

* The archives of the United States Marine Corps record the casualties suffered by the two battalions who took part in this gruelling march under the headings *Detached, Placed on Junks, Sent to Hospital, Missing, Dead*. Their total losses were 198, including one marine dead.

of the column, when a halt became due, often found all the available shade occupied by the leading troops.

Ever since they arrived in North China, each contingent had been scrutinising the bearing and equipment of the others with professional curiosity. It was as though Mars was holding a mannequin parade. One of the two types of rifle with which the Americans were armed—the Krag-Jorgensen—was much admired; the other, the Lee, was not. The Russians excelled at living off the country; 'they had nothing, yet lacked nothing,' as somebody put it. But their sanitary arrangements 'left much to be desired,' and their aimless brutality to civilians made it difficult for everybody else to get coolie labour. The train of camp-followers which formed an integral part of the Indian regiments—the sweepers, syces, blacksmiths' bellows-boys and the rest—came in for criticism; but between the Royal Welch Fusiliers and the United States Marines a bond of friendship was formed which endures to this day.* Japanese bravery was acknowledged by all; their only detractor was General Frey, who said that they took a positive pride in suffering casualties and added, unworthily and inaccurately, that this 'led them to sacrifice without a moment's hesitation hecatombs of men in order to gain for Japan the leading role in an action.' Both in the Siege and on the march to Peking the Japanese had, by reason of their racial and linguistic affinities with the enemy, a marked advantage over their allies in collecting intelligence.

In the early hours of 12 August the Japanese blew up the South Gate of Tungchow. The Chinese garrison had fled. The Allies marched in, and there was much looting of that peculiarly wanton kind indulged in by victorious troops who, lacking

* The United States Marines and the Royal Welch Fusiliers still exchange telegraphic greetings on anniversaries of traditional importance to the one or the other. In 1930 Sousa, then in charge of the Marines' musical arrangements, composed a march called 'The Royal Welch Fusiliers.' In 1937 the 2nd Battalion once more lay alongside the Marines in China, during a crisis in Shanghai. In 1957 the Corps and the regiment exchanged trophies dating back to, and commemorating, their first encounter before the walls of Tientsin.

the means to carry away more than a fraction of their booty, nevertheless pilfer and destroy from a kind of lust. In this looting the less reputable citizens of Tungchow joined with a will. The same thing had happened at Tientsin and was to happen in Peking; the foreign troops had at least the excuse that anything they left untouched would be plundered by its owner's compatriots.

The Relief Force spent the 12th resting and replenishing their supplies. A large American mission station in the city had been sacked by the Boxers in the early days of the Rising, and in its ruined but extensive compound General Gaselee decided to establish a market for local produce. On his staff was a Chinese-speaking missionary, pressed into service as an intelligence officer, and him General Gaselee desired to write a suitable notice, inviting the populace to return home and trade peacefully with their conquerors. The man of God thought poorly of this scheme; it would be far more to the point, he suggested, to use the compound as the site of a huge, minatory bonfire whose flames would be visible from Peking. 'Well, you know,' said Gaselee mildly, 'we do not wish to antagonise the 350 millions of China.' The missionary found this reply characteristic; the General was 'kindness itself.' *

In the ranks of the Imperial forces chaos now reigned. On 11 August, the day before Tungchow fell, the bitterly anti-foreign Li Ping-hêng painted in a despatch to the Court this picture of disintegration:

> I have retreated from Matou to Changchiawan. For the past few days I have seen several tens of thousands of troops jamming all roads. They fled as soon as they heard of the arrival of the enemy. As they passed the villages and towns they set fire and plundered, so much so that there was nothing left for the armies under my command to purchase [sic], with the result that men and horses were

* In Gaselee's obituary—he was fifty-six in 1900 and died at the age of seventy-four—*The Times* paid tribute to his unfailing consideration for others. It was one of the causes of his popularity with the rank and file.

Field-Marshal
Count von
Waldersee

Tableau Vivant
Germany's 'East Asiatic
Corps' poses for the photo-
grapher before embarka-
tion. An officer (on foot,
wearing sword) gesticu-
lates with the rifle issued
to his mounted orderly.
Both men wear straw
slouch hats decorated with
cockades

The Yellow Peril

This picture, by the artist Knackfuss, was commissioned by the Kaiser in 1895 and presented to the Tsar

hungry and exhausted. From youth to old age I have experienced many wars, but never saw things like these. . . . Unless we restore discipline and execute the retreating generals and escaping troops, there will be no place where we can stand. . . . The situation is getting out of control. There is no time to regroup and deploy. But I will do my utmost to collect the fleeing troops and fight to the death, so as to repay the kindness of Your Majesties and to do the smallest part of a Minister's duty.

Next day he took poison. Yü Lu, the time-serving Viceroy of Chihli, had blown out his brains in a coffin-shop five days earlier. The rout went on.

Yet it was not in high hopes of saving the Legations that the Allied commanders-in-chief met in conclave on the morning of 12 August. Tungchow was full of rumours that the foreigners in Peking had been murdered. From the first many had feared, and some had prophesied, that the approach of the Relief Force would seal the doom of the besieged, if indeed any of them were still alive. On 8 August General Gaselee and General Chaffee had received identical cypher messages, dated the 6th, from Sir Claude; these were accompanied by a sketch-map and gave directions about the best way of reaching the Legations. Various other messages had come to hand since then. Though they expressed a guarded confidence, all made it clear that the Legations were in acute peril.

However, the cavalry reported no signs of organised resistance between Tungchow and the walls of Peking, and it was resolved to press on with the minimum of delay. General Lineivitch maintained that his men were too tired to carry out an assault immediately after completing the approach march; and at his instance it was agreed to do the operation in two phases. The Allied contingents, each directed on a different gate in the walls, would advance along parallel axes; they would halt and bivouac three miles from Peking; and the entire force would put in a co-ordinated assault on the morning of the 15th. For the first time the Allies had a plan of operations which was simple, which gave every nationality a place of equal prominence in the line of battle, and which allowed each contingent enough elbow-room to manoeuvre without obstructing its neighbours. We shall see in the next chapter what effects stemmed from this egalitarian deployment.

It would be wrong to leave the expedition, thus poised for a supreme effort, without noting that there were now five runners in the race, not four. The indomitable Frey, with a few hundred exhausted troops at his heels, had caught up with the main body. What is more, he expected the rest of his Order of Chivalry to arrive at any moment. Soup was being boiled for them.

His orders on the 13th laid down that 'this evening the German, Austrian and Italian columns will lie alongside the French troops. Tomorrow, under the walls of Peking, when the foreign national anthems are played, a complete silence will be maintained; each anthem will be heard with respect.* When the French national anthem is played, it will be sung as loudly as possible, in tune, by the whole of the French Expeditionary Corps. Our compatriots and the occupants of the foreign Legations beleaguered on the other side of the walls of the Chinese capital will know, when they hear our noble warchant, that deliverance is at hand.'

This was finely conceived. But, alas, the Germans, the Austrians and the Italians did not arrive until several days later; the French contingent lost its way in the darkness; and the severe test to which General Frey proposed to subject Tonkinese lungs, Pekinese acoustics and his own knowledge of municipal topography was never carried out.

* Including, of course, the detested *Heil dir im Siegerkranz*.

# CHAPTER THIRTEEN

# The Relief

Men! That's no Chinese crowd!
Men! That's no heathen roar!
Hark! Now the trampling's loud—
Christ! They are at our door!
            From an anonymous contemporary poem.

LI PING-HÊNG, whose suicide in the moment of defeat the last chapter recorded, seems to have been largely instrumental in bringing the unofficial truce with the Legations to an end.

He was a man of strong character, a violent hater of foreigners and all their works, including railways, post offices and paper currency. He had been Governor of Shantung when the murder of two missionaries provided the Germans with a pretext for their seizure of Kiaochow; afterwards German pressure secured his removal from this post. He was now Imperial Inspector of the Yangtse Naval Forces, and when the Taku Forts fell he hurried to Kiangyin, a coastal stronghold covering the approaches to Shanghai, and prepared—much to the alarm of the pacific southern Viceroys—to bombard any foreign warships that might come within range.

He had a certain angry integrity, and was one of the few men of note to respond with enthusiasm to the Edict of 21 June, which declared war and ordered the Provinces to send reinforcements to Peking. The Court showed a keen anxiety to secure his services. On 24 June a Decree summoned him to the capital. A second, which he received en route, bade him make all haste. A third ordered him to travel day and night, thus doubling his speed. He reached Peking on 26 July.

The Empress Dowager received him in audience without delay. There were as yet no signs of an Allied advance from Tientsin; nor did anyone in Peking suspect the incapacity of the commanders and the cowardice of the troops holding the southward approaches to the capital. Li urged aggression; 'only when one can fight can one negotiate for peace.' Almost immediately firing broke out again round the besieged Legations.

The Empress Dowager had a weakness for strong men and firm, decisive actions. It was she who had sent for this paladin; her intuition had (by means of the telegraph which he disliked so much) accelerated his coming. Now that she had seen him, she was more than ever certain that she had done the right thing, that with him as her champion she could yet save China. There was a sanguine streak in the Empress Dowager's character; when, little more than a fortnight later, they came to tell her that in the Temple of Heaven there were several hundred black soldiers wearing turbans, 'she did not betray the least emotion but said: "Perhaps these are the reinforcements from Turkestan, anxious to engage in battle with the foreigners?" '

Li Ping-hêng was granted by Decree the rare privilege of riding a horse inside the Forbidden City and using a sedan chair borne by two persons in the Winter Palace. Four armies were placed under his command. An access of debilitated jingoism swept through the Manchu Court. One is reminded of some huge, brackish aquarium. When a new fish is dropped in, the others lose their glazed vacuity, abandon their lethargic and accustomed circuits, slough off their derelict air. There are flurries of activity; the sand spurts up, the blowsy vegetation undulates; the denizens quiver, gulp, emit long streams of bubbles, whisk to and fro with an air of purpose. Then gradually the old order is re-established. Flaccid, bulbous, goggling, the multi-coloured fish sink back into apathy and take up again the empty ritual of their rounds.

To all the moderates Li's advent was a severe and to some a

lethal blow. On 28 July Hsu Ching-ch'eng, a former Minister at St Petersburg and President of the Imperial University, and Yuan Ch'ang, a member of the Tsungli Yamen, were executed; a fortnight later three other men of like stamp, including the President of the Board of War, paid with their heads for their timid advocacy of peace. All had been critics of the Boxers, all had had amicable truck with foreigners; one had suggested that von Ketteler's corpse ought to be given a coffin. As a Decree put it, 'they really have committed the crime of gross disrespect.' They met their deaths with composure.

Although the truce had ended, the Chinese attacks were for some days only intermittent, and a sortie under a German ex-officer, von Strauch, enlarged the British perimeter by seizing and fortifying some houses in a dangerous sector of the Mongol Market. Except for women whose small children were wasting away before their eyes, the morale of the besieged was high; on 2 August M. Pichon dumbfounded his hearers by expressing a guarded confidence in the outcome. During the truce Mr Gamewell and his coadjutors had greatly strengthened and improved the fortifications. More important, the besieged were now in communication with the outside world; the forlorn suspicion that they had been abandoned to their fate no longer nagged them.

Apart from Sir Claude's correspondence with the Yamen, which continued to pursue its unfathomable course, they were by courtesy of their would-be butchers sending and receiving cypher telegrams. Several couriers arrived with letters from Tientsin. On 10 August a note from General Gaselee, dated two days earlier, caused transports of joy: '*Strong force of Allies advancing. Twice defeated enemy. Keep up your spirits.*' Later that day an even more recent message from General Fukushima to the Japanese Minister gave ampler details of the Relief Force's progress, and forecast its arrival at Peking on the 13th or 14th.

Within the perimeter an almost end-of-term atmosphere prevailed. A large cache of dollars was discovered in one of the buildings in the Fu, and part of it was offered as a prize for the best design for a medal to commemorate the Siege. Many felt that '*Mene, Mene, Tekel, Upharsin*' would make an appropriate motto, but one man thought poorly of the idea. 'After all,' he pointed out, 'not everybody knows Latin.'

Casualties were still occurring. On the evening of the 12th the French Captain Labrousse remarked to a companion that with relief so near at hand it behoved everyone to take especial care of their safety; a moment later he was shot through the head and killed. He had played a leading part in the heroic defence of the French Legation, and Sir Claude MacDonald paid tribute to his qualities in his official despatch. Privately he found him 'a good officer but a bit dotty.'

A fresh division from Shansi, whose commander had sworn to take the Legations in five days, was reported in the line. He and twenty-six of his men were shot down when a barricade collapsed. The Yamen sent a furious protest ('This is far from being a friendly procedure') and cancelled a meeting which had been arranged to discuss arrangements for the journey to Tientsin.

On the 13th, with the Relief Force under the walls of the capital, the Chinese made, as they had been expected to make, a supreme effort to overwhelm the defences. All day a stream of fire poured into the Legations, reaching a crescendo towards nightfall. From the British Legation activity was observed in an emplacement high up in the wall of the Imperial City; this had been unused since the truce ended, but now the picquets reported the glint of brass mountings, which suggested that a modern gun was being moved into position.

Sir Claude called up the American Colt and the Austrian Maxim, and as dusk fell had them trained on the embrasure at ranges of 350 and 200 yards. At eight o'clock the volleys on every side reached a climax, and the new gun joined in. It proved to be a two-inch quick-firing Krupp; 'in ten minutes this gun did more damage than the smooth-bores had effected in a five weeks' bombardment.' * But the two machine-guns

* *Journal of the Royal United Services Institute*, Vol. LIX, No. 437, August 1914: 'Some Personal Reminiscences' by Sir Claude MacDonald.

were promptly in action, firing through the darkness over fixed sights, and the Krupp was silenced after the seventh round. Had it not been, the consequences would have been serious. The timely siting of the machine-guns was Sir Claude's last tactical decision as commander-in-chief. It was a sound decision, and is a reminder that the besieged owed more than most realised to his military training and fighting instincts.

The war-trumpets blared. From all round the perimeter came howls of 'Kill! Kill!' Officers could be heard frantically ordering their men forward (they invariably, somebody noted, used the verb 'go', never the verb 'come'). The volleys were incessant. From the Bell Tower the alarm clanged out. 'Every weapon in the Legation was distributed', a missionary recalled. 'Even Mr Norris and myself, who had never been armed before, were provided with revolvers. Everyone was prepared for a grand assault.' Wounded were carried in on stretchers. Runners brought urgent demands for reinforcements. The confidence of the last few days fell away, and people were seized with terrible misgivings. Was help, after all, going to come too late?

The day had been heavily overcast. As the Relief Force moved in four parallel columns towards Peking many of the soldiers took the distant crash and rumble of the Chinese fusillades for thunder; fire so continuous and sustained was beyond their experience. But the old campaigners knew it for what it was. They suspected that their own arduous operations were even now provoking a massacre of those whom they had come to save; and like all soldiers in all ages they masked such anger or sorrow as they felt behind a callous cynicism. This is what they had said from the first would happen; this is what always happened. They pressed on.

The Allied plan for the final assault was straightforward and is shown in diagrammatic form on the next page. The four main columns advanced astride the Imperial Canal. The Russians on the right flank were to make for the Tung Chih Men. The Japanese, using the great paved road which ran immediately

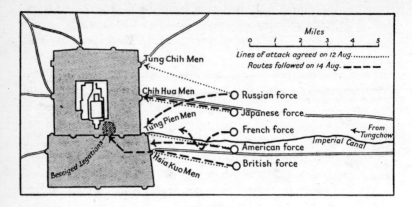

to the north of the canal, were directed on the Chih Hua Men. On the other side of the canal the Americans and, on the extreme left, the British were to attack the Tung Pien Men and the Hsia Kuo Men respectively. The French were sandwiched in between the Americans and the Japanese. It was agreed that all contingents would halt for the night at a distance of three miles from the walls, so that a concerted attack could be mounted on the 14th and put in on the 15th.

Up till now topography had exerted upon the competitive instincts of the Allies the same sort of restraining influence that a straitjacket exerts upon a madman. Tethered in any case to the river and the slow flotillas of supply-junks, the detachments could not even jockey for position once the order of march had been decided; on the narrow tracks along which they had advanced from Tientsin there simply was not room to do so.

For this last lap, however, their deployment might have been specifically designed to promote a race. There was no advance-guard, no reserve; everyone had an equal chance and a clear run to his objective.

In the course of 13 August the Relief Force moved off from Tungchow, fanned out, and plodded forward along roads made slippery by rain. It was intensely hot. The Bengal

Lancers, with long maize-leaves tucked under their helmets and hanging down to their waists, looked like figures in some fantastic masque. The countryside, dotted with little villages, clumps of trees, fields of *kaoliang*, pagodas, irrigation channels and sunken roads, was intricate and confusing; but before they bivouacked most of the detachments had sighted, black against the horizon, the long walls and the massive gate-towers of Peking. From beyond them came still the sound of heavy, continuous firing. Night fell, and with it a torrential rain.

Towards midnight rifle-fire was heard from the direction of the Tung Pien Men, the American objective immediately to the south of the canal. It grew in volume, and artillery joined in. The Japanese were nearer than anyone else to the scene of this unexpected action, and it soon dawned on them that the Russians were no longer under starter's orders. They had stolen a march on their allies. It was they who, on the ground that their troops were tired, had asked that the assault should be delayed. Now, without a word to anyone, they had broken their undertakings and pushed on single-handed along the path to glory—and along the wrong path at that.

The Russians' conduct was hotly criticised both on the battlefield and in accounts of the battle. They had not only attacked at least twenty-four hours ahead of an H-hour which they had had the chief voice in fixing, but they had cut diagonally across the Allied front and attacked not the next objective to their own but the next but one. Everyone assumed—the more naturally since the Tung Pien Men was the nearest of the four to the Legations—that General Lineivitch had deliberately tricked his allies, hoping, if all went well, to gain the lion's share of kudos by being the first into Peking.

The facts hardly warrant an explanation so sinister or so simple. During the 12th and 13th the Russians had done a lot of reconnaissance; their scouts were excellent, and with them rode a Norwegian adventurer called Munthe who had been a cavalry instructor in the Chinese Army and spoke the language fluently. On the evening of the 13th the scouts reported that they had got to within 200 yards of the Tung Pien Men before being fired on and that the wall in that sector appeared to be lightly held. Whether or not General Lineivitch understood which gate they were talking about (he may possibly have confused the Tung Pien with his own objective, the Tung Chih), he sent forward an advance-guard of one battalion and half a battery, whose role was to secure the undefended approaches to the gate and thus pave the way for an advance by the main body on the next day; it was, in other words, to act as what used to be called a standing patrol. The Russian chief of staff, General Vassilievski, was in command of this detachment, and Munthe went with him.

Vassilievski was a brave and enterprising man. He may or may not have known—it was a dark night—that he was at the wrong gate, but behind it he could hear the Legations being heavily fired on; and when the rain started, he saw the chance of a *coup de main*. Undetected, he led a party of men across a narrow bridge which spanned the moat, surprised the occupants of the outer guardhouse, and killed them all.

The alarm was given. Fire was opened from the wall but went wide in the darkness. The Russians brought up two guns and after a score of shots punched a hole in the iron-clad outer gate. Vassilievski and Munthe—the first men to enter Peking—went through it; the leading company of infantry followed.

Between the outer and inner gate in a Chinese city wall there is normally a courtyard, often surmounted by a tower of which it forms in effect the basement. The object of this arrangement is to ensure that enemies who penetrate the first gate will be caught in a death-trap before they can force the second; and this is what happened to the Russian spearhead, upon whom fire was poured from above at point-blank range.

However, the troops still outside managed to break in through a postern, and the Russians, though they lost heavily, had made themselves masters of the Tung Pien Men before sunrise. They hung on to the short and exposed sector of the wall which they had captured until their main body appeared at about 10 a.m. on 14 August.

There followed several hours of confused and bloody fighting on the wall and in the streets behind it, in the course of which Vassilievski was seriously wounded and all the horses of one artillery-troop were killed. It was not until the evening that the Russians joined hands with the Americans, who had scaled the wall on their left, and made their way to the Legations, where the first Allied troops had arrived in the early afternoon.

From this summary it will be clear that the legend of Russian duplicity is of questionable status. Vassilievski may have been over-bold, may have exceeded his orders; but it is scarcely conceivable that he was privily encouraged to do so by General Lineivitch. If he had been, the main body of the Russian contingent would not have taken nearly twelve hours to follow up the limited and costly success achieved by its small advance-guard. It is indeed the tardiness rather than the impetuosity of General Lineivitch's own movements which is the most striking feature of the Russian operations on 13–14 August. The din of a furious battle in which his advance-guard, under his chief of staff, was involved began to assail his ears before midnight on the 13th; yet it was not until ten o'clock on the 14th that his leading troops arrived before the gate which had been breached. It is at least as likely that in the darkness nobody really knew what they were doing or where they were as that the Russian deviation was a deep-laid plan; and if it was a deep-laid plan it was badly carried out.

'Owing to the premature advance of the Russians,' General Gaselee wrote in his despatch, 'the intended concentration was abandoned, and the troops were all hurried forward to assault the city of Peking.'

The Japanese had hard fighting all day before the Chih Hua Men. Although they brought up the whole of their artillery— fifty-four guns in all—and fired over 1000 shells, it was not until after dark that their engineers were able to make a breach with high explosive. Their main body did not enter Peking until the 15th.

The Americans, led by the 14th Infantry, succeeded in scaling the wall to the south of the Tung Pien Men—the first man up was Trumpeter Calvin P. Titus, 'a young soldier noted for his unspotted character'—and thus relieved pressure on the Russians, who had suffered severely and were more or less pinned down in the area of the gate-tower.

On the extreme left the British were not in action until noon. Only a few rifle-shots greeted their advance-guard as it approached the Hsia Kuo Men. Two guns of the 12th Regiment Royal Field Artillery were brought up (by a coincidence the same unit had served in the campaign in 1860) and shell-fire quickly drilled a hole in the gate. Roger Keyes, who had managed to get himself taken on by General Gaselee as a naval ADC, scaled the wall and hoisted *Fame*'s white ensign which he had providently brought with him.* Soon the main body was making an unopposed entry into Peking.

As they pressed forward through deserted streets the silence ahead of them seemed ominous. They were fired on from the great tower over the Ha Ta Men. Beyond it, on the wall, they could see three flags—the American, the British and the Russian. But it was the fact that they heard no firing from the Legations that weighed most with them. After the ceaseless fusillades of the previous night this deathly calm could, they persuaded themselves, mean only one thing. 'We had never been more hopeless of finding them alive than when we were actually in the Chinese City,' Keyes recorded. 'We feared,' wrote another member of Gaselee's staff, 'that the worst had happened and the flags were only a ruse to lead us on.'

But as they moved cautiously forward a signaller appeared on the ramparts. His blue-and-white semaphore flags crisply wagged out a message in Morse: '*Come in by sewer.*' He pointed to the foot of the wall directly below him.

The leading files surged forward. A seven-foot-high tunnel came into view. From the inside American Marines cleared away obstacles while the Rajputs broke down the rotten iron-work of a great grille. Within a few minutes the sepoys and their officers were scrambling through the black, viscid mud of the sluice and debouching into Canal Street, while on the Wall

* It is still among the regimental trophies of the 1st Sikhs.

above them United States Marines and Russian sailors, in a
last wild charge, bore down on the Chinese defenders of the
Chien Men and overwhelmed them.

It was between two and three o'clock on the morning of the
14th that the besieged first heard the guns of the Relief Force.
A series of dull booms were followed by 'a sound like tapping
quickly with one finger on the table.' 'The scene in the
British Legation was indescribable,' Sir Claude MacDonald
wrote. 'Those who, tired out, had fallen asleep were wakened
by these unwonted sounds, and there was much cheering and
shaking of hands. The enemy, too, had heard it. For a moment
there was silence; then the rifle-fire broke out more angry
and deafening than before, instantly responded to by the
rattle of our sharp-shooters and the grunt of the five-barrelled
Nordenfelt.' For the fourth time that night the tocsin was
rung.

Towards dawn the Chinese volleys grew ragged; one diarist
remembered only 'the occasional phut of a bullet and the
sustained rasp of the cicadas.' From the vantage-point of the
American barricades on the Wall Mr Squiers sent almost
hourly reports to the British Legation. They were written on
visiting cards bearing the address *Margarethenstrasse 1, Berlin.*
As time passed and the sound of firing came no nearer, a
disagreeable American called Pethick did his best to plunge
the whole community in despair. He had for some years
been secretary to Li Hung-chang and was an acknowledged
expert in Chinese matters. He was a know-all, ever anxious to
prove others wrong, and he now produced the theory that the
sounds of battle were nothing to do with a Relief Force. He
managed to convince Squiers, who wrote to Sir Claude: 'No
sign of the approach of our troops beyond the firing of machine-
guns. The other guns were *certainly* Chinese. Pethick tells me
Li Hung-chang in '95 bought some 50 Maxims, a number of
which were issued to the troops.' The tiresome quidnunc
enjoyed his little moment of ascendancy.

The hours dragged by. The mid-day meal of pony-meat was

eaten without appetite. Many people, exhausted, fell asleep. Polly Condit Smith debated with her lady's-maid whether or not to take a bath. Mr Gamewell, conscientious to the last, toured the defences on his bicycle. On his mattress in the hospital Dr Morrison, under conditions of appalling inconvenience and discomfort, wrote his lapidary account of the Siege: 'Gibbon could not have told the story better,' said the *Spectator* when it appeared in *The Times*. In the crowded Fu Chinese women flapped weakly at the flies which settled on dying babies.

Suddenly, at about half-past two, the uneasy torpor of the compounds was shattered. In a dozen languages the cry went up: 'They are coming! They are here!' People rushed up to the Wall; those on the Wall rushed down. Somebody said the troops were Germans. Then, all at once, the tennis-court in the British Legation was covered with Sikhs and Rajputs. As the besieged crowded round them, a kind of sobbing cheer went up, a strange uncontrollable sound like the baying of excited hounds.

Led by their British officers, more and more sepoys poured through the Sluice Gate, up Canal Street and on to the tennis-court—tall, turbanned, sweating men, their legs coated with the mud they had waded through, their faces strained by fatigue. Women crowded round them, touching them, patting them, even trying to kiss them. The soldiers' fierce eyes rolled alarm. '*Pani*,' they said humbly, pointing to their mouths, '*pine ki pani*.' Hands shaking with eagerness sought to imperil their souls with champagne.

There was a clatter of hooves outside. General Gaselee, dismounting, popped up on the tennis-court like the demon king in a pantomime. All knew him well by sight; a stern, bemedalled photograph had been cut out of an illustrated paper and posted on the Bell Tower several days earlier. Now he seemed not stern at all, with his joyous smile and his misty eyes; he found it difficult to speak at first, but stood there shaking hands and clearing his throat while the sweat ran down his neck on to the collar of his tunic.

Perhaps the last twelve hours had drained the besieged of emotion. Although 'one or two of the ladies could not appear in public,' it was the rescuers rather than the besieged whose feelings choked them. All accounts agree on this. 'There was not so much excitement among those rescued as might have been expected,' noted the Royal Welch Fusiliers when they followed the Punjabis through the Sluice Gate into the now seriously overcrowded compound. 'The dainty toilettes of the ladies' put some in mind of a garden party, and certainly snap-shots of the scene (which are unfortunately all very bad) show a number of parasols and some remarkable hats. One war-correspondent wrote: 'To us they looked as if they had just come out of a band-box. They had speckless linen on; some of the non-fighting men wore starched shirts with extra high glazed collars, fancy flannel suits, and vari-coloured ties.' He contrasted these elegants with 'the jolly guards with their bronzed faces,' thus giving some air of substance to Putnam Weale's characteristically ill-natured observation: 'People you had not seen for weeks, who might have, indeed, been dead a hundred times without your being any the wiser, appeared now for the first time from the rooms in which they had hidden and acted hysterically.'

Of all who recorded their memories of this extraordinary scene, two especially seem to recapture moments of truth. One was the lady who, after eating Mongol ponies for more than a month, was principally struck by 'what a treat it was to see a real horse again.' The other was the youthful Roger Keyes. 'Lady MacDonald looked very charming and nice and might have been our hostess. She said [to Keyes and another officer] that she didn't know who we were but was simply delighted to see us.' At that moment firing broke out. A Belgian woman was hit and fell screaming to the ground. 'So then they went in under cover, as one would out of a shower of rain.'

The British had won the race. 'It was a tremendous score our people being in first,' Sir Claude MacDonald wrote in a confidential letter to Mr Bertie at the Foreign Office, 'and I nearly burst with pride when I introduced old Gaselee to the Russian, French and Japanese Ministers and their wives.'

To be the first to reach the Legations was an achievement equally devoid of military and of political significance. Unlike the other contingents, the British did not fight their way into Peking (their only fatal casualty died from heat-stroke); they walked, they almost sauntered in. Their cheap success was not the reward of cunning or superior intelligence; it was due to luck, and to the ineptitude of the disintegrating Chinese command. But war has its childish side. It was as natural that the British should take pride in reaching the Legations an hour or two ahead of any other nationality as that the Rajputs should be elated by the equally fortuitous achievement of beating the Sikhs to the Sluice Gate by a few yards.

It is easy to argue, as all contemporary writers do, that the premature Russian attack acted as a diversion, that the defenders of Peking scurried northward along the Wall to deal with this threat, and that the Hsia Kuo Men was thus denuded of its garrison. But the Russian attack developed in the middle of the night, during a rainstorm. It is impossible to imagine more unlikely conditions for the swift redeployment of Chinese infantry, let alone artillery, even supposing a headquarters with the authority to deploy them was in effective existence. Several unmanned cannon were found in the embrasures of the Hsia Kuo Men; and it is far more probable that the officer responsible for its defence was well on his way out of the capital with the pay-chests than that he had marched along the Wall to the sound of the Russian guns.

General Chaffee and the 14th United States Infantry reached the Legations about 4.30 p.m., and General Lineivitch an hour or so later. General Fukushima arrived some time that evening. His main body was still battering away at its allotted gate; it occurred to nobody to call off an attack which, since the next two gates to the south were now wide open, no longer had much purpose.

It was not until the morning of the 15th that the French appeared. Their harrowing experiences during the assault are

too complex to describe in detail. In the small hours of
14 August they bumped into the Americans, who were bivouacked. Here they learnt that they were on the south bank of the
canal; they should have been on the north bank. They
floundered on, then halted. Some Bengal Lancers rode past
them in the darkness. The men were narrowly restrained from
opening fire, but in the excitement most of their coolies disappeared.

Then the Americans marched through them. General Chaffee
was disagreeable; he suspected General Frey of making an un-
authorised dash for Peking and reminded him that he was on
the wrong side of the canal. The French found a sluice-gate and
with great difficulty crossed to the north bank. It was by now
10 a.m. on the 14th. The men, who although they had done no
fighting had been brought up from Tientsin by forced marches,
were exhausted.

General Frey's object was to find the Russians. In an interview with General Lineivitch on the previous day he had concerted (or hoped he had concerted; there had been no interpreter present) pregnant plans concerning the occupation of
Peking, the considerate treatment of the Imperial Court and
other not strictly military matters. The Allies' arrangements
had provided for a conference of commanders-in-chief during
the 14th; and General Frey, whose voice had not been raised at
these conclaves since he went back to Tientsin a week earlier,
was pardonably anxious to reassert France's right to a hearing.
Since Lineivitch was the senior general, the conference would
be held in his camp; and to a quest for this camp General Frey,
whose stamina must have been remarkable, devoted the rest of
the day.

The French Expeditionary Corps had only one map; it was
obsolete and useless. Their few Shetland-pony-sized chargers
were on their last legs; Frey was virtually destitute of scouts or
even mounted orderlies. He did eventually find the Japanese
commander-in-chief; but neither General Yamaguchi nor anyone else present could speak a language other than their own,
and Frey was given an escort to take him forward to the

Japanese chief of staff, General Fukushima, who was something of a linguist and would put him in touch with the Russians, now believed to be well inside Peking.

So, it turned out, was General Fukushima. Frey had a long, lacerating wait at Japanese advanced headquarters outside the Tung Pien Men. At nightfall he sent Captain Bobo back to bring up part of the French contingent; and thus, to use his own words, 'our national prestige was safeguarded, for the French Commander-in-Chief and a small detachment of infantry and artillery passed through the Tung Pien Men (in other words entered Peking) on the same day as the other Allies—the 14th of August, before midnight.'

By 4 a.m. on the 15th they were advancing cautiously in a deluge of rain through the deserted streets, clutching the muzzles of their rifles to prevent the bayonets rattling. A halt was called on the outskirts of the Legation Quarter. Colours were unfurled, buglers marshalled to the front; their entry was to be a ceremonial victory march. Commands were given incisively. The brave notes rang out. The small, tired soldiers stepped off briskly. The sodden Tricolor flapped. But alas, the going was not suited to their purpose. 'The column, obliged to cross barricades, trenches and other obstacles became somewhat strung out and disorganised.'

In every race somebody loses. The French were last in this one. It was greatly to the credit of their Commander-in-Chief that they finished in the first five and did not straggle in three days later with the also-rans, who were even worse provided than they by the Governments who sent them to risk their lives in China. In these pages the achievements and the tribulations of the French Expeditionary Corps have been followed because its records reveal, more nakedly than those of any other force, the international jealousies underlying a chivalrous enterprise.

CHAPTER FOURTEEN

# The Beleaguered Cathedral

*Wednesday 15 July. At 0500 hrs. a violent explosion was caused by the detona-
tion of the mine against which countermining was in progress. So far 16 killed, 25
wounded. The effect on our defensive arrangements is negligible. (Later) 21 dead
have been identified. Cartridges fired: 6. In hand, 6,866.*

From the War Diary kept by Enseigne de Vaisseau Paul Henry.

THE Siege had lasted fifty-five days. Sixty-six foreigners had
been killed, two adults and six babies had died, and over 150
had been wounded; Chinese casualties within the perimeter
were not recorded.

Its longed-for end produced a moment of pure rapture, but
this did not endure. A feeling of deflation settled quickly on the
Legations. Their strange little microcosm of danger and
privation—on which they now found themselves looking back
with a jealous, almost affectionate pride, whose realities (they
had begun to suspect) no one but themselves would ever
properly comprehend—had vanished. They were still on the
stage, but they had played out their parts; the scenery had been
struck and the lights turned up, the drama was over. Partly,
perhaps, it was the subconscious sense that their own importance had diminished overnight that made the survivors so
tetchy.

There were, too, more obvious, more material causes for
their disenchantment. They had been saved, they had been
freed; why then should life have suddenly become so much
more inconvenient and unsettled? 'In twenty-four hours,'
wrote Allen, 'the whole aspect of the British Legation had
changed, and the moral atmosphere was as changed as the

outward aspect. The crowd had been great before, but by long residence it had become settled and orderly. Then each one had his own place, his own work. . . . Now the whole compound was in a turmoil. Officers on horseback, parties of Lancers, companies of infantry, guns, ammunition waggons, baggage-trains, carts, filled all the ways. The lawn was crowded with soldiers and civilians, every corner packed with camp-followers and coolies. There was no room to move where everyone was moving. There was no longer the regular routine of watch and other duties for the besieged. The daily ration of flour, rice and horse-flesh to which we had grown accustomed ceased; everyone had to forage for himself. We had hoped that the arrival of the Relief Force would restore order and bring us plentiful supplies. For the moment it seemed as if confusion was worse confounded, and supplies more difficult and scanty than ever. Already men in small parties were beginning to go out in search of loot. . . . There was a good deal of jealousy among the Allies, and many were found to prophesy that they could not remain long together without strife.'

The Manchu Court had fled, the Chinese Government had disintegrated, the Imperial armies were melting away, the streets were littered with scarlet trappings discarded by the Boxers. But one urgent military task remained to be performed. This was the relief of the Peitang, two miles to the north-west of the Legations, where Bishop Favier, his priests, his converts and his small guard of French and Italian sailors were assumed, from the intermittent sounds of bombardment, to be holding out. No news had been received from them since the Siege began, and no gunfire had been heard from that quarter for several days.

The defence of the Peitang, or North Cathedral, was on several counts a more remarkable feat of arms than the defence of the Legations. The besieged enclave was indeed more compact than that which sheltered the diplomats; but in relation to its tiny garrison of two young officers and forty-one sailors it appeared unmanageably large. Besides the Cathedral itself the compound walls enclosed a miscellany of premises—an orphan-age, the bishop's house, a convent, a dispensary, several schools, a printing press, a chapel, a museum, as well as stores, stables and other buildings.

Though the perimeter was shorter, the number of people inside it was larger than in the Legations, and the proportion of *bouches inutiles* a good deal higher. Out of some 3400 men, women and children, less than a hundred were Europeans. There were twenty-two Sisters of Charity and 850 Chinese schoolgirls; the exact number of small children is uncertain, but 166 were buried during the siege.

For all these people there was not enough to eat. Foreseeing trouble, Favier had laid in supplies, but his calculations were upset by the great influx of refugees who at the last moment sought asylum from the Boxers. In the Peitang the cornucopia of Imbeck's and Kierulff's abandoned shops was lacking; there were no strings of racing ponies, only a few bony mules. By 6 July the daily ration for each adult had been reduced to a pound of rice, beans or millet; three weeks later it was cut to a third of this meagre amount; and on 10 August, after 400 pounds of rice and the last mule had been set aside for the fighting men, there was virtually nothing left. The leaves off the trees were eaten; a kind of soup was concocted from the roots of dahlias and lilies.

But the main reason why the Cathedral's ordeal was more severe, and its deliverance more surprising, than the Legations' lies in the fact that the unofficial truce, which gave the latter so invaluable a respite, did not extend to the Peitang. Here, although their violence fluctuated, the Chinese attacks went on relentlessly for eight whole weeks. It has been surmised that the sack of the Cathedral and the slaughter of its inmates were originally assigned to the Boxers as a kind of special treat; and certainly they played a more prominent part in this lesser siege than they did before the Legations, where after the first few days almost all the fighting was done by Imperial troops. But in their endeavours against the Peitang the Boxers had ample support from regular forces; on one day as many as fourteen cannon were in action—a weightier concentration of artillery than was ever brought to bear on the Legations.

From first to last the defenders of the Peitang received no news of any sort from outside. There were no chinks in the wall of their cell. A messenger sent out in the early days was skinned alive before being decapitated; his skin and his poor ravaged head were displayed like a scarecrow before the main gate. Sometimes they heard firing from the direction of the Legations; that was as near as they came to having contact with the world to which they belonged. Theirs was a most desolate situation.

By comparison with the Peitang the British Legation was a haven of security. For its occupants and defenders life was hard and uncertain; but at least they had enough to eat, they were not surrounded at close quarters by piteous sufferings which they could do nothing to alleviate, after a month they enjoyed a lull, and when that ended they had some reason to hope that the worst was over. In the Cathedral a longer, harsher agony was endured with no such alleviations.

Yet the story of this other siege has a simple nobility which does not continuously illumine the tale of the Legations, where the antique virtues are often obscured by petty grievances and international jealousies. There seem to have been no Pichons, and no Putnam Weales, in the Peitang: no shirkers, no *embusqués*, no panics. The Bishop presided, serene and sagacious, over a flock between whom and martyrdom stood only forty-three French and Italian sailors with (initially) 300 cartridges each.

The Siege of the Legations has no single hero; all accounts of the fight for the Peitang are dominated by the figure of Paul Henry, the twenty-three-year-old Breton officer who commanded the small French naval detachment. He inspired a remarkable confidence and affection not only in his thirty men but, as time went on, in the Chinese converts whom he armed with pikes and trained to act as look-outs and to do other auxiliary duties. He was not merely a good officer, well liked though a strict disciplinarian; he was a resourceful and imaginative fighter.

On the second night of the siege he led a sortie and captured a cannon. His aggressive attitude and his contempt for danger communicated themselves to his men, mostly Bretons like himself, and to the handful of Italians serving alongside them; and the tiny garrison, which under less positive leadership might, hypnotised by the odds against it, have crouched glumly and ineffectively behind its barricades, was on its toes all the time, seeking with relish for opportunities to punish the Chinese. A mile away to the south-east the French Minister, who had nothing to do, noted every evening in his diary the number of shells fired by the enemy cannon. In the Peitang his young compatriot, who was tirelessly active all day and most of the night, found time to keep a similar but less otiose record:

> *9 juillet. Cartouches tirées 54. Restent 7357.*
> *10 juillet. Cartouches tirées 124. Restent 7233.*

He husbanded his precious ammunition with care and controlled his fire-power coolly; in one early attack the corpses of twenty-seven uniformed Boxers and twenty adherents who had come to see the fun were counted after the French had fired fifty-eight cartridges in two volleys. Much of the ground round the Peitang was open, and its attackers relied less on siege-works and barricades than did their comrades round the Legations; it seems quite possible that Henry and his men killed more Chinese than all the other detachments put together.

Henry was mortally wounded by a bullet through the throat on 30 July. He had seemed so indispensable to their protection that many of the besieged gave themselves up for lost; but from that date, although the bombardment went on, attempts to storm the Cathedral almost ceased. In these the Chinese had lost heavily and achieved nothing; they were now relying on a different method of attack for which elaborate preparations were in hand.

They had already—on 18 July—exploded a mine under one of the crowded buildings in the compound, causing some fifty casualties and much damage. On 12 August an enormous charge was detonated beneath the infants' crêche and the quarters occupied by the nuns. Five of the Italian sailors were killed as well as about 100 Chinese, including almost all the babies. On the next day another terrible explosion caused more havoc; but although eighty yards of the outer compound wall were destroyed the Chinese lacked the courage to force an entry, and confined themselves to yelling hideously and firing on the dazed rescue-workers.

Next day their standards had vanished from the wall of the Imperial City, and the guns of the Relief Force could be heard thundering at the gates of Peking. Rescue had suddenly ceased to be a mirage.

We had, earlier in this chapter, a glimpse of the confusion reigning in the Legations after the arrival of the troops. It partly explains, but hardly condones, the tardy, almost negligent manner in which arrangements for the relief of the Cathedral were concerted.

One would have expected the French Minister, once the Legations were relieved, to have lost no time in organising the rescue of his compatriots in the Peitang, little more than a mile away. He did in fact mention the matter to the British and American Ministers some time on 14 August; both undertook to provide troops for the operation, but for some odd reason it occurred to nobody in the Allied advance guard to tell M. Pichon of the French contingent's existence. He was still in bed when its bugles echoed down Legation Street next morning.

General Frey, according to his own account, took the matter in hand as soon as he reached the Legations on the morning of the 15th and was actually giving out his orders for an advance on the Peitang when General Chaffee informed him that he was about to attack the Imperial City. Since the whole American contingent would be committed, no troops could be detached to support the French at the Peitang; and its relief was accordingly put off until the following day, the French being too weak to attempt it unaided.

This is a lame story. The Legation Quarter now swarmed with troops, and the Japanese in particular were already

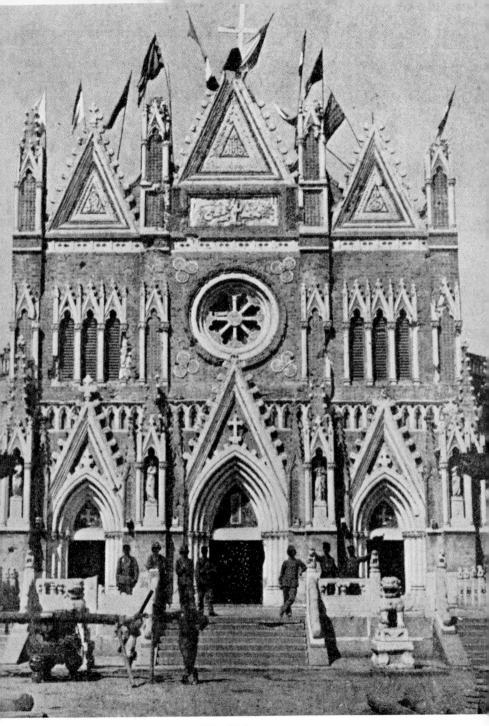

The Peitang

Sepoys of the 1st Sikhs scale the walls of Peking after taking off their boots

The Sluice-Gate

Lt.-General Sir Alfred Gaselee

Lt.-General Adna Chaffee

working through the Tartar City in the general direction of the Cathedral. It would not have been difficult to raise a rescue party of adequate strength; and there was every reason to suppose that the need for one was urgent.

But *la gloire* beckoned. To forgo French participation in an enterprise as momentous and dramatic as the storming of the Imperial City was a prospect as repugnant to M. Pichon as to General Frey. The French infantry were as usual in a state of collapse; but a mountain battery of four guns was manhandled up a ramp on to the Tartar Wall, where some diplomats and a number of ladies assembled to watch the proceedings.

M. Pichon pointed out the targets. General Frey gave the orders. The ladies clapped their hands to their ears. The guns fired. When the shells burst far away among the delicate and brilliant roofs there were cries of admiration. 'The whole affair,' wrote a war-correspondent, 'was pretty enough.'

Almost immediately, however, there arrived upon the Wall an American staff officer with an urgent message from General Chaffee, '*qui fait connaître au général Frey que son tir le gêne beaucoup.*' Frey replied that the bombardment, so far from impeding General Chaffee's operations or endangering his men, 'was, rather, calculated to enhance his prospects of success'; and the four little guns continued amid squeals of feminine excitement to distribute their shells in accordance with the whims of M. Pichon.

Half an hour later the American officer returned with what Frey describes, euphemistically, as 'a pressing request' from General Chaffee. The *feu de joie* ceased forthwith. 'This man,' Polly Condit Smith wrote of Chaffee, 'is instantly obeyed.'

The American assault on the Imperial City was a gallant but somewhat aimless affair. General Chaffee was a dour cavalryman who had risen from the ranks during the Indian Wars: a rugged rather than a sympathetic character, to whom inter-allied co-operation was a novel and distasteful concept. He was not much liked by his troops. On the march he imposed a strict but not always enlightened discipline. 'Some officers,' wrote one of his infantry colonels darkly, 'can march a column of troops to the designated point with the loss of only the feeblest; others will exhaust and disintegrate their commands during the first hour of the march.' Certainly the Americans left many stragglers and much discarded equipment behind them; and by compelling his column to bivouac in the airless, insect-haunted millet-fields instead of on open ground General Chaffee did nothing to improve the men's stamina or raise their spirits.

To the United States Marines he was anathema. They had been almost two months in North China before the first Army units disembarked; they had endured the hardships and perils of the Seymour expedition and the Siege. Yet on the march to Peking Chaffee allotted them humble and unrewarding roles as garrisons for staging-posts and guards for baggage-trains; and when he reached Peking he gave (until his orders were counter-manded as a result of protests in Washington) the privilege of guarding his country's Legation to the Army, not to the Corps which had saved it from destruction. He even despatched the home-made cannon 'Betsey,' which the Marines had improvised and manned, to the Army's collection of trophies at West Point; and in 1901 he tried—unsuccessfully—to get Colonel Waller, a Marine officer who had served under him with distinction in China, convicted of murder by an Army court martial after a mutiny of native guides in the Philippines. It will be seen that General Chaffee had not an accommodating disposition.

It is not clear (and in so fluid a situation and so heady an atmosphere it would be surprising if it was clear) why, without consulting his allies, he launched his assault on the high pink walls which enclosed the Imperial precincts. It seems to have been an impulsive, self-centred, bull-in-a-china-shop operation, embarked on with scant consideration of the need for intelli-gence, planning and special equipment such as scaling-ladders. 'There is the gate!' his staff officer told the colonel of the 14th United States Infantry, who led the assault. 'My duty ceases, yours begins.' Even Chaffee's complaints to Frey, whose little mountain guns were peppering pagodas in the middle distance, sound in retrospect frivolous.

At seven o'clock in the morning the Americans began their advance from the Chien Men with Captain Reilly's battery supporting them from the tower above that gate. With the help of battering-rams they forced their way into what proved to be the first of several spacious forecourts leading to the South Gate of the Imperial City. In each they came under heavy fire and suffered casualties; but they pressed doggedly on, two guns firing at point-blank range into a succession of massive gates. At last, with the help of ladders carried by Japanese coolies, the wall of the Imperial City was scaled and the Stars and Stripes hoisted on it. 'When the first plucky devil sat astride the parapet and waved the colours, we underneath cheered ourselves hoarse,' wrote a British war-correspondent.

Three gates now remained to be stormed before that most fabulous of military objectives, the Forbidden City, lay within their grasp. The Americans had forced two of them, for a total loss of fifteen killed and many more wounded, when General Chaffee suddenly ordered a withdrawal. 'It was hard,' wrote an eyewitness, 'on these magnificent men, who had fought like tigers, to be compelled to march away (barring the swearing) like so many lambs!'

The Russians, supported by the French, were the chief advocates of a lenient and conciliatory attitude towards the Manchu Court, and it was their influence, exerted at a commander-in-chiefs' conference at four o'clock that afternoon, which led to the American attack being called off. The Russians believed that to violate by force the sacred precincts of the Forbidden City would leave an indelible scar on Chinese susceptibilities, a consequence which for political reasons they were anxious to avoid; and this view, though not shared by all the Powers, prevailed. After a day spent in fighting their way through a series of death-traps to no purpose, the Americans found themselves back where they started. They cursed General Chaffee; it can hardly be held that they did so without cause.

Their bitterness was increased by the death of Captain Reilly, who during this futile action had been shot down while directing the fire of his guns; he was a much-loved officer, held in high esteem by all the contingents. He was buried the same afternoon with full military honours in the Legation compound. As the rough coffin was lowered into the grave Mr Conger stepped forward and, remarking that there was a serious shortage of American flags in Peking, prepared to salvage the Stars and Stripes in which it was shrouded. 'Don't touch that flag!' bellowed General Chaffee. 'If it's the last American flag in China it shall be buried with Reilly.' Mr Conger desisted.*

Early on the next day, 16 August, a strong force set out for the Peitang. There was no good reason why it should not have started twenty-four hours earlier. If it had, it would not have passed the severed head of a European displayed on a lance-point outside a yamen newly evacuated by Tung Fu-hsiang's men. Père Addosio had been rescued from the sack of the South Cathedral before the Siege began. The sights he had seen had turned his hair and beard prematurely white and made him wander-witted. The day after the Legations were relieved he mounted a donkey and rode off to find out what had happened to his Bishop. Nobody knows whether he intended a gesture of protest at the soldiers' neglect of an urgent humanitarian duty, or whether he was too simple-minded to apprehend the dangers he courted. Whatever the motive of his sortie, it had a savage end.

The French, supported by strong Russian and British detachments, advanced cautiously through the abandoned streets and captured without difficulty a gate in the Imperial City wall which gave access to the environs of the Peitang. Alas, anti-climax continued to dog the endeavours of General Frey. 'What was our surprise,' he wrote, 'to see ahead of us between

* Though lacking in respect for the dead, the American Minister's motives were above reproach from a utilitarian point of view. In the early days of the Occupation flags were indispensable as a means of staking *de facto* claims to palaces, banks and other desirable properties. No nationality had enough of them; and the Stars and Stripes, unlike the Tricolor and the Rising Sun, was not easily improvised.

250 and 300 Japanese whose presence nobody could explain.'
The Cathedral had already been relieved.

But Monseigneur Favier seized a bugle and sounded *La Casquette du Père Bugeaud*, the soldiers cheered, there was a little skirmish, M. Pichon wept, converts kissed General Frey's hand, and as the besieged greeted their compatriots a surge of warm, generous emotions made it easy to forget about the Japanese.

CHAPTER FIFTEEN

# The Riddles

*Who would be so foolish as to cast missiles at a rat in the vicinity of a priceless piece of porcelain?*

Li Hung-chang in a Memorial to the Throne, late July 1900.

PERHAPS it is because the Siege had so many strange aspects that the strangest of all has been overlooked. Why did it take place? Thousands of pages in a dozen languages have been written about the defence of the Legations. On only one of them * is the question asked: Why were the Legations attacked?

It was not, in the nature of things, the sort of question that people asked themselves in 1900. The diplomats were taken by surprise; the world was shocked; but nobody was puzzled. Emotions ran high. The Chinese were devils incarnate, embodiments of the motiveless malignity which Coleridge found in Iago. What need to look further than their bloodlust for an explanation of their actions? It is true that several of the besieged recorded in their diaries the conviction that the Chinese were behaving, in their own wider interests, like imbeciles. But nobody pondered the problem of why they were doing so. The Chinese capacity for folly as well as for evil was regarded as boundless, and the Siege was accepted as an act of God, like an earthquake or a storm at sea.

It was nothing of the sort. It was a project to which for two months the Empress Dowager and the Manchu Court devoted their main energies, much thought and a large army. Their purpose was never in doubt; it was to annihilate the entire

* C. C. Tan: *The Boxer Catastrophe*, p. 96.

foreign community in Peking, together with some 5000 Christian Chinese. They wavered in this purpose during the short-lived truce; but in general they pursued it with diligence in the face of remonstrances from the Viceroys, protests and threats from the Powers, warnings from their diplomatic representatives, and a growing volume of evidence that the whole world regarded their conduct as monstrous.

What the Chinese Government was attempting was a barbarous crime not only by the rules of international usage but by the precepts of their own sages and the traditions of their race. It involved the murder of eleven foreign envoys with their staffs and families. No state of war existed between China and the Powers whom these envoys represented; their Governments were repeatedly assured, while Chinese troops poured shot and shell into the Legations and dug mines underneath them, that the Throne was doing its utmost to protect the lives and property of the diplomats.

The Chinese efforts to overrun the Legations and butcher their inmates failed, and China was severely punished for making them. What if they had succeeded? The consequences for China must have been infinitely worse. Singlehanded, the most junior of the eleven Powers concerned had heavily defeated her in war only five years earlier; the whole world would have been at her throat to avenge the atrocious, unforgivable deed to which for two months her rulers devoted their best efforts. This was not a risk, but a certainty; and the fact must have been obvious not merely to the shrewd, experienced Empress Dowager but to the most purblind backwoodsman among her advisers.

Why, then, was the Siege relentlessly prosecuted? In the ferment of those days right and wrong went for little at the Imperial Court; but to profit and loss, advantage and disadvantage, a total blindness can hardly be assumed. It is easy to imagine various modified versions of the Siege which neither outrage probability nor reflect—as the reality does—an Imperial policy which is wholly unaccountable.

One can, for instance, readily visualise an attack on the Legations being made as an impulsive reprisal for the capture of the Taku Forts, to be abandoned later in the light of threatening international developments. Or Boxers, possibly stiffened by regulars in Boxer attire, might have been encouraged to see what they could do, the fiction being maintained that they were beyond the control of the authorities. Finally, given the circumstance of a full-dress siege by Imperial troops, the besieged might have been used as hostages, who would be massacred unless the Relief Force halted its advance and negotiations for an amicable settlement were put in hand. Each of these expedients would have had its dangers and disadvantages; none had the suicidal implications of the course actually followed.

Like a brightly coloured illustration in a child's history book, the Siege has its recognised place in the past, a conspicuous landmark in the wide no-man's-land between China and the rest of the world. The only historian to note, in passing, that the problem of why it ever happened demands an answer cannot provide one from the Chinese sources which he has widely surveyed. 'While it is evident,' writes Tan, 'that the attack upon the Legations was authorized by the Imperial Court, it is not clear why such an attack should have been made.' He concludes that the Court's motives must have been complex and may have included the following:

(1) Sheer hatred of the foreigners.
(2) The desire to stimulate patriotism.
(3) A genuine fear of the 400 Legation guards.
(4) The need to exterminate all independent witnesses of the Court's and the Boxers' misdeeds.

But the references with which he supports these suggestions are themselves only suggestions, made in Memorials submitted to the Throne by two grandees and one censor; there is no evidence that they influenced the Empress Dowager; and though all four motives were doubtless present in the minds of the Court they do not, even collectively, provide a valid explanation for its recourse to desperate measures in which success was bound to prove even more fatal than failure.

The mystery, unperceived for half a century, is likely to remain a mystery for ever. Anyone can play patience with the faded Imperial cards—the need to give the Boxers an outlet, the ravening hatred of foreigners, the impulse to strike hard at what seemed most vulnerable in the hated, the reluctance to lose face by calling off the attacks, the death-wish—the *après-nous-le-déluge* attitude—of a doomed dynasty, the scarcely measurable depths of fatuity which underlay so many proceedings of the Manchu Court, a woman's confidence in the assurances of men about military arrangements. The pack can be reshuffled, the cards rearranged again and again; but the game of patience will never come out, for the ace of truth is missing. The historian can do no more than draw attention to the fact that, of all the extraordinary occurrences connected with the Siege, the most extraordinary was the occurrence of the Siege itself.

Only less strange than the launching of the Chinese attacks was their failure. 'Had we been fighting such people as the Zulus or Dervishes we should have been polished off in two or three days,' reflected a young diarist; and similar opinions are echoed in almost all the annals of the Siege. Smith was convinced that 'a few hundred Chinese, willing to throw away their lives to ensure the capture of the Legations, could have taken them at any moment during the first month of the Siege.'

The long, inadequately fortified perimeter was sparsely manned by tired men who were consistently short of ammunition. A co-ordinated onslaught on the whole of it was perhaps beyond the capacities of the Chinese command. But no such ambitious project was called for; one breach, made preferably at night and exploited with reasonable resolution, would have brought the affair to an end. However low we rate the courage of the Imperial troops and the competence of their officers, the fact that for two whole months so large a force of well-armed infantry did no more than nibble into the flimsy defences

P                      225

covering their objective is a mystery of which no satisfactory explanation exists.

Equally baffling is the sparing and ineffective use of artillery by the attackers. After the Siege hundreds of guns were discovered in arsenals in and around Peking; many were modern, some were still in the packing-cases in which Krupp had consigned them from Europe. There was no lack of ordnance; the Chinese had the means to pulverise in a day or two all the foreign barricades. Why then were the Legations subjected only to a lackadaisical, intermittent bombardment by a few guns? The Chinese are estimated to have fired 3000 shells and cannon-balls into the defences during the Siege. There was nothing to prevent them firing a like number every day. If they had, the Legations would have become untenable in no time.

To this mystery of the artillery there are some faint and indirect clues. Tung Fu-hsiang was by common consent an ogre. All sources, Chinese and foreign, testify to his zeal in furthering the design of massacre and to the ferocity of his Moslem troops. They held the sectors opposite the northern and western sides of the perimeter; it was they who burnt down the Hanlin.

But Tung was subordinate to Jung Lu, the Commander-in-Chief, whose own personal army invested the rest of the perimeter, and there is some evidence that Jung Lu deliberately kept him short of artillery, an arm with which one would not expect an ex-freebooter from the distant province of Kansu to be well-provided from his own resources.

One account describes an audience which Tung had of the Empress Dowager on 23 June, the third day of the Siege, at which he complained that 'Jung Lu has the guns which my army needs; with their aid not a stone would be left standing in the whole of the Legation Quarter.' The Empress Dowager, who had been painting a design of bamboos on silk when the warrior was announced, dismissed him with contumely. 'Your tail,' she said elliptically, 'is becoming too heavy to wag.' Ching-Shan mentions Tung's grievance about guns a week later.

In those days, and indeed for several subsequent decades,

the sinews of war were regarded by Chinese commanders as personal possessions or perquisites. They were the counters with which the game for power was played and, even when the exigencies of war seemed to demand it, were not lightly placed under the control of a subordinate, particularly one with a forceful character. The picture, faintly glimpsed, of a lack of co-operation between the two generals principally concerned in the Siege has thus a natural air.

But why did Jung Lu not use the guns himself? A good deal of evidence suggests that Jung Lu's attitude throughout the Siege was of cardinal importance, and that it was to his restraining or stultifying influence on the Chinese attacks that the foreigners owed their preservation.

Before the Throne openly extended its patronage to the Boxers, Jung Lu favoured their suppression. In a telegram to a senior official on 2 June he summarised the military measures he had put in hand to this end (they were later countermanded from above) and concluded: 'To forestall conflicts with the foreign Powers, we must hasten to purge the metropolitan area of the Boxers. This is important.'

A further telegram, despatched to the southern Viceroys during the first week of the Siege, sets forth his views with such clarity that it is worth quoting at length:

> If one weak country fights more than ten powerful countries, danger and ruin will follow at once. Moreover, when two countries are at war, it has been customary from far antiquity not to injure the envoys. The founding of the Dynasty by our forefathers was an arduous task; how can it now be lightly thrown away by believing in the heretical brigands? It requires no particular sagacity to know all this. I have argued with all my efforts, but without in the least succeeding in saving the situation. Later I was ill and could not move; still during my leave I submitted seven Memorials. . . . Death I do not mind, but the guilt I shall bear for all ages! Heaven alone can testify to my heart. What a grief!

This avowal of unfashionable and indeed dangerous convictions has all the marks of sincerity. It was certainly accepted as sincere by the men to whom it was addressed, for the southern Viceroys continued to urge the northern Commander-in-Chief to support by his personal intervention at Court the moderate counsels contained in their telegraphed Memorials. But Jung Lu knew that the Empress Dowager's mind was closed; to show his hand would be not only futile but perilous. He continued to direct the Imperial forces in an operation of which, on grounds alike of principle and of expediency, he strongly disapproved. The Siege, he once said, 'is worse than an outrage, it is a piece of stupidity which will be remembered against China for all time.'

There is no conclusive evidence to prove that Jung Lu, powerless to avert the attacks on the Legations, took it upon himself to procure their ill-success. It is true that on his deathbed, three years later, he wrote in a Valedictory Memorial 'I was able to avert the crowning misfortune which would have resulted from the killing of the Foreign Ministers;' but such documents were concerned rather with decorum than with ultimate truth, and claims made by their authors are not necessarily well founded.

After the Siege Jung Lu was, or affected to be, surprised that he was not *persona grata* with the foreigners; but his name was not—as was, for instance, Tung Fu-hsiang's—on the Allies' list of what would today be called 'war criminals,' whose punishment was one of the conditions of peace. He is known to have arranged the short cease-fire on 25 June, and later, during the truce, he took every opportunity of establishing his own channels of communication with the Ministers, in addition to those opened by the Tsungli Yamen. Finally, shortly before her death the Empress Dowager is said to have 'placed on record her opinion that he had saved the Manchus by refusing to assist in the attacks on the Legations.'

Though powerless to alter the Court's policy, Jung Lu (and nobody else) was in a position to render its military designs abortive. The Court had made known its purpose unequivocally on 23 June; 'the work now undertaken by Tung Fu-hsiang' was to be 'completed as soon as possible.' The work went noisily on, week after week. Is it surprising that it was not completed by an overseer who was telling the southern Viceroys 'If we can save the foreign Ministers, it will be good for the future?'

Sir Robert Hart, writing immediately after the event and without the benefit of much evidence which has since come to light, saw that someone must have played behind the scenes the part which history now allots to Jung Lu. His reconstruction of what had to be assumed is remarkably perceptive:

'That somebody intervened for our semi-protection seems, however, probable. Attacks were not made by such numbers as the Government had at its disposal—they were never pushed home, but always ceased just when we feared they would succeed—and, had the force round us really attacked with thoroughness and determination, we could not have held out a week, perhaps not even a day. . . . Somebody, probably a wise man who knew that the destruction of the Legations would cost the Empire and Dynasty dear, intervened between the issue of the order for our destruction and the execution of it, and so kept the soldiery playing with us as cats do with mice, the continued and seemingly heavy firing telling the Palace how fiercely we were attacked and how stubbornly we defended ourselves, while its curiously half-hearted character not only gave us the chance to live through it, but also gave any relief forces time to come and extricate us, and thus avert the national calamity which the Palace in its pride and conceit ignored, but which someone in authority in his wisdom foresaw and in his discretion sought how to push aside.'

A more accurate diagnosis could hardly be made today. In China, foreigners were fond of saying at that period, everything is topsy-turvy, the opposite of what you would expect; and certainly it is difficult to think of another country in which a garrison besieged for two months by overwhelming odds would have been likely to owe its deliverance to the patriotic instincts of the opposing Commander-in-Chief.

Every siege is a harsh test of the human spirit. One of the things that makes it so is the sense of isolation, of being cut off from friends and surrounded by enemies. I have tried to show how keen, how almost overmastering, was the Legations' hunger for news from outside: how easily their spirits were raised or lowered by barely specious rumours: how indignant they became at the receipt from an authoritative source of vague and unilluminating tidings.

Yet the more closely one studies the events of that summer in North China, the more forcibly one is struck by the advantages which human beings in desperate and obscure situations may derive from having no method of communicating with each other. It is not going too far to suggest that if anybody, at almost any stage, had known accurately what was happening to anybody else the results might have been disastrous. Half a dozen efficient wireless transmitters could hardly have failed to change for the worse the pattern of events.

Seymour (for instance), burdened with casualties and seriously short of ammunition, began his retreat down the river on 18 June. On that day Tientsin came under heavy attack, and its situation grew steadily more critical until it was relieved on the 23rd. Tientsin had no idea of Seymour's whereabouts, let alone of the straits he was in; Seymour knew no more about the position at Tientsin than his ears, which heard the mumble of gunfire, could tell him. If the Admiral had been able to exchange messages with the garrison, it is at least questionable whether he would have persisted in a course which led, in the event, to his salvation.

The Powers were playing upon the plain of Chihli a game of Blind Man's Buff. Under its rules the complete annihilation of Seymour's expedition would have made no difference to the Legations, since they would have been unaware of it. But supposing that, when the Corps Diplomatique met to consider the original Chinese ultimatum on 19 June, its members had been apprised of the true state of affairs: had known that Seymour's force (which they assumed to be irresistible and believed to be within striking distance of Peking) had foundered, that its base at Tientsin was in jeopardy, and that communications between Tientsin and the coast had been severed. How, then, would they have answered an ultimatum which, as it was, only the brutal impact of von Ketteler's assassination nerved them to reject?

Speculations of this sort are normally a waste of time. But the defence of the Legations provides, as do all sieges, a study in human endurance; and in an age when communications are almost invariably excellent and render possible if not obligatory the reference of every decision to a higher authority, it seems worth pointing out that in 1900 daunting situations were faced without such amenities and, had they existed, might not have been weathered.

# CHAPTER SIXTEEN

# Flight to the West

*When our Imperial Chariot departed in haste from the Forbidden City, the moaning of the wind and the cry of the heron seemed to our startled ears as the tramp of an advancing enemy.*

From a Penitential Decree issued at Sian on 13 February 1901.

IN the early hours of 15 August the Manchu Court prepared, tardily, for flight. Few things better illustrate its near-lunacy than the fact that nothing, absolutely nothing, was ready for a long, difficult journey, the imminent necessity for which had been obvious to everyone in the Forbidden City for the best part of a week.

The Empress Dowager donned the coarse dark-blue clothes of a peasant woman, cut her long, lacquered nails and dressed her hair for the first time in the Chinese style. While she was doing this (she told Wu Yung) 'we heard bullets flying, making noises like the crying of cats', and one of these bullets came through the window and bounced about on the floor. At that moment yet another alarming report of barbarian military activity was brought to her.*

She summoned the Emperor. According to one account he had been taking part in the religious rites prescribed for the day and was wearing elaborate pearl-studded robes and a red tasselled hat. These were swiftly changed for less conspicuous

---

* *The Flight of an Empress.* Even if Wu Yung were an unimpeachable source, which he is far from being, this Imperial reminiscence would need to be treated with reserve. No fighting was in progress anywhere near the Winter Palace at the time.

attire, and the august pair, attended by a small, frightened retinue of Grand Councillors, eunuchs and other myrmidons, prepared by torchlight to make their departure in three common carts.

At the last minute the Imperial concubines appeared (in what numbers it is not related) to pay their respects; they had been forbidden by Decree to accompany the Throne, and there was in any case no room for them in the carts. The Pearl Concubine, the Emperor's favourite, had the temerity to suggest that the Emperor ought to remain in Peking or, alternatively, that she should be allowed to accompany him in flight.

The Empress Dowager did not like the Pearl Concubine. Whether, as one source maintains, she cried to the eunuchs 'Throw this wretched minion down the well!' or whether, as another suggests, she merely said, 'If you are not satisfied, why do you not throw yourself down a well?' it is no longer possible to establish. What is certain is that, despite the frantic entreaties of the Emperor, the Pearl Concubine was then and there wrapped up in a carpet by two eunuchs and dropped down a capacious well outside the Ning Shou Palace. The Empress Dowager proceeded to give out her orders for the start of the expedition with a crisp lucidity which was much admired.

A mile away to the east the Japanese field-pieces were still hammering away at the Chih Hua Men. The rain which, earlier in the night, had enabled the Russians to surprise the picquets at the Tung Pien drummed on the hoods of the little Peking carts as they creaked northward through the Gate of Military Prowess, heading for the Summer Palace. Without luggage, without a change of clothes, without even a pair of chopsticks, the Empress Dowager left the great capital upon which she had brought misery and shame. It was forty years since, as a young concubine, she had fled by this same road from the thunder of barbarian guns. Then, as now, the reigning Emperor had been a weak and useless individual. Then, as now, his precipitate decampment had been attended by panic and confusion. Now, as then, it was officially described as an 'autumn tour of inspection.'

In the Winter Palace, a British diplomat's wife noted a few days later, 'Tzü Hsi's room was just as she had left it. On the rich coverlet of the bed lay an embroidered coat of black satin; beneath, a pair of Manchu shoes. Nearby were two large boxes of silk handkerchiefs, overturned: one box of pale yellow handkerchiefs and one of pale blue. A handful had been hurriedly snatched from each. In the adjoining rooms, along the walls, were huge camphor-wood boxes, filled to the top with coats and trousers of every colour, embroidered with gold and with pearls. In other boxes were rich sable coats lined with white fox fur. . . . On a long table, the length of one room, were dozens of foreign clocks, some handsome, others hideous, all ticking cheerfully, regardless of the ominous silence around.'

Two days after she had forsaken these amenities, Wu Yung, the magistrate of a small town on the road to the north, met the Imperial fugitive. It was raining again. Tzü Hsi was wet, cold and in tears. She and the Emperor looked like 'dejected jackals.' They were parched with thirst, for all the wells were defiled with decapitated human heads. They were famished, for Boxers and fleeing soldiery had stripped the countryside. Not without difficulty, Wu Yung procured for them bowls of coarse porridge and one pair of chopsticks. Waiting anxiously outside their wretched room in the wayside inn, he was immensely relieved to hear 'the sound of swift eating, and of porridge being drunk with inhaling breaths, as if the food were good.' When the bowls were emptied, the worthy official acquired still further merit by finding five eggs in a deserted house. He boiled them and sent them in. Presently Li Lienying, the villainous Chief Eunuch, emerged and announced: 'The Empress Dowager enjoyed the eggs very much. Of the five you sent she ate three, the remaining two she gave to the Lord of Ten Thousand Years.* The light' (this life-long gourmet added with chagrin) 'was shed on no one else.' The Empress Dowager

* A conventional way of referring to the Emperor.

now wished to smoke a water-pipe. Could Wu Yung produce any paper lighters?

'Who could ever have believed,' Tzü Hsi is credibly reported to have said when she put on her peasant clothes, 'that it would come to this?'

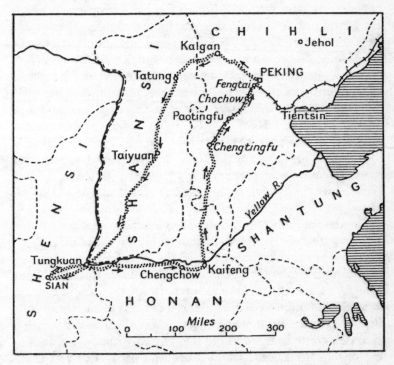

Those first days on the road marked the nadir of the Court's fortunes. The Imperial Chariot rolled slowly north-west to Kalgan, on the edge of the Mongolian plateau, then altered course south-west for Sian, the capital of the mid-western province of Shensi. The journey of 700 miles was completed in two months; but with each stage its inconveniences and anxieties decreased. The fear of pursuit (which the Allies never seriously considered and from which they were in effect debarred by their lack of cavalry) receded as mountain ranges were laboriously crossed and theoretically reliable garrisons left behind to hold the passes. Millet porridge was replaced by bird's-nest soup. A panic-stricken bolt became a stately progress.

The retinue grew larger as more and more of the leading reactionaries caught up with the strange caravan. Mule-litters and sedan chairs were substituted for the Peking carts, which are vehicles of an excruciating discomfort. As they drew away from the capital the trail of disorder and devastation left by the rebels and the broken armies petered out; the locust-swarm of grandees, bannermen and hangers-on emptied the treasuries and granaries by more orderly methods.

A halt of three weeks was made at Taiyuan, the capital of Shansi province. Here the Empress Dowager was accommodated in the Yamen of the Governor, Yü Hsien, where she took pride and pleasure in using the magnificent gold and silver tableware prepared in 1775 for the Emperor Ch'ien Lung's progress (which in the end he never made) to the sacred mountain of Wu T'ai Shan.

She showed, too, a keen interest in a more recent page of the Yamen's history. In its main courtyard, six weeks earlier, Yü Hsien had ordered and supervised the greatest single massacre of foreigners which took place during the Boxer troubles. 'Your Majesty's slave,' he told the Empress Dowager, 'caught them as in a net, and allowed neither chicken nor dog to escape.' While Prince Tuan's fifteen-year-old son, the loutish and dissipated Heir Apparent, pranced round the courtyard gleefully brandishing one of the swords which had been used, Tzü Hsi cross-questioned Yü Hsien on the details of a crime which had taken a whole day to perpetrate. 'You did splendidly,' she said, 'in ridding Shansi of the whole brood of foreign devils.'

In my narrative the fate of missionaries in the interior has been touched on only in general terms. In many cases what had happened to them did not become known until after the Relief of Peking. Since the horrible stories had, through their impact on world opinion, an effect on the climate in which the peace negotiations opened, it may be well to insert here an account of the events of 9 July at Taiyuan, with a reminder that these events were exceptional in only two respects: the large number of victims butchered in the same place on the same day, and the direct participation of a provincial governor.*

The evidence came, Smith wrote, from 'an unwilling witness—a Baptist convert whose story has been confirmed from other sources. He saw the foreign pastors and their wives and children, the Roman Catholic priests and nuns, and several Chinese Christians, taken to the Governor's Yamen. Hearing that they were to be killed, he vainly endeavoured to get out of the crowd, but was borne along by it, and witnessed the massacre.'

This is what he saw:

'The first to be led forth was Mr Farthing (English Baptist). His wife clung to him, but he gently put her aside, and going in front of the soldiers knelt down without saying a word, and his head was struck off with one blow of the executioner's knife. He was quickly followed by Mr Hoddle and Mr Beynon, Drs Lovitt and Wilson, each of whom was beheaded by one blow of the executioner. Then the Governor, Yü Hsien, grew impatient and told his bodyguard, all of whom carried heavy swords with long handles, to help kill the others. Mr Stokes, Mr Simpson, and Mr Whitehouse were next killed, the last by one blow only, the other two by several.

'When the men were finished the ladies were taken. Mrs Farthing had hold of the hands of her children who clung to her, but the soldiers parted them, and with one blow beheaded their mother. The executioner beheaded all the children and did it skilfully, needing only one blow, but the soldiers were clumsy, and some of the ladies suffered several cuts before death. Mrs Lovitt was wearing her spectacles and held the hand of her little boy, even when she was killed. She spoke to the people, saying 'We all came to China to bring you the good news of the salvation by Jesus Christ; we have done you no harm, only

* In all, about 250 missionaries (including more than fifty of their children) were murdered in China during the year 1900.

good, why do you treat us so?' A soldier took off her spectacles before beheading her, which needed two blows.

'When the Protestants had been killed, the Roman Catholics were led forward. The Bishop, an old man with a long white beard, asked the Governor why he was doing this wicked deed. I did not hear the Governor give him any answer, but he drew his sword and cut the Bishop across the face one heavy stroke; blood poured down his white beard, and he was beheaded.

'The priests and nuns quickly followed him in death. Then Mr Piggott and his party were led from the district jail which is close by. He was still handcuffed, and so was Mr Robinson. He preached to the people till the very last, when he was beheaded with one blow. Mr Robinson suffered death very calmly. Mrs Piggott held the hand of her son, even when she was beheaded, and he was killed immediately after her. The ladies and two girls were also quickly killed.

'On that day forty-five foreigners were beheaded in all, thirty-three Protestants and twelve Roman Catholics. A number of native Christians were also killed. The bodies of all were left where they fell till the next morning, as it was evening before the work was finished. During the night they had been stripped of their clothing, rings, and watches. The next day they were removed to a place inside the great South Gate, except some of the heads, which were placed in cages on the city wall. All were surprised at the firmness and quietness of the foreigners, none of whom except two or three of the children cried, or made any noise.'

Although the Empress Dowager listened with evident approbation to Yü Hsien's account of this carnage, she warned him that he might have to be punished to appease the wrath of the barbarians. A few days later his name was included in an Expiatory Decree which dismissed from office nine of the senior officials most closely implicated in the Boxer movement. When it became clear that the Powers would insist on more drastic penalties for the offenders, she remarked in passing to Yü Hsien that 'the price of coffins is rising,' a delicate hint that he should commit suicide. In the end he was executed. 'Now,' Wu

Yung recorded, 'some of the Shansi people praise him, pity him, and think he was wronged. I cannot understand why this is so.'

From Taiyuan (where Jung Lu as well as many less sage advisers joined it) the Court journeyed on to Sian at the end of September; this move was prompted by false rumours that the Allies were mounting a punitive expedition to avenge the missionaries. Save for the much shorter flight to Jehol in Manchuria forty years ago, this was the first time since childhood that the Empress Dowager had visited the interior of her vast domains. As the long, banner-gay cavalcade wound its way through the valleys in the mellow autumn sunshine the old lady took a lively interest in the peasants, the petty officials and the local worthies. Everything was almost as fresh and strange to her as it would have been to a foreigner. 'Tour of inspection' may have been a euphemism; it was not a misnomer.

The Court wintered, in some state, at Sian. Intrigues and impeachments were the order of the day. Tribute poured in and the eunuchs lined their pockets. The conduct of the Heir Apparent caused scandal in the city. The Empress Dowager suffered intermittently from indigestion and continuously from anxiety for the vast treasure buried in the purlieus of the Winter Palace; she was incensed by reports that her personal quarters had been desecrated by the foreign soldiery, her throne hurled into the lake, and the walls of her bedroom defiled with 'lewd and ribald drawings.'

Wu Yung has left us this eldritch picture of the Emperor, who was treated 'as a puppet that is pulled by strings. . . . If he was idle and had nothing to do, he would sit down on the floor and amuse himself with the eunuchs. He liked to draw pictures on paper of a big head and long body and of the different kinds of demons and spirits. When he had finished a drawing he would tear it to pieces. Sometimes he would draw a large tortoise,* write the name of Yüan Shih-k'ai on its back

---

* By reason of its supposed homosexual tendencies the tortoise is an opprobrious symbol in China. During the Siege the Russian sailors taught themselves enough Chinese to answer their assailants' yells of 'Kill the foreign devils!' with shouts of 'Kill the tortoise eggs!'

and stick it on the wall. With a small bamboo bow he would shoot at the picture, then take it down and cut it to pieces with scissors, and throw the pieces into the air like a swarm of butter-flies. His hate of Yüan Shih-k'ai [whose treachery had sparked off the *coup d'état* of 1898] was apparently very deep. He did this almost every day as though it was a task he must perform. . . . The sound of his voice was light and thin like the hum of a mosquito.'

To this poor shadow of a ruler were addressed the telegrams and Memorials which streamed in from Peking and elsewhere about the peace negotiations with the Powers. They were, needless to say, taken direct to the Empress Dowager.

The conquerors: *Above*, General Gaselee and his staff

*Below*, General Frey and his staff (Captain Bobo with helmet)

General Chaffee and his staff

The victory parade

# CHAPTER SEVENTEEN

# The Last Word

*After a long discussion of the situation with Yin Ch'ang, I directed him to write in German to* [Chinese rendering of a German name] *requesting his friendly intervention at the Berlin Foreign Office with a definite explanation that China could not possibly agree that the Expiatory Mission should be received kneeling, that Germany had nothing to gain from insisting on such a procedure, and that the only result of a fiasco would be to make both countries appear extremely ridiculous. . . . After the ceremony the German Emperor came to call on me. He was very cordial and . . . begged me to remain longer in Berlin, suggesting that I should visit the arsenals and inspect the fleet under Prince Henry at Stettin. I could scarcely decline these polite attentions. . . . Thanks to the glorious prestige of our Empire, matters have thus been satisfactorily settled.*

From a telegram sent by Prince Ch'un to the Chinese Peace Plenipotentiaries, 26 September 1901.

'It is easier,' says a Chinese proverb, 'to gain a victory than to secure its advantages.' The Relief of the Legations and the flight of the Court created a vacuum in North China. The victorious Allies found themselves at a loss. All their main problems had become insoluble overnight. No one was left for the generals to fight, no one for the diplomats to make peace with. This unforeseen aftermath of anticlimax they devoted, in the main, to petty quarrels and extensive looting.

The conquered capital was divided into zones, each of which was garrisoned by a different nationality; the French complained, probably with justice, that they were allotted the worst sector but succeeded, thanks to the gullibility of Mr Conger, in enlarging it at the Americans' expense. The population had shrunk to a quarter of its normal size; in the chaos of the past weeks thousands had been murdered and tens of thousands had fled. The demeanour of those who remained was abject and obsequious. 'Grovelling curs,' a British student interpreter called them, and deplored the fact that 'an idiotic spirit of mercy pervades everyone.'

The citizens made haste to improvise little flags (the Japanese, being the easiest to copy, was at first the commonest), which they displayed on their persons and houses. Notices appeared on all premises still occupied—'Pray officer excuse. Here good people,' 'Noble and good sirs, please do not shoot us,' and so on.

These precautions were no safeguard against the looters who roved the corpse-littered streets. The city had already been extensively plundered by the Boxers, by the Imperial troops and by its own criminal class, the ranks of which were swollen by the troubled times. Now it was ransacked again by the foreigners, civil and military. Some of the Chinese still in Peking had stayed behind to loot; but though these were relieved of ill-gotten gains, more were robbed, often with great brutality, of their lawful possessions. It seems to be a natural law that in these matters the tail of an army has fewer scruples than its teeth, and as the administrative services caught up with the men who had done the fighting, and as people got to know their way about and native informers came forward, more and more caches were unearthed. Considerable fortunes were made by those who knew what they were at, and the world was, or affected to be, shocked by newspaper reports of the sordid scramble.

This vandalism was no doubt deplorable. But a spirit of revenge was abroad, the city was in disorder and half-abandoned, and it may be questioned whether it was humanly possible to prevent looting in the first place, still less to stop it once it had started. It went squalidly on for months, with each nationality blaming some other for setting a bad example and claiming that its own hands were clean.* It was common knowledge that the highest as well as the lowest plundered.

'It was rumoured,' wrote a leading Russian statesman, 'that Russian army officers took part in the looting, and I must say,

---

* Cf. von Waldersee: 'Every nationality accords the palm to some other in respect to the art of plundering, but it remains the fact that each and all of them went in hot and strong for loot.'

to our shame, that our agent in Peking unofficially confirmed these rumours to me.  One lieutenant general, who had received the Cross of St George for the capture of Peking [presumably Lineivitch], returned to his post in the Amur region with ten trunks full of valuables from the looted Peking palaces.  Unfortunately, the general's example was followed by other army men.' * In October a British officer wrote home: 'Lady MacDonald was out with the small force left behind in Peking [during a punitive expedition in Chihli] and devoted herself most earnestly to looting.'  Everyone was in it.

After the Relief the soldiers' blood tended to cool while the pent-up indignation of the diplomats made them vociferous in the demand for reprisals.  At a joint meeting of Ministers and Generals at the Russian Legation on 18 August the would-be avengers were overruled by the partisans of appeasement and, in particular, a proposal to raze the Imperial Palace and the city walls was rejected.

The motives which divided the Allies are too complex for detailed analysis in these pages.  The prime movers in the more aggressive faction were the Germans.  They wanted to exact retribution for von Ketteler's murder, and they were perhaps even more cogently influenced by the fact that a strong German expeditionary force and a German Supreme Commander were still at sea, thirsting for glory, while the tiny German contingent actually in North China had not yet reached Peking (where it arrived on the 19th).  A policy of reprisals meant an extension of military operations in which German arms would play a leading part; a policy of conciliation would involve German prestige in an anticlimax not far removed from fiasco.

The Russians had reasons at once subtler and more compelling for assuming the role of an honest broker, an altruistic benefactor who was prepared to forgive the erring Dynasty and give the other Powers a lead in setting it on its feet again.  From the first, Russia—who, incidentally, had no stake and thus no

* *The Memoirs of Count Witte*: edited by A. Yarmolinsky.

liabilities in the field of missionary endeavour—had seen in the Boxer Rising a pretext which could be used to further her territorial designs. On the day when the first news of the outbreaks reached St Petersburg, the Minister of War, Kuropatkin, expressed his delight to the Minister of Finance, Count Witte. 'I am very glad,' he said. 'This will give us an excuse for seizing Manchuria. We will turn Manchuria into a second Bokhara.' *

By mid-August these aspirations were well on the way to being realised. Strong Russian forces, ostensibly despatched to suppress the rioters and protect Russian lives and property, were in effective occupation of all three provinces of Manchuria. Throughout the period Russia's policy was to trade diplomatic good offices in North China for territorial and economic concessions in Manchuria; if you earn the gratitude of a half-drowned man by successfully applying artificial respiration, there is a chance that he will overlook the fact that you have stolen his wallet in the process, or will at least allow you to retain part of its contents.

It was reasoning on these lines which caused the Russian Government to announce, immediately the Legations had been relieved, that it would withdraw its Minister and its troops from Peking to Tientsin with the least possible delay. Its soldiers had achieved their objective; its diplomats, whose purpose was now to help in establishing a legally constituted central government and in the restoration of order, could do little to the purpose while the Court was on tour. This sop to Chinese susceptibilities made small impression on its intended beneficiaries, in whom the brutal behaviour of the Tsar's troops on both sides of the Great Wall was arousing fear and revulsion; but the departure of M. de Giers added slightly to the atmosphere of unreality and cross-purposes now pervading the Legation Quarter.

Though it rejected the idea of reprisals, the military-diplomatic conference of 18 August resolved to stage a Victory

* The Central Asian Emirate of Bokhara, though allowed to retain a titular independence, had recently been brought under Russian control.

March through the Imperial City, 'lest' (as Sir Claude Mac-
Donald put it) 'the Chinese, with their infinite capacity for
misrepresentation, should infer that some supernatural power
had intervened, so that the Allied forces had been affected by
fear of the consequences of invading the sacred precincts.'

An inter-Allied ceremonial parade is at all times difficult to
arrange. Few can have presented as many problems as this
one. Lacking a common alphabet, the eight nations represented could not invoke the impersonal arbitrament of alpha-
betical order to decide their respective stations in the line of
march. It was agreed that precedence should go by numerical
strength. The Japanese was in fact the largest contingent, but
the Russians blandly asserted that they had more men than
anybody else. To impugn their good faith was out of the
question, to prove them wrong impossible; they led the march
on 28 August.

For some inscrutable reason attempts were made to exclude
the journalists, but General Lineivitch, who headed the procession and took the salute, allowed one British war-correspondent, Henry Savage Landor, to ride beside him. To him
we owe a parting glimpse of the Corps Diplomatique:

'In front stood prominent the lumbering, bony figure of Sir
Claude MacDonald, in an ample grey suit of tennis clothes and
a rakish Panama slouch hat. He walked jauntily and with
gigantic strides, moving his arms about as if preparing for a
boxing match. To his right the Russian Minister seemed
reposeful by contrast. He was clad in dark clothes, and bore
himself with dignity. Next to him came the representative of
the French Republic, in a garb which combined the requirements of the Bois de Boulogne on a Sunday with the con-
veniences of tropical attire on a weekday. Mr. Conger, the
American Minister, strode ponderously behind, dressed in
white cottons and military gaiters. The march through the
Palace being a military affair, it seemed as if the Ministers were
sulky and attached 'no importance to the occasion. In fact,
some appeared quite bored.'

Ever since the commanders of the Allied warships off Taku

had begun to exchange courtesy visits, the campaign in North China had been a bandmaster's nightmare. The Russian band, which played the contingents past the saluting base, made a sad hash of the Japanese national anthem as the sturdy little men in their white tunics (only the British and Americans wore khaki) trudged past; it found the bagpipes of the Sikhs disconcerting; and it was still playing the Marseillaise when the troops of monarchist Italy swung into view. The German goose-step aroused stifled mirth in the spectators. The French 'seemed so much exhausted that they could scarcely walk'; their commander-in-chief had to admit that their uniforms were 'still very dirty.'

After this display of military might the diplomats and senior officers were escorted by eunuchs round the various palaces, with whose more portable treasures many of them openly stuffed their pockets as they went along.

The peace negotiations got under way slowly. Before she fled the Empress Dowager had appointed Li Hung-chang as China's plenipotentiary. For thirty years this shrewd man had played a dominant part in his country's affairs. He was now Viceroy at Canton, where the first of twelve Edicts summoning him urgently to Peking had reached him as long ago as 18 June. The worse things got, the more the Court felt the need for his guidance. Li gave it liberally by telegram, but, seeing that the reactionaries were invariably successful in setting it aside, he judged it useless and perhaps imprudent to repair in person to Peking. Disregarding orders from the Throne and entreaties from the southern Viceroys, he stayed where he was.

The occupation of the capital and the departure of the Court created a breach into which only Li could step. 'If you do not go to Peking, no negotiations can be held,' one of the Yangtse Viceroys telegraphed on 18 August; on the following day came an Edict saying 'This minister has been well known for his loyalty and respected by the foreigners. Now that the country has come to such a situation, how he should exert himself!'

Yet still Li Hung-chang tarried. His reasons for playing a

waiting game are obscure, and he can hardly have realised how well his tactics suited the Germans, who were not in the least anxious for peace negotiations to begin and who, when Li at last took ship for the North, toyed with the idea of intercepting him on passage and holding him prisoner at Tsingtao. The Russians, by contrast, gave him every encouragement to embark on his duties as plenipotentiary and even offered to place a warship at his disposal. Li knew that he was regarded, particularly by Britain, as pro-Russian, and in the end he sailed for Taku in a Chinese ship. He did not want, he said, to 'arouse suspicions' which, he might have added, were ill-founded. He had no more love for Russia than for Germany and once described them both as 'equally pernicious and brutal.' He arrived at Tientsin on 18 September and did not move up to Peking until three weeks later.

The peace negotiations were complex, protracted and unedifying; to follow their whole course would be beyond the scope of this book.

It was four months before the foreign Ministers, representing the eleven Powers, held on Christmas Eve their first meeting with the two Chinese plenipotentiaries, of whom, Li Hung-chang being ill, only Prince Ch'ing was able to attend. This long delay was due partly to inter-Allied differences, resolved at Government level, about the form and content of the demands to be made upon China; but in fact these differences were relatively trivial,* and much of the time was lost over an academic point of protocol. This concerned the credentials of the Chinese plenipotentiaries. Who, it was asked, did they represent? The Emperor? He was notoriously a puppet. The Chinese Government? It was composed of rabid xenophobes

---

* Endless telegrams, for example, were exchanged about the use of the epithet 'irrevocable,' which sounds slightly stronger in English than it does in French, and when translated from French into Chinese might, it was feared, sound stronger still. Mr Conger was instructed by Washington to oppose the use of this word with the utmost vehemence, but owing to a mistake in decyphering he did exactly the opposite, thus (when the error was discovered) still further prolonging the debate.

who were likely to repudiate or dishonour any agreement reached. What authority, in any case, could the plenipotentiaries produce to show that they represented anyone?

These nice problems were thrashed out with more diligence than they deserved, and at last the Powers agreed to leave the validity of the Chinese credentials to be assessed, when they were presented, by their representatives in Peking. Prince Ch'ing, therefore, after taking his place at the conference-table in the Spanish Legation, offered with courteous bows eleven large envelopes to the eleven Ministers. They were accepted, opened. The texts were perused (in translation), the vermilion seals vaguely scrutinised.

'The Prince then asked the Representatives to produce their full powers in return.' Alas, no-one except the German Minister had any form of document authorising him to negotiate, 'and the meeting was declared to be closed.' * China had won the first round on points.

Two main issues dominated the negotiations: the punishment of 'war criminals' (though they were not so called) and the size of the indemnity to be paid by China.

At first the Allies, led by Germany, made an abortive attempt to insist that peace negotiations would begin only after Prince Tuan and the other ring-leaders had been delivered up to the Allies for punishment. But the Empress Dowager, acting in response to strong recommendations from Li Hung-chang, adroitly forestalled them. On 25 September she issued an Edict degrading and dismissing from their posts nine Princes and Ministers. On 13 November a further Edict imposed heavier punishments on them; and when it became clear that the Powers would be satisfied with nothing less than the death penalty for the worst offenders, two Edicts on 13 and 21 February 1901 delivered the *coups de grâce*.

Prince Tuan and Duke Tsai Lan were exiled to Turkestan

* Sir Ernest Satow to Lord Lansdowne, 24 December 1900. Satow had succeeded MacDonald in Peking, and Lansdowne Salisbury at the Foreign Office.

(Tuan actually went to Manchuria). Prince Chuang, Ying Nien and Chao Shu-chiao were ordered to commit suicide. Yü Hsien and Hsu Cheng-yu were condemned to decapitation, Kang Yi (who had died) and Li Ping-hêng to posthumous degradation. Tung Fu-hsiang, who was popular in West China and whose still formidable army was deployed about Sian, was regretfully allowed by the Powers to suffer dismissal only. One hundred and nineteen minor officials were sentenced, mostly to death, for crimes committed in the interior.

Those condemned had long known, almost for certain, that the Court would be forced to sacrifice them in the end. It is a tribute to Chinese stoicism, and to the strong sense of loyalty to the Throne permeating even the least admirable members of an official class which in most respects was wholly unprincipled, that not one of these men attempted to evade his doom. Most were at liberty, all were powerful; several could have slipped away and vanished into a distant province. None did.

The sentences were carried out at the end of February, some of them untidily. Chao Shu-chiao, a strong and vigorous man, duly took poison when the Edict was read out to him, but it had no effect and he continued to discuss affairs with the friends who crowded into his room. At length the Governor of Shensi ordered opium to be administered. This produced negligible results. A strong dose of arsenic brought on terrible pains, but the hour at which his death was to be reported to the Empress Dowager had passed and Chao was still alive. It was only after his nostrils and mouth had been stuffed with screws of paper on which spirits were poured that life became extinct. Equally indecorous, though less public, was the end of Ying Nien; after a day spent in solitary and unbecoming lamentations he choked himself to death by swallowing mud.

Haggling over the size of the indemnity, and arguments about the best way to exact a large reparation without bankrupting China, went on into the summer of 1901. Abstruse and arbitrary calculations fixed China's total liability at

£67,500,000; only America (who, von Waldersee crossly observed, 'seems to desire that nobody shall get anything out of
China') tried to stand out for a reduction of this large sum by
more than a third. On 26 May an Imperial Edict guaranteed
payment in full; the process would take thirty-nine years.

Of the eleven Powers concerned, China was to become,
within less than half that period, the enemy in a major war
of three, the ally of seven. Thereafter the country was rent by
civil strife; its currency became worthless, its reserves of specie
exhausted and its credit bad. All these things disrupted the
system under which the instalments of the Boxer Indemnity
were supposed to be paid. Britain ploughed her share back,
and the money was spent under joint Anglo-Chinese super-
vision on education, scientific research, health services and
other sorely needed amenities. Most of the other Powers
followed suit.

At long last the protocol of the Peace Treaty assumed its final
form. Its principal provisions—closely foreshadowed in a
Joint Note addressed by the Powers to China in January—were
these:

(1) Prince Ch'un was to convey to the German Emperor
the Chinese Emperor's regrets for the assassination of
Baron von Ketteler, upon the scene of which a suitable
monument would be erected.

(2) Official examinations were to be suspended for five years
in all cities where foreigners had been murdered or
maltreated. (This was to remind the official class of its
responsibility.)

(3) An emissary was to apologise to the Emperor of Japan
for the assassination of Mr Sugiyama.

(4) Expiatory monuments were to be erected in the foreign
cemeteries which had been desecrated.

(5) China was to prohibit the importation of arms and
armaments.

(6) The Legation Quarter was to be placed under foreign
control and might be fortified.

(7) The Taku Forts were to be razed.

(8) Twelve places between the capital and the coast were to be garrisoned by the Powers so as to safeguard communications with their envoys.

(9) Membership of any anti-foreign society was to be punishable by death. Officials failing to repress anti-foreign outbreaks would be dismissed instantly and never again re-employed.

(10) The Tsungli Yamen was to be elevated to the status of a Ministry of Foreign Affairs. Court ceremonial governing the reception of diplomats was to be modi-fied.

There were in all twelve articles and nineteen annexes.

The treaty was signed on 7 September 1901, over a year after the Legations had been relieved. Of the thirteen pleni-potentiaries assembled in the Spanish Legation only five * could remember that day in June when, sitting round the same table, they had felt, to the sound of detonations, the chill im-pact of the Chinese ultimatum, ushering in the sequence of extraordinary events to which they had now come to write *Finis*.

It may be doubted whether, at a meeting 'characterized by genial and friendly congratulations on all sides,' the five veterans of the Siege were much tempted to ruminate upon that earlier, less auspicious conclave. If they recalled it, it must have seemed further away in history than it was in time. Their presence in the Spanish chancery was not the climax of a sentimental pilgrimage. They had been immured in it for ten months, groping their way towards those bright uplands of 'constant peace and perpetual friendship' which had now—as Prince Ch'ing wound up their long business by erroneously claiming—been attained. It seems unlikely that they had thoughts to spare for anything beyond the intoxicating prob-

* Apart from the doyen, Señor Cologan, MM. Joostens (Belgium), Sal-vago Raggi (Italy), Knobel (Netherlands) and de Giers (Russia) were still *en poste* at Peking.

ability that meetings in the doyen's chancery would henceforth be irregular and brief.

The last troops of the international garrison left Peking ten days after the treaty was signed. China has always had a propensity for corrupting her conquerors, and the occupation of her capital is, at best, a lacklustre episode in the history of the armies that took part.

Indiscriminate looting was gradually brought under control or at least driven underground. In April American deserters were leading Chinese robber bands; two of them were captured but escaped. Higher up the social scale comparable activities were conducted more urbanely: as when it suddenly occurred to the French that some of the world-famous instruments in the Imperial Observatory, established two centuries earlier by Verbiest, had been made in France and presented to the Emperor K'ang Hsi by Louis XIV. General Voyron, who had relieved Frey, formally requested from the Supreme Commander permission to remove these treasures, most of which were of unmistakably Oriental workmanship.

The Observatory stood in the German sector. 'The instruments,' von Waldersee wrote in a despatch to the Kaiser, 'were without a doubt the property of the Chinese State,' but 'in accordance with the custom universally prevailing here were to be regarded as German war-booty'; they could moreover 'be regarded as an equivalent for at least a small portion of the war indemnity, the whole of which is not likely to be paid.' Despite however what seemed to him the overwhelming legality of Germany's claim to these unique works of art, the Field-Marshal was reluctant to offend the French; the instruments were divided up between the two Powers (France being represented in this transaction by Colonel Marchand, of Fashoda fame) and shipped to Europe. Germany was forced by the Treaty of Versailles to restore her share.

The incident elicited a protest in writing from General Chaffee; it was couched in strong terms and included a veiled reminder that German troops had not been present at the

Relief. The Supreme Commander returned this missive with a curt intimation that he was unable to receive it, whereupon Chaffee apologised and was asked to luncheon. The atmosphere in Peking was unpropitious to moral indignation.

Field-Marshal von Waldersee wanted a run for his money. News of the Court's flight, which reached him while he was still on his way to China, came as a great relief. 'Had they [the Emperor and Empress Dowager] been taken prisoners in Peking,' he wrote, 'there would have been no trouble about making peace, I should have arrived too late, and probably we should have been able to play no decisive part in the peace negotiations.' When he at last—in early October—reached Peking he threw himself heart and soul into the organisation of punitive expeditions; 'the only thing that worries me,' he said, 'is our slackness with the Chinese,' and he claimed that a large-scale Allied foray to Paotingfu, where the murder of some missionaries was avenged by the execution of officials and other reprisals, 'is exerting a moral influence of far-reaching importance.'

But these punitive expeditions, never seriously opposed and seldom opposed at all, were unrewarding enterprises, yielding little glory. 'It is safe to say,' General Chaffee told a journalist, 'that where one real Boxer has been killed since the capture of Peking, fifteen harmless coolies or labourers on the farms, including not a few women and children, have been slain.' His estimate is borne out by a British officer writing home in October: 'We fired about 2000 rounds, mostly at inoffensive people I believe, and killed about fifteen of them.' From von Waldersee's point of view this sort of thing was better than peace, but it hardly constituted war. It was gratifying to read, in a letter written by the Kaiser's own hand: 'How glad I am to hear of the satisfactory working of our heavy howitzers! Our whole Field Artillery is cock-a-hoop over this;' but the Field-Marshal could not help feeling that these admirable guns deserved to be more worthily employed than in bashing down conspicuous pagodas. 'A resumption of larger operations may shortly become necessary,' he wrote on 15 February 1901 in an order decreeing that the Allied contingents must review their transport arrangements, for spring, 'a favourable season,' would soon be here; but in the end he went away from China without fighting a battle.

The Press and—outside Germany—the humourists made great play with an 'asbestos hut' which, it was announced soon after his appointment, von Waldersee would use as his field headquarters in China. Whether this novelty was ever assembled and occupied we do not know; but there was, unhappily, nothing incombustible about the palace in which he was living in the spring of 1901. It caught fire one night and his chief of staff was burnt to death.

If there is nothing particularly attractive about the first Allied Supreme Commander of modern times, it is probable that if the appointment had not existed, or if it had been filled by a less positive personality, the tiffs and animosities which ceaselessly embittered the relations between the contingents in North China would have assumed serious proportions. As it was, an Anglo-Russian dispute over the railways brought the two nations perilously close to an open conflict; the original Russian contingent, which included a strong detachment of railway engineers, had been allotted operational control of lines which were the property of British bond-holders and for a long time refused to relinquish it. There were countless other minor incidents, and it is at least partly to von Waldersee's credit that nothing came of them.

Resilience is a leading Chinese characteristic. If a graph could be drawn comparing the fortunes of the Allies after the capture of Peking, it is probable that the Chinese line after plummeting sharply downwards would show a steady upward curve, while the Allied line would follow a directly opposite course.

The Allies were successful in relieving the Legations. They exacted a large indemnity. They virtually dictated the terms of peace. But the *de jure* material gains which they collectively acquired as a result of punishing China for her misdemeanours

# THE LAST WORD

were derisory when compared with the *de facto* exactions which they had individually practiced on China during the preceding years. Russia alone obtained in Manchuria benefits which seemed substantial; but she did not keep them long, and her brief enjoyment of them led to, and was brusquely ended by, her disastrous war with Japan in 1904. The Chinese Empire, which had seemed on the point of being partitioned when the Boxer Rising started, had in some odd way become secure from such a fate after the disturbances had been suppressed.

In North China the conduct of the conquerors was unbecoming, and they knew it. Their garrisons bickered; the troops suffered from inactivity and boredom; venereal disease thinned their ranks. The population, though outwardly compliant, became less hangdog. Small deceptions and swindles began to be practised on the barbarians. Terra-cotta figurines, depicting with great realism soldiers of the different contingents in savage and repellent postures, came into circulation, and were soon so ubiquitous that the Supreme Commander felt obliged to order that the moulds should be confiscated and destroyed.* The victorious flags flew bravely from palace and pagoda; but the streets beneath were seamy with corruption, violence and intrigue. The smell of corpses had gone, the smell of scandal remained.

This aroma was inseparable from the day-to-day life of the Manchu Court, whose sojourn in Sian was no more edifying than had been its residence in the Imperial City. But those destitute, humiliating August days of rain-lashed Peking carts, millet porridge and borrowed chopsticks were far behind; the Empress Dowager's nails were once more assuming

* Pierre Loti: *Les Derniers Jours de Pékin*. The novelist was on the staff of the French Admiral Pottier and spent the winter in Peking. Though he is not a particularly reliable witness, some idea of the atmosphere prevailing may be gained by the epithets on which he principally relies. They include: *funeste, infecte, affreux, ténébreux, louche, sournois, lugubre, maussade, épouvantable*. In writing of the 'statuettes accusatrices' he claims that the French soldier alone was depicted in an inoffensive and even benign manner; he was shown playing with a Chinese baby.

THE SIEGE AT PEKING

elegant proportions, the line of the graph was curving up-
wards.

Though the news from St Petersburg and from Manchuria
was consistently bad, that from Peking was less alarming than
anyone had expected. At times some among the Powers (and at
almost all times America) felt that the terms imposed on China
were over-harsh; the Chinese, judging matters from an Oriental
standpoint, found them astonishingly lenient.

It had come as a welcome surprise to the Empress Dowager
to find that the Imperial Chariot was not pursued. It was
almost a shock to learn that the Allies made no demand for her
own punishment; and it would have been wholly unlike her to
have any qualms about decreeing death for those of her advisers
whose blood the Powers were determined to have. Though the
financial indemnity was a heavy one, it could be raised; and
the discovery that no surrender of territory was included in the
conditions of peace was a great and unlooked-for relief.

Deferentially but ably conducted by the two Chinese plenipotentiaries, the negotiations in the Spanish chancery dragged
on, and it gradually (as Bland and Backhouse well put it)
'became clear to the Empress Dowager that along the well-worn
path of international jealousies she could return unpunished,
and even welcomed, to Peking.' Ever since her flight she had
been tidying up the disordered and equivocal position of the
Dynasty. In a series of Expiatory Decrees she rearranged the
past in a decorous perspective, showing in the performance of
this pious duty as little regard for the truth as do modern
Russian historians when required to revise the annals of their
country. She rehabilitated the memories of the five moderate
Ministers who had been decapitated during the Siege; she
performed a like office for the Pearl Concubine, praising the
qualities which had 'led her virtuously to commit suicide when
unable to catch up the Court on its departure from Peking.'
She disinherited the Heir Apparent; apart from the fact that his
behaviour had become intolerable, he was Prince Tuan's son
and in view of his father's guilt was likely to prove a liability in
the capital.

Li Hung-chang

Victims of the Taiyuan Massacre: Dr and Mrs Lovitt with their son and Mrs Lovitt's father

Chinese soldiers

The Chien Men before its destruction

# THE LAST WORD

By June 1901 it was clear that the Peace Treaty would soon be ready for signature, and a Decree was issued in the Emperor's name:

> Our Sacred Mother's advanced age renders it necessary that we should take the greatest care of her health, so that she may attain to peaceful longevity; a long journey in the heat being evidently undesirable, we have fixed on the 19th day of the 7th Moon (1 September) to commence our return journey and are now preparing to escort Her Majesty by way of Honan.

This announcement was welcomed throughout the Empire; even the foreigners felt vaguely that a confused picture was being brought into focus, that they would now know better how things stood.

In the event reports of bad road-conditions caused by the summer rains delayed the Court's start until 24 October. It was, improbably but according to Wu Yung, in 'entire silence and perfect order' that the gigantic caravan set out from Sian, the Imperial party borne in yellow sedan chairs in the centre of a procession which included two thousand carts and ten thousand flags, with a swarm of cavalry and mounted officials hovering on its flanks.

There can have been few stranger, few more barbarically beautiful sights seen in the last sixty years than this long file of animals and men and caparisoned vehicles crawling to the screech of axles and the blare of trumpets through bright sunlight along a narrow road between the bare, harsh, dun-coloured mountains of West China. Even Wu Yung, who bore heavy responsibilities for supervising entertainment and accommodation at the halts, and for organising what we should call traffic control and he called 'decorum on the road,' enjoyed most of the 700-mile journey. 'Men looked like ants walking up the hills. A wooden bridge was built over the river. The water was white and clear; there were no waves, and the sky could be seen as in a mirror. The houses on the hillsides looked like stars. The Imperial outing was attended by many soldiers and was as pleasant as the hunting trips of the Han Dynasty.' There was nothing woebegone, nothing remorseful, about the Throne's return to the capital.

The Chariot rolled slowly on. The weather grew colder; overhead the wild geese were flying south. The Court crossed the Yellow River in a splendid barge, built to represent a dragon. As they drew nearer to the capital, parties of missionaries were here and there seen among the crowds who gathered to watch the great procession pass; and it was noticed that the Empress Dowager went out of her way to show them signs of affability.

On crossing the borders of the metropolitan province of Chihli she issued Decrees commanding that foreigners should not, as was customary, be forbidden to watch her progress through the streets of Peking, and announcing that immediately on his arrival the Emperor would receive the envoys in the central Throne Hall, and that she herself was eager to renew acquaintance with their consorts. Under the terms of the Peace Treaty the Emperor was obliged to hold diplomatic audiences in the Throne Hall instead of, as formerly, in a building less hallowed and commodious; but few of his subjects were aware of this, and the Decree thus produced the impression that the Emperor was showing unexampled condescension to the barbarians in spite of their disgusting behaviour.

The last lap of the journey, from Chengtingfu, was completed by railway. Four freight trains were needed to carry the less personal items of the Imperial baggage, such as the accumulation of tribute and archives; and eventually, at an hour deemed auspicious by the astrologers, the Emperor and the Empress Dowager took their places in the luxuriously appointed 'fire-cart' provided for them by the Belgian railway authorities.

They had never travelled in a conveyance of this type before, but all went well. Bursting with Princes, Grand Councillors, eunuchs, concubines, mules, cooks and other members of the retinue, upholstered with yellow silk, furnished with two thrones and several opium pipes, and decorated with valuable curios, the train rattled over the plain towards Peking. The

Belgian railway official in charge of the arrangements was decorated with the Order of the Double Dragon (second class).

At Fengtai the Imperial circus, mules and all, transferred to a British train. The Empress Dowager, who despite the intense cold had been in almost hilarious spirits throughout the railway journey, now showed signs of fretting; it was of the utmost importance that she should reach Peking at the hour set by the soothsayers, and although the timetable of her special train had been arranged to this end, her awe of the spirit world was deeper-rooted than her faith in the engine-driver.

They arrived, however, exactly on time. Since the Siege the railway had been extended from Machiapu (where the Legation guards had detrained eighteen months earlier) to a terminus inside the city. But the Imperial party alighted outside the walls and, after an inevitable interlude of confusion, entered the Chinese City through the Yung Ting Men—the scene of Sugiyama's murder—and proceeded up the wide central avenue to the Chien Men, before which they halted to perform the prescribed rites at a shrine.

The great tower over the Chien Men had, it may be remembered, been destroyed in the disastrous fire which gutted the commercial quarter in the early days of the Siege. But a lunette, a kind of fortified balcony, still jutted out over the huge tunnel-like entrance to the gate through which the Emperors, emerging from or returning to the Tartar City, had always made ceremonial progress; and on this coign of vantage many of the foreigners in Peking had gathered to watch an event which some felt to be momentous and all hoped would be picturesque.

One of them, an Italian, described it thus: 'There was a strong wind and much dust, but all Peking had collected on top of the wall. We could not have chosen a better place to watch it from. First to arrive were the Manchu bannermen on their fiery little horses. Next came a group of Chinese officials in ceremonial robes, and finally the Imperial palanquins, which advanced at an almost incredible speed between two ranks of kneeling soldiers. The higher the rank of the person carried in the palanquin, the faster he should go. The Court chairs seemed to move as fast as the Tartar cavalry.

'When they reached the enclosure between the wall and the outer lunette, the chairs halted and the Emperor and Empress Dowager stepped down to carry out the ceremonies prescribed by the Book of Rites for a homecoming, that is to say, to burn incense and recite prayers in the tiny temple built up against the side of the wall. In that temple there is a shrine to the tutelary god of the Manchus.

'As she got out of her chair, the Empress Dowager looked up at the smoke-blackened walls and saw us: a row of foreigners, watching her arrival from behind the ramparts. The eunuchs seemed to be trying to get her to move on, as it was not seemly that she should remain there in full view of everybody. But the Empress was not to be hurried, and continued to stand between two of her ladies who held her up under the arms on either side, not because she needed any support but because such is the custom in China.

'At last she condescended to move, but before entering the temple where the priests were all ready to begin the ceremony, she stopped once more and, looking up at us, lifted her closed hands under her chin and made a series of little bows.

'The effect of this gesture was astonishing. We had all gone up on the wall in the hopes of catching a glimpse of the terrible Empress, whom the West considered almost an enemy of the human race. But we had been impressed by the magnificence of the swiftly moving pageant and by the beauty of the picturesque group, by the palanquins of yellow satin flashing with gold. Something told us that the return of the Court to Peking was a turning-point in history, and in our breathless interest we forgot our resentment against the woman who was responsible for so much evil.

'That little bow, and the graceful gesture of the closed hands, took us by surprise. From all along the wall there came, in answer, a spontaneous burst of applause. The Empress Dowager appeared pleased. She remained there a few moments longer, looking up and smiling.'

Above her, against the winter sky, the ruins of a once noble pagoda stood out black and jagged. It had been burnt through her folly. From emplacements in its gutted base Jung Lu's cannon, on her orders, had thrown shrapnel and roundshot at some of those who now, putting down their binoculars, clapped their fur-gloved hands, waved to her, and smirked.

She stood below them like a great actress taking her curtain call with all the hazards of an awkward first night behind her: bowing to everyone and to no one, smiling a secret smile, masking her pride behind a show of humility, savouring the moment.

And there, in the centre of the stage, we must leave her, and allow the curtain to fall.

# BIBLIOGRAPHY

ALLEN, Rev. Roland: *The Siege of the Peking Legations* (London, 1901)

ASAKAWA, K.: *The Russo-Japanese Conflict* (Cambridge, Mass., 1904)

ASPINALL-OGLANDER, Cecil: *Roger Keyes* (London, 1951)

BACON, Admiral Sir Reginald: *The Life of John Rushworth, Earl Jellicoe* (London, 1936)

BARNES, Captain A. A. S.: *On Active Service with the Chinese Regiment* (London, 1902)

BAZIN, René: *L'Enseigne de Vaisseau Paul Henry* (Tours, 1905)

BEATTY, David, Earl: See Chalmers

BIGHAM, Clive: *A Year in China* (London, 1901)

BLAND, J. O. P., and BACKHOUSE, E.: *China Under the Empress Dowager* (London, 1911)

BREDON, Juliet: *Sir Robert Hart* (London, 1909)

BROOMHALL, M.: *Martyred Missionaries of the China Inland Mission: with a Record of the Perils and Sufferings of Some who Escaped* (London, 1901)

BROWN, The Rev. Frederick: *From Tientsin to Peking with the Allied Forces* (London, 1902)

CARL, KATHERINE A.: *With the Empress Dowager of China* (London, 1906)

CARTER, Major-General W. H.: *The Life of Lieutenant-General Chaffee* (Chicago, 1917)

CASSERLY, Captain Gordon: *The Land of the Boxers* (London, 1903)

CHALMERS, Rear-Admiral W. S.: *The Life and Letters of David, Earl Beatty, Admiral of the Fleet* (London, 1951)

CHEMINON (with FAUVEL-GALLAIS): *Les Événements Militaires en Chine* (Paris, 1902)

CHING-SHAN: *Diary.* Translated by J. J. L. DUYVENDAK (Leyden, 1924)

CHIROL, Valentine, *The Far Eastern Question* (London, 1898)

CLEMENTS, Paul H.: *The Boxer Rebellion* (New York, 1915)

COLLIS, Maurice: *Foreign Mud* (London, 1946)

COLTMAN, The Rev. R.: *Beleaguered in Peking* (Philadelphia, 1901)

CONGER, Sarah Pike: *Letters From China* (London, 1909)

# BIBLIOGRAPHY

CORDIER, Henri: *Histoire des Relations de la Chine avec les Puissances Occidentales.* 3 vols. (Paris, 1901)

DAGGETT, Brigadier-General A. S.: *America in the China Relief Expedition* (Kansas City, 1903)

DIX, Lt C. C., RN.: *The World's Navies in the Boxer Rebellion* (London, 1905)

FREY, Général H.: *Français et Alliés au Pé-tchili* (Paris, 1904)

HART, Sir Robert: *These From the Land of Sinim* (London, 1901)

HEWLETT, W. Meyrick: *The Siege of the Peking Legations* (Harrow-on-the-Hill, 1900)

HOOKER, Mary: *Behind the Scenes in Peking* (London, 1910)

HOOVER, Herbert: *Memoirs* (London, 1952)

JOSEPH, Philip: *Foreign Diplomacy in China, 1894–1900* (London, 1928)

*The Kaiser's Letters to the Tsar.* Edited by N. F. Grant (London, 1920)

KEN SHEN WEIGH: *Russo-Chinese Diplomacy* (Shanghai, 1928)

KENT, P. H.: *Railway Enterprise in China* (London, 1907)

KEYES, Roger: See Aspinall-Oglander

LANDOR, Henry Savage: *China and the Allies.* 2 vols. (London, 1901)

LANGER, William L.: *The Diplomacy of Imperialism, 1890–1902.* 2 vols. (New York, 1935)

LAUR, F.: *Siège de Pékin: Récits Authentiques des Assiégés* (Paris, 1904)

LOTI, Pierre: *Les Derniers Jours de Pékin* (Paris, 1901)

LYNCH, George: *The War of the Civilizations* (London, 1901)

MARTIN, W. A. P.: *The Siege in Peking* (London, 1900)

MORRISON, Dr G. E.: *An Australian in China* (London, 1895)

OLIPHANT, N.: *A Diary of the Siege of the Legations in Peking* (London, 1901)

PICHON, Stephen: *Dans La Bataille* (Paris, 1908)

PUTNAM WEALE, B. L.: *Indiscreet Letters From Peking* (London, 1906)

QUEEN VICTORIA: *The Letters of Queen Victoria, Vol. III. 1896–1901.* Edited by G. E. Buckle (London, 1932)

RANSOME, Jessie: *The Story of the Siege Hospital in Peking* (London, 1901)

ROSEN, Baron: *Forty Years of Diplomacy.* 2 vols. (London, 1922)

RUSSELL, S. M.: *The Story of the Siege in Peking* (London, 1901)

SERGEANT, Philip W.: *The Great Empress Dowager of China* (London, 1910)

SEYMOUR, Admiral Sir Edward: *My Naval Career and Travels* (London, 1911)

SMITH, Arthur H.: *China in Convulsion.* 2 Vols. (New York, 1901)

STEWART, Major-General Sir N.: *My Service Days* (London, 1908)

SWINHOE, Robert: *Narrative of the North China Campaign of 1860* (London, 1863)

TAN, Chester C.: *The Boxer Catastrophe* (New York, 1955)

THAYER, W. R.: *The Life and Letters of John Hay* (London, 1915)

THOMSON, H. C.: *China and the Powers* (London, 1902)

VARÈ, Daniele: *The Last of the Empresses* (London, 1936)

VAUGHAN, Lieutenant-Colonel H. B.: *St George and the Chinese Dragon* (London, 1902)

WALDERSEE, Alfred, Count von: *A Field-Marshal's Memoirs* (London, 1924)

WEN CHING: *The Chinese Crisis From Within* (London, 1901)

WITTE, Count: *Memoirs*. Edited by A. Yarmolinsky (London, 1921)

WOLSELEY, Lieutenant-Colonel G. J.: *Narrative of the War with China in 1860* (London, 1862)

WU YUNG: *The Flight of an Empress* (London, 1937)

### REGIMENTAL HISTORIES.

*History of the 1st Sikh Infantry, 1846–1902.* (Madras, 1903)

*Regimental Records of the Royal Welch Fusiliers.* Vol. II. (London, 1923)

### FOREIGN OFFICE DOCUMENTS.

*China (No. 3) 1900:* Correspondence respecting the Insurrectionary Movement in China

*China (No. 1) 1900:* Further Correspondence respecting the Affairs of China

*China (No. 4) 1900:* Reports from HM Minister in China respecting Events at Peking

*China (No. 3) 1901:* Further Correspondence respecting Events at Peking

*China (No. 1) 1901:* Correspondence respecting the Disturbances in China

*China (No. 5) 1901:* Further Correspondence respecting the Disturbances in China

*China (No. 6) 1901:* Further Correspondence respecting the Disturbances in China

*China (No. 1) 1902:* Correspondence respecting the Affairs of China

### STATE DEPARTMENT DOCUMENTS.

*Papers Relating to the Foreign Relations of the United States.* (Washington, 1902)

# Index

R 2

# INDEX

Broomhall, M., *Martyred Missionaries of the China Inland Mission*, 42–3
Bruce, Admiral, 130, 133
Buddhism, 24, 38
Burma, Upper, 27, 31
Butler, Lieut. Smedley, 190

Campiche, Dr P., 'Notes sur la Carrière d'Auguste Chamot,' 67 n
Canton, 25, 26, 132 n
Carl, Miss K. A., 57
Carles, Mr, 130; and Yü Lu, 84 n; Sir Claude and, 102, 174; his letter to the Legations, 174–6
Carving Knife Brigade, 115
Cassini Convention, 29 and n*, 30
Cathedrals, the burning of, 94
Cavalry, in the International Relief Force, 182 and n†, 183, 193
Chaffee, General, 181, 193, 208; and the storming of the Imperial City, 216–20; and the Imperial Observatory incident, 252–3; and reprisals, 253
Chamot, M., and Mme Auguste, 19, 67 and n, 94, 110, 118 n†
Changchiawan, 189, 192
Ch'anghsintien, destruction of, 67
Chao Shu-chiao, 249
Chefoo Convention, 31
Ch'ien Lung, Emperor, 236
Chien Men, 123, 124, 141, 205, 219; destruction of, 96, 259; the Empress Dowager re-enters, 259–61
Chih Hua Men, 200, 203, 233
Chihli, 83, 90, 230, 258; Boxer Rising in, 23, 51, 52, 54–5
China, effect of Japanese war on, 19, 28–9; the Manchu Dynasty and, 24–6, 46–7; foreign aggression on, 26–32, 36, 43; British requirements in, 31; impact of the missionaries on, 37–43; Roman Catholic secular pretensions in, 41–2; Sir Robert Hart and, 65–6; the capture of the Taku Forts and, 83; her attitude to the Siege of Peking, 134; the Boxer movement and, 165–6; peace negotiations and, 247–51, 254–5
China, North, 82 n; Boxer Rising in, 23; in a state of anarchy, 53; Beatty on, 90; the focus of world attention, 129, 131, 133–9, 182; after the Relief of Peking, 24 ff, 255
Chinese, the, and the Deity, 17 and n*; not naturally religious, 38; and Roman Catholic secular rights, 41–2; and the advent of the railways, 43–4;

and opium traffic, 45; and secret societies, 48; fire the Hanlin, 121–3; their sparing use of artillery, 124, 226; the besieged's impressions of, 149; their barricades and artillery, 156; and the International Relief Force, 184 ff; reasons for the Siege and its failure, 222–9; massacre of their converts, 237, 238; their conduct after the Relief, 241–2
Chinese City, 16 n
Chinese Customs Service, 20 and n
Chinese Government, 17; and the Boxer Rising, 24, 34, 54; and European encroachments, 32 and n, 33; demand the evacuation of the Legations, 100; and von Ketteler's murder, 107; give assurances concerning the Legations, 134; makes overtures to the besieged, 159–61, 162; its disintegration, 212; attempt to murder the envoys, 223; and peace negotiations, 247 ff
Chinese Post Office, 19, 71 n
Ch'ing, Prince, 104; replaced by Prince Tuan, 66, 159 n; Sir Claude MacDonald and, 71, 159, 161, 165; and peace negotiations, 247, 251
Ching-Shan, his Diary of the Siege, 114 and n*, 127, 226
Chirol, V., *The Far Eastern Question*, 32 n
Christianity, and the Deity in China, 17 n*; the Boxers and, 21, 35–43, 54; recognised in China, 37; ridiculed in China, 40–1; rescue of Chinese converts in Peking, 99; efforts to wipe out the converts to, 223
Chuang, Prince, 249
Ch'un, Prince, 241, 250
Clements, P. H., *The Boxer Rebellion*, 25
Cockburn, Mr, 49, 152
Collis, M., *Foreign Mud*, 132 n
Cologan, Señor, 102, 145, 147, 251 n
Confucianism, 38
Conger, Edwin, 19, 95, 241; the Americans and, 71, 92; and the Yamen's ultimatum, 103, 104–5; conduct during the Siege, 119, 141, 142, 147, 148; and the Stars and Stripes, 220 and n; in the Victory March, 245; and peace negotiations, 247 n
Conger, Mrs, 148–9
Cordes, Herr, and von Ketteler's murder, 106–7, 108
Cordier, H., *Histoire des Relations de la Chine . . .*, 26, 29

266

# INDEX

# INDEX

pedition, 133; attack Tientsin, 163, 164–5; and the International Relief Force, 178 and n, 179, 180, 181, 182–3, 186, 189, 190, 191, 199–201, 203, 233; and the relief of the Peitang, 216–17, 221; in the Victory March, 245, 246

Japanese Legation, 17
Jardine, Matheson, 19
Jellicoe, Capt. John, 75 and n, 82 n, 87
Jesuits, 17 n*, 24
Joostens, M., 19, 251 n
Joseph, P., *Foreign Diplomacy in China, 1894–1900*, 23, 28, 31
*Journal of the Principal Events Connected with China*, 180
Jung Lu, directs the Siege, 96, 127–8, 151, 154, 159, 226, 228, 261; his sparing use of artillery, 226–9; and the Boxers, 227; joins the Empress in flight, 239

Kaiser, the, 250; and the Relief of Peking, 29, 134, 135–6, 178–9; and von Waldersee, 179–80, 253
K'ang Hsi, Emperor, 38, 94, 252
Kang Yi, 249
Kansu, Mohammedan forces from, 68, 69, 79, 91, 126, 226
Kempff, Admiral, 81, 178
Keyes, Roger, 82 n, 187, 204, 207
Kiangyin, 195
Kiaochow Bay, Germany seizes, 29–30, 51, 195
Kierulff's, 19, 145
Knobel, M., 145, 147, 251 n
*Koreetz*, the, 80
Kowloon, 27
Kuang Hsü, Emperor, deposed by his aunt, 21, 32, 56; flees from Peking, 232–4, 239–40; returns to Peking, 258
Kuropatkin, 244
Kwangchouwan, France seizes, 30
Kwangsi, 30
Kwangtung, 30

Labrousse, Capt., 198
Landor, H. S., 187, 245
Langer, W. L., *The Diplomacy of Imperialism 1890–1902*, 33
Langfang, 76, 77
Lansdowne, Lord, 248 n
Legation Quarter, creation of, 17; Sir Robert Hart and, 65; its isolation, 71–2; refugees in, 92; and the Yamen's ultimatum, 102; explosions

in, 158; International troops in, 216; after the Relief, 244; the Peace Treaty and, 250
Legation Street, 16, 69, 92, 115
Legations, the siege of, 11–12, 110–28, 140–61, 168–76, 197–9, 205–7; situation of in Peking, 17–20; their ignorance of danger, 62–6, 71–2, 100; send for guards, 68–9; and the missionaries, 71; atmosphere of crisis in, 92, 98; isolation of, 95, 101, 230; exodus of non-Christian servants from, 98–9; and the Chinese converts, 99–100; receive the Yamen's ultimatum, 101–12; armed strength of, 114–15, 123; fortification of, 123–4; a lull in the Siege, 124–8; Press reports of their fate, 134–9, 177; atmosphere in during the Siege, 140–6, 152–4; conduct of the Ministers, 146–8; subject to rumours, 153–5; their desperate position, 155–8; receive overtures from Prince Ch'ing, 158–61, 169–73; during the truce, 168–76; attempt to make contact with Tientsin, 173–6; the International Relief Force and, 178–9, 193, 197, 205–8; resumption of the Siege of, 197–9; their defence compared with that of the Peitang, 212–14; reasons for the Siege of, 222–5; causes of its failure, 225–9; and the Peace Treaty, 251
Li Hung-chang, 28, 205, 222; appointed plenipotentiary, 246–7, 248
Li Lien-ying, 234
Li Ping-hêng, 51, 192–3; commits suicide, 193, 195, 259; summoned to the Manchu Court, 195–7
Lineivitch, General, and the International Relief Force, 181, 188, 190, 193, 201, 203, 208, 243; and the Victory March, 245
*Lion*, the, 80
Lofa, 75, 76
Looting, in Peking after the Relief, 242–3, 246, 252
Loti, Pierre, *Les Derniers Jours de Pékin*, 255 n
Lovitt, Dr and Mrs, 237

MacDonald, Lady, 15, 62, 123, 145, 207, 243; the Empress Dowager and, 57
MacDonald, Sir Claude, 13, 15, 19, 21, 70, 97 n, 103, 116, 130; and Putnam Weale, 20 n; and Chinese unrest, 22; ignores the danger signals, 53, 64–6,

269

# INDEX

# INDEX